The Constitutional Amending Process in American Political Thought

THE
CONSTITUTIONAL
AMENDING PROCESS
IN AMERICAN
POLITICAL
THOUGHT _____

John R. Vile

PRAEGER

New York
Westport, Connecticut
London

342.7303
V699c
1992

Library of Congress Cataloging-in-Publication Data

Vile, John R.
   The Constitutional amending process in American political thought
/ John R. Vile.
        p.   cm.
   Includes bibliographical references and index.
   ISBN 0-275-94280-5 (alk. paper)
   1. United States—Constitutional law—Amendments—History.
   2. Political science—United States—History.   I. Title.
   KF4555.V55   1992
   342.73'03—dc20
   [347.3023]   91-43441

British Library Cataloguing in Publication Data is available.

Library of Congress Catalog Card Number: 91-43441
ISBN: 0-275-94280-5

First published in 1992

Praeger Publishers, One Madison Avenue, New York, NY 10010
An imprint of Greenwood Publishing Group, Inc.

Printed in the United States of America

The paper used in this book complies with the
Permanent Paper Standard issued by the National
Information Standards Organization (Z39.48-1984).

10 9 8 7 6 5 4 3 2 1

Copyright Acknowledgments

The author and publisher gratefully acknowledge permission to reprint all or parts of the following articles:

John R. Vile. "The Amending Process: Alternative to Revolution." *Southeastern Political Review* 11 (Fall 1983): 49–95.

John R. Vile. "American Views of the Constitutional Amending Process: An Intellectual History of Article V." *The American Journal of Legal History* 35 (January 1991): 44–69.

John R. Vile. "Ideas of Legal Change: Precursors to the Constitutional Amending Process." *Southeastern Political Review* 15 (Fall 1987): 3–26.

John R. Vile. "Jefferson's Views on Governmental Change: An Alternative Perspective on Prevalent Madisonian Caution." *Texas Journal of Political Studies* 12 (Fall/Winter 1989–90): 48–75.

John R. Vile. "John C. Calhoun and the Constitutional Amending Process: Article V and the Theory of Concurrent Majorities." *Midsouth Political Science Journal* 9 (1988): 64–76.

John R. Vile. "Limitations on the Constitutional Amending Process." *Constitutional Commentary* 2 (Summer 1985): 373–88.

To twin blessings,
Virginia and Rebekah

Contents

Preface

I have been writing and thinking about the constitutional amending process for more than a dozen years, a time during which no national amendments have been ratified but scores of good articles and books have been published on the subject. Many of these publications suggest that my fascination with the topic of amendments has been justified and that a proper understanding of the amending process illuminates such topics as the nature of the American political system, the balance that it embodies between natural rights and popular sovereignty, the relation between the judiciary and the elected branches of government, and a host of other important issues.

While I have profited immensely from existing scholarly work on the amending process, I believe that this literature has given inadequate attention to the work of prior theorists in this field. Most writings, understandably prompted by modern concerns, jump from a quick review of statements in colonial charters and/or statements made at the U.S. Constitutional Convention to a discussion of an individual amendment or amendments or to one or another modern day controversy, with little attention to what happened in between. In conducting my own research, however, I have discovered that there is a rich legacy of commentary on the constitutional amending process that more clearly illuminates this topic and that casts further light on the historical development of the Constitution.

While Americans tend to think of the amending process as unique, they sometimes forget that political theorists had been discussing legal change and stability for centuries; such views, and their possible influences, are the subject of Chapter 1 of this book. Chapter 2 follows with a discussion of events at the Constitutional Convention and arguments, most notably by James Madison and Alexander Hamilton under the pen name Publius, that were advanced in defense of the amending process during the debates over ratification of the U.S. Constitution. Such debates are further illuminated in the next two chapters by examining the views of George Washington, which seem fairly representative of contemporary sentiment, and of Thomas Jefferson, whose views differed in some important particulars from those of many of his contemporaries, including James Madison, his friend and political ally. Adding further diversity to the mix of American opinions on the amending process are the views in Chapter 5 of John C. Calhoun, a prominent Southern political theorist and apologist for slavery; in Chapter 6 of Sidney George Fisher, a Philadelphia lawyer who wrote during the Civil War and who favored congressional adaptation of the Constitution over amendment; and in Chapter 7 of Christopher Tiedeman, a law professor and defender of laissez-faire economics who wrote a back in 1890 encouraging judges to adapt the Constitution through interpretation. These chapters are followed by two others: Chapter 8 discusses a number of Progressive spokesmen who wanted to liberalize the amending process, and Chapter 9 analyzes their conservative counterparts who hoped, in the wake of four new amendments, to find implicit constitutional restraints on the kinds of alterations that could be adopted. While it is my hope that these nine chapters compose a coherent whole, I also hope that scholars interested in a single thinker or time period discussed here will find that they can profit from individual chapters on occasions where they cannot read the entire account.

Obviously, many scholars have written about the amending process since the time period covered in this book. Indeed, as the patient and resourceful interlibrary loan librarians at Middle Tennessee State University can testify, there is rarely a monthly issue of the *Index to Legal Periodicals* that does not contain at least one new article directly relevant to the amending process, and other pieces regularly appear in journals and books directed to political scientists and historians. Were all such pieces to be treated, they would require another volume. Were they to be ignored, it might be difficult to see the relevance of this volume to contemporary debates. My solution has been to treat some of the most important modern theorists in the conclusions of the chapters in this book (particularly the latter chapters) and thereby to show, whenever possible, how old debates and issues are reflected in modern controversies. Such a treatment must necessarily be more suggestive than it is complete, but it is my hope that the parallels that are drawn will both point to areas for future research and show the relevance of understanding past debates to analyzing modern controversies.

Acknowledgments

Although I formulated the outline for this book fairly recently, I now realize that this volume has been in the making for more than a dozen years. During this time I have accumulated many intellectual debts, a good number of which I acknowledged in an earlier work. I would like to repeat my thanks here to all those who have befriended, nurtured, instructed, challenged, and inspired me.

Again I should like to extend special thanks to Professor Henry Abraham at the University of Virginia and to Professor Walter Murphy at Princeton University. I will always be under deep obligation to Professor Alpheus Mason of Princeton, whose memory I would like once again to honor. I would also like to thank those who first taught me political theory—Professor Roger Smith at the College of William and Mary and Professors Dante Germino, Delba Winthrop, Robert Morgan, and Sidney Pearson at the University of Virginia. I owe special thanks, which I am pleased to acknowledge, to Middle Tennessee State University, which has continued to extend research support to me; to my colleagues and students at this institution (especially those in the Political Science Department) who have provided such a congenial and stimulating work environment; and to librarians—especially Betty McFall, Peggy Colflesh, and John Marshall—who have done so much to aid my research efforts. McNeese State University, where I was previously employed, also extended research support for some of the projects that now appear in this book.

I should add special thanks to the editors at Praeger, especially James Dunton, John Roberts, and Debra Greinke. I also want to thank the editors of the various journals acknowledged here for refining ideas that were first advanced in earlier articles and that have been further elaborated in this manuscript. None of those listed above bears any responsibility for errors of fact or for expressions of opinion in this book.

My life at home has been considerably enhanced during the years of researching and writing this book by the presence of twin daughters who, while frequently diverting me from purely scholarly pursuits, have added immeasurably to the range of my life experiences and to my general happiness. This book is affectionately dedicated to them, the equally important contributions of my wife having been recognized in my dissertation and the role of my parents having been acknowledged in an earlier book.

Chapter 1

The Philosophical Heritage

CONTEMPORARY APPROACHES TO THE AMENDING PROCESS

The contemporary understanding of the origins of the amending process has been dominated by discussions of the deliberations at the U.S. Constitutional Convention, either singly or against the backdrop of the idea of revolution and earlier state charters and constitutions. While the analysis in Chapter 2 will confirm that this approach casts some important light on the origins of the amending mechanism, the method suffers both from the paucity of the comments on the amending mechanism at the Constitutional Convention,[1] and from the failure to consider the way that New World mechanisms might have been shaped by, or related to, previous discussions of legal change.

Widening the field of search, the noteworthy exception to this approach is an essay by Edmond Cahn contrasting the amending mechanism in the Constitution with earlier documents that either omitted such a provision or specifically declaimed against it.[2] Cromwell's Instrument of Government is an example of the first approach, while Locke's proposed constitution for Carolina is an example of the second; Locke not only provided for "perpetuity" but also prohibited any "comments and exposition" of the document.[3] For Cahn, Cromwell and Locke represented the stance toward constitutional amendment prior to the U.S. Constitution.

Cahn's approach, like others, presents the view of American exclusiveness: Prior to 1787 no national constitution other than the Articles of Confederation contained a formal mechanism for constitutional change; before this time, indeed, written constitutions had essentially not been invented. However, in stressing the uniqueness of the amending mechanism in Article

V of the Constitution, it is important to remember that this provision was designed to address the issue of legal change. Contrary to what the doctrine of American exceptionalism might suggest, a number of important political philosophers had recognized that legal changes were sometimes necessary and must be permitted. However, most also agreed that changes in laws must not be precipitate. In short, many earlier philosophers called for the kind of balance between stability and change that the proponents of the amending process claimed to have provided.

To see Article V as a solution to a perennial problem of political thought is hardly to denigrate its importance. Indeed, this approach may give even greater credit to the genius of the American Founders than discussions that omit this background. There is, of course, always the danger of interpreting past thinkers in light of a specific mechanism about which they did not and could not have known, but an initial caveat should be adequate to guard against this risk. Moreover, there is greater danger of portraying past thinkers as ignorant or naive simply because they had yet to develop a constitutional mechanism that is now taken for granted.

There are additional reasons for considering treatments of constitutional change as components of a much larger discussion. Given the impact of judicial review[4] and the development of informal customs and usages,[5] amendments are but part of the story of constitutional change even in America. Moreover, the Constitution is a form of law to which discussions of the pros and cons of legal flexibility should apply with particular force. Most importantly, however, setting the thought of the Founders against the backdrop of earlier theories of legal change demonstrates that here, as elsewhere,[6] the Founders' contribution to government was not in the realm of abstract political theory but in the creation of specific mechanisms translating earlier theories of legal change into reality. To this extent at least, existing studies of the amending process will not only be challenged but vindicated.

BIBLICAL HISTORY

The Founders knew about Hebrew history from the Bible and about classical history from a variety of sources.[7] Both time periods would suggest that laws needed to express enduring principles and to avoid excessive rigidity. If ever a set of laws was considered to be permanent, it was certainly the Ten Commandments that Moses brought down from Mount Sinai.[8] Those familiar with the New Testament, however, had certainly come to view the numerous explanations and emanations of these commands as excessively rigid. Many health, dietary, and ceremonial provisions followed by the Hebrew people seemed clearly tied to an earlier tribal life-style,[9] while Jesus had indicated that excessive interpretations of provisions such as the prohibition of work on the Sabbath could defeat the spirit of the command.[10] Moreover, attentive readers of the Old Testament would be familiar with two stories, those recorded in the books of Daniel and Esther, that would caution against overly rigid laws. In each case, a king found himself bound by the unchangeable laws of the Medes and Persians to a policy with potentially disastrous consequences for his friends.[11] In Daniel's case, God's direct intervention was required to close the lions' mouths and save his life,[12] while in the case of Esther, the Jews who were to be slaughtered under the first unalterable decree were permitted by a second order to assemble and defend themselves.[13] Both stories demonstrated that unchangeable laws might have unintended consequences.[14]

CLASSICAL HISTORY

Greek and Roman history both offered examples of long regimes, but even the most enduring hardly survived without major alterations. Thus, Founders reading the histories of either period would probably conclude that, while safeguards could sometimes preserve constitutions, change was inevitable. Plutarch reported that Solon mandated that his laws remain in force for one hundred years[15] and left Athens for a decade after proclaiming the laws in the hope that the people would become accustomed to them during this time.[16] When Solon returned, however, his laws proved incapable of preventing a transfer of power to Pisistratus, who ruled the city like a tyrant.

Like Solon, Lycurgus took measures to make his laws unalterable. After extracting the promise not to change the laws until he returned, Lycurgus left Sparta and martyred himself.[17] Adding some balance are reports that Lycurgus neither put his laws into writing nor legislated on matters which were, according to Plutarch, "better left unprescribed by written laws, or rigid customs, but adaptable to circumstances and the judgments of educated men."[18] Moreover, after reporting that Sparta's laws lasted for over five hundred years, Plutarch immediately indicated that the importation of gold and silver under King Agis resulted in changes that fundamentally altered the state.[19] Neither Solon's example nor that of Lycurgus, then, suggested that unalterable laws were an effective expedient, and both might be taken as warnings against an inflexible constitution created by trickery. At least one Anti-Federalist, writing under the title of the "Old Whig," later drew this conclusion.[20]

By the same token, another example drawn from Greek history suggested that laws should not be too flexible either. Leoni has stated that the Greeks were for a time so obsessed with innovations in their laws that a special group of magistrates called the *nomotelai* were charged with defending old laws against innovations; furthermore, those proposing changes in the laws were legally liable for any resulting ill effects and could even be sentenced to death.[21] Classical history, then, cautioned both against excessive constitutional flexibility and rigidity.

PLATO

While Platonic philosophy had no direct influence on most of the American Founders, who took their inspiration largely from other sources,[22] Plato's thought had a major impact on the development of Western philosophy and was familiar to many of the Founders. Plato was undoubtedly aware of the tensions in Greek thought represented by Heraclitus, who taught that everything was in constant flux, and Parmenides, who stressed continuing elements of stability.[23]

As much as any thinker, Plato emphasized legal stability, a stance evident in his discussion of children's games in *The Laws*. Plato argued that children accustomed to changes in the games they played would also expect changes in their government, thinking that there is "no permanent agreed standard of what is becoming or unbecoming."[24] Shortly thereafter, Plato asserted: "Change . . . except in something evil, is extremely dangerous. This is true of seasons and winds, the regimen of the body and the character of the soul—in short, of everything without exception (unless . . . the change affects something evil)."[25] His ideal state established, Plato wanted the people's soul to be "filled with such respect for tradition that it shrinks from meddling with it in any way."[26]

With all of Plato's reservations about change, he suggested a mechanism by which change might occur, namely the Nocturnal Council. While its central role was that of "keeping the legal code intact,"[27] it was to do so by consulting those who had traveled and observed the laws of other states.[28] Apparently, the Council would have authority to change the constitution when the need became clear. Like those wise men permitted to travel, one would expect each guardian to act both for "the strengthening of the customs of his country which are soundly based, and the refurbishing of any that are defective."[29]

ARISTOTLE

Aristotle treated legal change in *The Politics* when discussing the pros and cons of Hippodamus's proposal to honor those who suggested worthwhile improvements to the state.[30] On the positive side, Aristotle noted that "change has proved beneficial" in fields such as medicine, physical training and other "arts and forms of human skill," among which politics could well be counted.[31] Referring to examples of earlier uncivilized conduct such as buying brides, Aristotle noted that it would be foolish to maintain such traditions.[32] Aristotle also commended some changes in written laws.

It may also be urged that to leave *written* laws unchanged is not a good policy. The reason is that in matters of political organization, as in the arts generally, it is impossible for every rule to be written down precisely; rules must be expressed in general terms, but actions are concerned with particulars.[33]

Having established that "in *some* cases, and at *some* times, laws ought to be changed," Aristotle stressed the need for "great caution," noting that laws rest upon habits that "can be created only by the passage of time" and that can be weakened by too readily changing "from existing to new and different laws."[34] Perceiving stability as an important good, Aristotle preferred to defer minor benefits to achieve it.

MARCUS TULLIUS CICERO

While Marcus Tullius Cicero's most comprehensive political work, *On the Commonwealth*, was unavailable to the American Founders, his major speeches were known and reflected themes developed in this more philosophical work.[35]

In these speeches, Cicero, like Polybius, emphasized constitutional stability and commended a mixed regime like Rome's for its capacity to resist the danger of simple forms of government to degenerate.[36] Cicero placed the "founding" and the "preserving" of states on a similar level, arguing that both "approximate the divine."[37] Cicero also suggested that the preservation and betterment of the state might require alterations. Thus, he favorably compared Rome to cities like Minos, Sparta, Athens, and Plato's Republic in speech by arguing that Rome "was the work of several men in several generations."[38]

If such themes commend continual constitutional adaptation, Cicero's belief in natural law argues for some constitutional unalterables. This law of right reason "which is in accordance with nature applies to all men, and is unchangeable and eternal," can neither be changed by "the senate nor the people" and will not vary from city to city.[39] While this law might serve to limit permissible constitutional changes, the distinction between natural and positive law suggested that the latter might be altered when it was not directly based on the former.

ST. THOMAS AQUINAS

St. Thomas Aquinas's discussion of law parallels Aristotle's. In asking "whether human law should be changed in any way," Thomas argued that changes in human laws may be prompted either by progress in human reason or by changes in a nation's citizens. Progress is to be expected.

Those who first endeavored to discover something useful for the human community, not being able by themselves to take everything into consideration, set up certain

institutions which were deficient in many ways, and these were changed by subsequent lawgivers who made institutions that might prove less frequently deficient
in respect of the common weal.[40]

Moreover, law may need to change "on account of the changed condition
of man, to whom different things are expedient according to the differences
of his condition."[41] Answering objections to change, Thomas distinguished
between the natural law, which is unchanging, and human law, which
"contains particular precepts, according to various emergencies."[42]

Thomas followed Aristotle's lead in answering the question of whether
human law should always be changed whenever something better occurs.
Like Aristotle, Thomas argued that change itself can be "prejudicial to
the common good because custom avails much for the observance of
laws."[43] Except in cases of clear injustice or harm, Thomas counseled
caution.

NICCOLO MACHIAVELLI

One of many republican thinkers who influenced the American Founders,
Niccolo Machiavelli tied the themes of constitutional change and renewal
to the tendency of governments to degenerate over time.[44] In his discussion
in *The Discourses* of the different types of republics, Machiavelli noted that
some begin with good laws and others do not. While Sparta's laws lasted
for 800 years without alteration, other cities have had to modify their laws
as their people changed or as defects surfaced. For Machiavelli, change is
rarely easy and often dangerous.

For the majority of men never willingly adopt any new law tending to change the
constitution of the state, unless the necessity of the case is clearly demonstrated; and
as such a necessity cannot make itself felt without being accompanied with danger,
the republic may easily be destroyed before having perfected its constitution.[45]

Believing that republics were particularly susceptible to change, Machiavelli, like Cicero, recommended a form of mixed government to avoid the
danger.[46]

Machiavelli drew connections between a state's constitution and her citizens' character, between good laws and good habits. The constitution must
change with the people.[47] Unfortunately, such a task is not easy. Constitutional amendment must occur "either all at once, or by degrees as each
defect becomes known," and both options "are equally impossible."[48] Even
wise men find it difficult to persuade others of the need for alterations,
while leaders capable of initiating major changes may be uninterested in the
public good.[49] Believing that people resist change, Machiavelli advised the
reformer to "retain the semblance of the old forms: so that it may seem to
the people that there has been no change."[50]

Machiavelli emphasized that governments and religions both needed to return periodically to "first principles."[51] Believing that fear could be a key to a state's renewal, Machiavelli recommended executions at least once every decade.[52] This practical, if harsh, suggestion notwitstanding, for Machiavelli constitutional renewal was, like religious revival, not easily adapted to fixed forms. The difficulty was that of assuring that men of sufficient "virtue," with all the ambiguity that this word had for Machiavelli, would arise in time to avert threatened dangers.

RICHARD HOOKER

An Anglican counterpart to St. Thomas, Richard Hooker's views were more accessible and familiar to American readers of Locke.[53] Moreover, Hooker further clarifies some of the legal lessons that Americans might have gleaned from Scripture.

Hooker distinguished a variety of laws, among them natural law and positive law.[54] The latter could be imposed either by God or man, and be either mutable or permanent.[55] To be just, human laws must not contradict "any positive law in Scripture,"[56] but commands in Scripture must be supplemented by human reason, and some biblical comments regarding "the regiment and polity of the Church" are subject to change.[57] In analyzing the laws of the Old Testament, Hooker divided them into "the moral, ceremonial, and judicial" categories.

If the end for which and the matter according whereunto God maketh his laws continue always one and the same, his laws also do the like; for which cause the moral law cannot be altered; secondly, that whether the matter whereon laws are made continue or continue not, if their end have once ceased, they cease also to be of force; as in the law ceremonial it fareth; finally, that albeit the end continue . . . yet forasmuch as there is not in all respects the same subject or matter remaining for which they were first instituted, even this is sufficient cause of change.[58]

While natural laws are therefore constant, positive laws may be adapted "to the place and persons for which they are made."[59]

Hooker emphasized both the organic unity of the state and the need for consent.[60] Hooker's attention to the organic unity of, and the human dependency upon, the state cautioned against precipitate or radical changes while his emphasis on consent argued for occasional alterations.

FRANCIS BACON AND EDWARD COKE

Of the large number of lawyers at the U.S. Constitutional Convention, many would no doubt have been aware of various controversies over law reform in the mother country. Sir Francis Bacon (1561–1626) and Sir Edward Coke (1552–1634), fierce rivals in their day, were among the best known names in this field.[61] The former had proposed throughout his life to rework the laws of England into a more systematic group of maxims, and he unsuccessfully petitioned the king to this end.[62] Coke was apparently leery of such schemes, writing years before Bacon's letter:

For any fundamental point of the ancient common laws and customs of the realm, it is a maxim in policy, and a trail by experience, that the alteration of them is most dangerous; for that which hath been refined and perfected by all the wisest men in former succession of ages, and proved and approved by continual experience to be good and profitable for the common wealth, cannot without great hazard and danger be altered and changed.[63]

Bacon himself seemed inclined to moderation, however, saying at one point that he did "not advise to cast the law into a new mould [sic]," explaining, "The work which I propound tendeth to proyning [sic] and grafting the law, and not to ploughing up and planting it again; for such a remove I should hold indeed for a perilous innovation."[64] In one of his brilliant essays, entitled "Of Innovations," Bacon acknowledged the advantages of sticking to long-standing customs while balancing these advantages against the inevitability of change.

All this is true if time stood still; which contraiwise moveth so round that a froward retention of custom is as turbulent a thing as an innovation; and they that reverence too much old times are but a scorn to the new. It were good therefore that men in their innovations would follow the example of time itself, which indeed innovateth greatly, but quietly by degrees scarce to be perceived.[65]

Bacon followed up this advice with the observation that "it is good also not to try experiments in states, except the necessity be urgent or the utility evident."[66]

MATTHEW HALE

Sir Matthew Hale (1609–76) was another lawyer whose writings were quite influential in America.[67] He illustrated the role of continuity and change in the English common law by comparing it to a ship and a body.

As the Argonauts [sic] ship was the same when it returned home, as it was when it went out, tho' in that Voyage it had successive Amendments, and scarce came back with any of its former Materials; and as Titius is the same man he was 40 Years since, tho' Physicians tell us, That in a Tract of seven Years, the Body has scarce any of the same Material Substance it had before [so is the common law].[68]

One of Hale's essays must surely still stand as one of the most thorough pieces ever penned on the subject of constitutional change. Beginning with the observation that legal reform was a "choice and tender business," he observed that it was "neither wholly to be omitted when the necessity requires, and yet very cautiously and warily to be undertaken."[69] Hale began with the dangers of reform. Old laws are, simply because of age, better known than new ones. Moreover, they have been tested by time, which adapts "new remedies" to "new inconveniences."[70] The introduction of new laws can bring "a great fluidness, lubricity and unsteadiness in the laws, and renders it upon every little occasion subject to perpetual fluxes, vicissitudes and mutations," and poses the danger of "perpetual motion."[71] Reforms may breed "seditious rebellions and tumults, and prepare people's minds for distempers."[72] Changes should be introduced only when clearly beneficial. Moreover, changes should "be not in foundations or principles, but in such things as may consist with the general frame and basis of the government or laws"; even then changes should be introduced gradually "and not too much at once."[73]

Hale traced the desire for excessive legal changes to unwholesome psychological qualities. There are those who are motivated by novelty in laws as in fashion and who possess "a giddy humor after something which is new, and possibly upon no other account but because it is new."[74] Those who are injured in some small particular by the existing laws sometimes advocate changes, as do those who are enamored with the possibility of formulating a perfect set of laws. Hale assures his reader that such perfection is impossible. True, the law God gave Moses was perfect "according to the use and end for which it was designed," but not for other peoples and circumstances;[75] indeed, even God allowed for a Sanhedrin to provide for special exigencies in the Jewish laws, and laws suited for one people may not serve adequately for others. Reform sentiment sometimes springs from ignorance of the true purposes of law and of the likely consequences of change. Again, reformers may be prompted by excessive love for "the product of their own hands," so that they are "like boys, that blow a bubble out of a walnut-shell, which when it is up, run after it with their eyes fixed only upon their bubble, and never consider what ditches they fall into or what breaches they run into in their pursuit."[76] Hale further tied the itch for legal change to the passions of "vain glory," "ambition," "fear," and "envy and malice."[77]

There are times, however, when change is needed, and so Hale proceeded to examine why some individuals oppose all changes. First and foremost was a "superstitious veneration" of the law, akin to that by which "the Romanists in point of religion" followed "ancient rites and ceremonies transmitted to them by their ancestors."[78] This was linked to fear of unforeseen "inconvenience" and to fear of displeasing existing legal authorities.

Others unduly feared that small reforms "shall be used like a little wedge put into a great piece of timber, which shall give opportunity to violent persons to drive greater after them, and cleave the whole in pieces";[79] others focus on previous miscarriages of legal reform.

Hale noted, however, that legal change was part of legal preservation, and in forceful comparison noted that laws "without due husbandry of them will die of themselves, like trees that want pruning."[80] Hale observed, moreover, that reform is often necessary to cleanse the law of corruption.

As all sublunary things are subject to corruption and putrefaction, to diseases and rust, so even laws themselves, by long tract of time gather certain diseases and excrescences; certain abuses and corruptions grow into the law, as close as the ivy unto the tree, or the rust to the iron, and in a little tract of time gain the reputation of being part of the law.[81]

Indeed, sometimes the original laws themselves require reform when, for example, "in their very constitution and fabric they are rotten and faulty, and unjust" or when the law has, over the course of time, become "obsolete and out of use, or weak and unprofitable to its end, or inconsistent with some new superinduction that time and variety of occasions have intro-duced."[82] Laws, like other human endeavors, must moreover, "receive new advantages and discoveries by time and experience."[83] Sometimes, too, the law grows so that "as the rolling of a snow-ball, it increaseth in bulk in every age, till it become utterly unmanagable."[84]

Hale thus returned to his warning of the two extremes and made a number of recommendations. As to matters to be reformed, Hale cautioned against any "alterations of the government in any measure," apparently, with les-sons learned during Cromwell's reign, referring to the form of the regime itself.[85] Similarly, nothing should be altered "that is a foundation or principal integral of the law"; as Hale explained:

We must do herein, as a wise builder doth with a house that hath some inconvenience or is under some decays. Possibly here or there a door or a window may be altered, or a partition made; but as long as the foundations or principals of the house be sound, they must not be tampered with.[86]

As to the manner by which the laws should be altered, Hale advocated deliberation and debate, with judges making some reforms and parliament others. Laws should not be retrospective, and, when discussed in parlia-ment, judges should be given an opportunity for debate there. Timing too was important, "It is not every parliament that is fit for such business."[87] Hale wrote:

When either the times are turbulent or busy, or when other occasions of state are many, great or important, that is not a season for such an undertaking; for it is not possible among such hurries of business, there can be that attendance upon and attention unto a business of this nature, as in truth it requires. It must be in such a time, when there is a great tranquility at home and little engagement abroad, that the parliament may resolvedly, patiently, attentively, and constantly apply itself to the work.[88]

Believing that the time of his essay might be such an occasion, Hale proceeded to discuss various reforms that might be fruitfully considered.

JOHN LOCKE

Few philosophers who influenced the American Founding Fathers are more widely known or studied than John Locke. While his draft of the Carolina Constitution opposed constitutional change, other features of Locke's thought are more compatible with it.[89] Thus in the *Second Treatise* Locke indicated that because "things of this World are in so constant a Flux," representation that was once fair can sometimes become unequal and unfair.[90] In such cases Locke commended executive remedies in preference to "certain and unalterable laws."[91]

Locke devoted little attention to formal constitutional mechanisms,[92] and he probably would not have drawn a fine line between constitutional amendment and the right of revolution, a right which Locke, in contrast to Hobbes,[93] clearly upheld. Countering criticism that popular consent was an unsteady foundation of government, Locke argued that people are conservative.

They are hardly to be prevailed with to amend the acknowledg'd Faults, in the Frame they have been accustom'd to. And if there be any Original defects, or adventitious ones introduced by time, or corruption; tis not an easie thing to get them changed, even when all the World sees there is an opportunity for it.[94]

Rebellion would not occur until discontent is general and visible since, "the People, who are more disposed to suffer, than right themselves by Resistance, are not apt to stir."[95] As one who affirmed a right of revolution, Locke could hardly quarrel with the lesser right implicit in an amending process.

WILLIAM PENN

William Penn's *Frame of Government for Pennsylvania* was the first to contain an amending mechanism.[96] Much like those philosophers who had earlier distinguished higher law from everyday law, Penn distinguished between "fundamental" laws and "circumstantial" or "superficial" laws. The first, consisting of basic rights of Englishmen, he considered to be unalterable; Penn believed most other laws should adapt to changes in conditions.[97] In the preamble to his *Frame of Government*, Penn noted "I do not find a model in the world that time, place, and some singular emergencies have not necessarily altered."[98] Moreover, Penn permitted alterations with "the Consent of the Governor his heirs or Assigns and six part of seven of the said freemen in Provincial Council and General Assembly,"[99] a formula virtually unchanged in succeeding versions.[100]

An alteration in the Charter of Privileges granted to Pennsylvania in 1701 built on Penn's distinction between fundamental and circumstantial law. Repeating his familiar amending formula, Penn limited its application, promising:

That the *First* Article of the Charter relating to liberty of Conscience, and every Part and Clause therein, according to the true Intent and Meaning thereof, shall be kept and remain, without any Alteration, invariably for ever.[101]

The American Founders subsequently used a similar expedient, albeit for arguably less noble purposes, when they guaranteed slave importation for twenty years and promised that states would not be involuntarily deprived of their equal suffrage in the Senate.[102]

JOHN TRENCHARD AND THOMAS GORDON

The essays by John Trenchard and Thomas Gordon, entitled *Cato's Letters* and first published from 1720 to 1723, were among the Whig writings that influenced the political theory of the Founders.[103] While none of Cato's essays focused exclusively on the issue of constitutional change, a number of them treated this and related subjects, drawing lessons from the decline of classical regimes.[104]

Cato emphasized the need to avoid the corrupting influence of unbalanced, unrestrained, and/or unchecked power on liberty. While laws and institutions are critical, men are so corrupt and crafty that laws must change as new evasions and threats to liberty surface. The laws of nature do not change, but positive laws must adapt to circumstances.

Positive Laws deriving their Force from the Law of Nature, by which we are directed to make occasional Rules, which we call Laws, according to the Exigencies of Times, Places, and Persons, grow obsolete, or cease to be, as soon as they cease to be necessary.[105]

Constitutional arrangements may also have to change. Thus, in describing Britain's unwritten constitution, Cato recognized that as one part changes, others must adjust.

The great Secret in Politics is mainly to watch and observe the Fluctuation and Change of natural Power, and to adjust the political to it by prudent Precautions and timely Remedies, and not put Nature to the Expense of Throws and Convulsions to do her own Work.[106]

When there is a dispute between the people and their magistrates, Cato, like Locke, recommended an appeal to heaven.[107] Cato also joined Locke in seeking to restrain such revolution. People should neither revolt over minor grievances nor overthrow a reasonably functioning government for another they imagine to be better.[108] Accordingly, in comparing the English government with more "popular" forms, Cato argued that the theoretically best constitution must yield to be the best practicable regime under the circumstances.[109]

BARON DE MONTESQUIEU

The Baron de Montesquieu so adeptly preserved tensions in his work that American Founders frequently quoted him on both sides of an issue.[110] Thus, Montesquieu upheld a form of natural law theory and the view that most laws must be adapted to the "climate . . . the . . . soil, . . . [the] situation and extent, to the occupations . . . the degree of liberty . . . to the religion of the inhabitants, to their inclinations, riches, numbers, commerce, manners, and customs."[111]

Montesquieu distinguished the immutable laws governing the physical world, from the "laws" to which men do not conform "so exactly."[112] Ideally, man is governed by reason and law, but these must accommodate to human variations.

The political and civil laws of each nation ought to be only the particular cases in which human reason is applied.

They should be adapted in such a manner to the people for whom they are framed that it should be a great chance if those of one nation suit another.[113]

Noting that laws should not be separated from their end, Montesquieu observed *"that sometimes it is proper the Law should amend itself"* or be eliminated altogether.[114] Montesquieu's survey of diverse legal practices from various historical epochs and civilizations and his emphasis on adapting laws to a people's circumstances pointed to the need for constitutional flexibility.

Montesquieu also believed that small changes might effect major consequences. Warning in one heading that *"the smallest Change of the Constitution"* may be accompanied by *"the Ruin of its Principles,"*[115] Montesquieu cautioned that "the spirit of a legislator ought to be that of moderation."[116] In short, Montesquieu sanctioned alterations in laws (and, by implication, in constitutions) in accord with changing times, mores, and circumstances, while warning against improvident, ill-conceived, or radical changes with unpredictable results.

JEAN-JACQUES ROUSSEAU

However at variance some of his opinions were with the views of the Founders, Jean-Jacques Rousseau's ideas were a part of the intellectual atmosphere of their day. In *The Social Contract*, Rousseau argued that, while the government was entrusted with the execution and application of law to specific circumstances, all law-making authority was rightfully lodged in the sovereign people who must meet periodically to maintain their power.

Besides the extraordinary assemblies which unforseen events may require, it is necessary that there should be fixed and periodical ones which nothing can abolish or prorogue; so that, on the appointed day, the people are rightfully convoked by the law, without needing for that purpose any formal summons.[117]

Americans have argued about the power of constitutional conventions. For Rousseau, whose conventions would consist of everyone, the power as first described appears plenary.

So soon as the people are lawfully assembled as a sovereign body, the whole jurisdiction of the government ceases, the executive power is suspended, and the person of the meanest citizen is as sacred and inviolable as that of the first magistrate.[118]

Rousseau did, however, believe that it was inappropriate for the people to pass particular acts; in addition to passing general laws, the convened sovereign could sanction or change the present government and its administration.[119] While the idea that the people should periodically revise their constitutions gained notice but not widespread favor in America, the Founders certainly shared Rousseau's belief that the people were the source of government.[120]

DAVID HUME AND EDMUND BURKE

David Hume was representative of the Scottish Enlightenment. While not always well spoken of in the colonies,[121] Hume's works influenced the Founders both directly and through his influence on Edmund Burke, who was well known in America.[122]

Hume traced the origins of government to "necessity, . . . natural inclination . . . and habit."[123] Acknowledging that consent and divine Providence may have played a part in the formation of government, Hume argued that habit, tradition, and familiarity, born from a sense of utility, were more likely to contribute to the perpetuation of individual governments.[124]

But as human society is in perpetual flux, one man every hour going out of the world, another coming into it, it is necessary in order to preserve stability in government that the new brood should conform themselves to the established consti-

tution, and nearly follow the path which their fathers, treading in the footsteps of theirs, had marked out to them.[125]

Hume conceded the need for occasional revolutions but warned about the dangers of revolution generally: "We shall become more scrupulous of putting into practice the doctrine of resistance. The common rule requires submission, and it is only in cases of grievous tyranny and oppression that the exception can take place."[126] Long or present possession, conquest, succession, and/or positive laws will justify the ruler's title where such rule is in the general interest. However, since such interests, rather than divine mandate, justify any particular ruler, his rights may cease when he fails to further these interests.[127] The justice of particular revolutions cannot be settled by a priori philosophical principles but must be resolved by those directly affected.

Hume's approach to constitutional change paralleled his stance on revolution and was articulated in his essay, "Idea of a Perfect Commonwealth," which is known to have been particularly influential on James Madison.[128] Hume rejected the analogy of government to other artificial contrivances "where trials may safely be made even though the success be doubtful."[129] Since most people are governed more by "authority" than by "reason," "an established government has an infinite advantage by that very circumstance of its being established."[130] Thus, Hume's ideas for a perfect constitution were not for immediate use but for an opportunity afforded "either by dissolution of some old government or by the combination of men to form a new one in some distant part of the world."[131]

Burke's views were similar to Hume's. His view of change, like that of the American revolutionaries, was more akin to that of the English Revolution (and the kinds of changes once advocated by Coke) than the French.[132] In commending the Glorious Revolution, Burke noted that "a state without the means of some change is without the means of its own conservation."[133] The changes he favored, however, were incremental—a "reparation as nearly as possible in the style of the building."[134] In short, Burke did not advise against all change, but he cautioned that change should occur slowly and only after due deliberation and consideration.

THE HERITAGE EXAMINED

A summary of leading views of legal change with which American Founders would have been familiar must recognize differing emphases and even some contradictions. For example, thinkers like Machiavelli and Rousseau attempted to institutionalize change through periodic reviews or renewals. Aristotle saw legal change chiefly as a means of introducing innovations pointed to by experience; Machiavelli, Gordon and Trenchard, and Montesquieu viewed constitutional change primarily as a matter of constitutional renewal or adaptation to changes in the habits of the people; and St. Thomas and Hale mentioned both. Plato, Penn, and Rousseau suggested mechanisms for constitutional change while Machiavelli (and possibly Plutarch) thought it could best be initiated by outstanding men. Locke, Trenchard and Gordon, and Hume did not clearly distinguish between legal change and revolutionary change, and, of the thinkers surveyed, only Rousseau and Penn appear clearly to have distinguished ordinary legal changes from constitutional changes, although Hale's suggestion that not every parliament should consider law reform was also a step in this direction.

Thinkers have differed as to whether human beings by nature seek change or avoid it. Plato, Aristotle, Aquinas, Hume, Coke, Hale, and Burke thought the matter was chiefly one of custom or training and feared that frequent legal changes would breed a desire for novelty and lead to political instability. For Machiavelli and Locke, human beings are disposed to oppose change except when necessity imposes it upon them. Cicero, Aquinas, Hooker, Hale, Penn, and Trenchard and Gordon distinguished unchangeable laws and principles from those that are subject to change, while others did not.

Whatever the differences of emphasis or outright disagreements, it is clear that the idea of accommodating and limiting legal, and by inference, constitutional, change was not unique to the American Founders but was characteristic of views taken by philosophers over the previous two thousand years. Apart perhaps from Hippodamus, about whom there is only secondhand information from Aristotle, no thinker surveyed appeared oblivious to the need for legal stability, nor, apart from Solon and Lycurgus, did any thinkers expect that a law or system once established could in all points remain permanent. In short, the consensus was that legal change should be both accommodated and limited. Given this consensus, it seems surprising that it took so long to translate discussions about change into a concrete mechanism.

Two major obstacles to the development of an amending mechanism were the belief that some principles were unalterable and the fear that changes in the law would undermine governmental stability by accustoming the citizens to perpetual innovations. This is surely a part of the genius of the constitutional system that would be established in America. It distinguishes between ordinary acts of legislation and provisions worthy of being placed in the Constitution in a way that mimics, but is not identical to, the distinction between positive and natural law.[135] By making the adoption of amendments so much more difficult than alterations of ordinary legislation, the American Founders ensured that the Constitution would not likely be disturbed by such continual innovations as to undermine faith in the structure and basic principles of the regime. In this way, the Founders achieved the kind of balance between stability and change that earlier thinkers had advocated. While Article V is a New World mechanism, its goals clearly have roots deep within Western political thought.

NOTES

1. Bill Gaugush, "Principles Governing the Interpretation of Exercise of Article V Powers," *The Western Political Quarterly* 35 (June 1982), p. 213.

2. Edmond Cahn, "An American Contribution," *Supreme Court and Supreme Law*, ed. Edmond Cahn (Bloomington: Indiana University Press, 1954), pp. 1–25. Another more recent work which also deserves some credit is Philip A. Hamburger, "The Constitution's Accommodation of Social Change," *Michigan Law Review* 88 (November 1989), pp. 239–327.

3. Cahn, "An American Contribution," pp. 6–7. Locke's attitude seems to epitomize the brand of hermeneutics that H. Jefferson Powell has identified with the Protestant Reformation. See Powell, "The Original Understanding of Original Intent," *Harvard Law Review* 98 (March 1985), pp. 889–94.

4. See Bruce A. Ackerman, "The Storrs Lectures: Discovering the Constitution," *Yale Law Journal* 93 (May 1874), pp. 1013–72, and Cahn, "An American Contribution."

5. Herbert W. Horwell, *The Usages of the American Constitution* (Oxford: Oxford University Press, 1925). Also see Don K. Price, *America's Unwritten Constitution: Science, Religion, and Political Responsibility* (Cambridge, MA: Harvard University Press, 1985). Michael Foley's *The Silence of Constitutions: Gaps, 'Abeyances' and Political Temperament in the Maintenance of Government* (London: Routledge, 1989) is also relevant.

6. Alpheus T. Mason and Gordon E. Baker, *Free Government in the Making*, 4th ed. (New York: Oxford University Press, 1985), pp. 4–6.

7. Forrest McDonald, "A Founding Father's Library," *Literature of Liberty* 1 (1978), p. 6.

8. Exodus 20.

9. See the explanations of Richard Hooker and Sir Edward Hale on this point later in this chapter.

10. Mark 2:27; Mark 3:4.

11. Justice Matthews would refer unfavorably to such rigid laws in *Hurtado v. California*, 110 U.S. 516, 529 (1884).

12. Daniel 6.

13. Esther 8.

14. For further reflections on the possibility of amending divine law, see Sanford Levinson, "On the Notion of Amendment: Reflections on David Daube's Jehovah the Good," *S'Vara: A Journal of Philosophy and Judaism* 1 (Winter 1990), pp. 25–31.

15. Plutarch, *The Rise and Fall of Athens: Nine Greek Lives*, trans. Ian Scott-Kilvert (Baltimore, MD: Penguin, 1960), p. 67.

16. Ibid., pp. 68–69.

17. Plutarch, *Selected Lives and Essays*, trans. Louise Ropes Loomis (Roslyn, NY: Walter J. Black, 1951), p. 29.

18. Ibid., pp. 12–13.

19. Ibid., p. 29.

20. Herbert J. Storing, ed., *The Complete Anti-Federalist* (Chicago: University of Chicago Press, 1981), vol. 3, p. 19.

21. Bruno Leoni, *Freedom and the Law* (Los Angeles: Nash, 1972), pp. 80–81.

22. McDonald, "A Founding Father's Library," p. 11.

23. One chronicler of Greek thought notes that Parmenides "was the exact reverse of Heraclitus." The author explains: "For Heraclitus, movement and change were the only realities; for Parmenides, movement was impossible, and the whole of reality consisted of a single, motionless and unchanging substance." See W. K. C. Guthrie, *The Greek Philosophers: From Thales to Aristotle* (New York: Harper & Row, 1960), p. 47.

24. Plato, *The Laws*, trans. Trevor J. Saunders (Baltimore: Penguin, 1970), p. 283.

25. Ibid., p. 284.

26. Ibid. It is interesting that Walter Bagehot would later observe that early society "covets fixity." In such ages, he argued, "men do not want to have their laws adapted, but to have them steady." He adds: "In the early stages of human society all change is thought an evil. And *most* change is an evil. The conditions of life are so simple and so unvarying that any decent sort of rules suffice, so long as men know what they are. Custom is the first check on tyranny." See Bagehot, *The English Constitution* (Garden City, NY: Doubleday, n.d.), pp. 281–82.

27. Plato, *The Laws*, p. 518.

28. Ibid., pp. 501–2.

29. Ibid.

30. Aristotle, *The Politics of Aristotle*, ed. Ernest Barker (New York: Oxford University Press, 1958), p. 72.

31. Ibid.

32. Ibid., p. 73.

33. Ibid.

34. Ibid.

35. Marcus Tullius Cicero, *On the Commonwealth*, trans. G. Sabine and S. Smith (Indianapolis: Bobbs-Merrill, 1976; reprint of 1929 edition), p. 1.

36. Ibid., p. 133. For Polybius's commendation of mixed government, see Hamburger, "The Constitution's Accommodation of Social Change," p. 250.

37. Cicero, *On the Commonwealth*, p. 112.

38. Ibid., p. 155.

39. Ibid., pp. 215–16.

40. Thomas Aquinas, *The Political Ideas of Saint Thomas Aquinas*, ed. D. Bigongiari (New York: Hafner Press, 1953), p. 79.

41. Ibid.

42. Ibid.

43. Ibid., p. 81. This argument is similar to the response that Madison gave to Jefferson's idea of changing the U.S. Constitution every generation. See Alexander Hamilton, James Madison, and John Jay, *The Federalist Papers*, ed. Clinton Rossiter (New York: New American Library, 1961), pp. 314–15. This is reviewed in Chapter 2 of this book.

44. See especially J. G. A. Pocock, *The Machiavellian Moment* (Princeton, NJ: Princeton University Press, 1975).

45. Niccolo Machiavelli, *The Prince and The Discourses*, intro. Max Lerner, (New York: The Modern Library, 1950), p. 111.

46. Ibid., p. 115.

47. Ibid., p. 168.

48. Ibid., p. 170.

49. Ibid., p. 171.

50. Ibid., p. 182.

51. Ibid., p. 398. John Pym, an important English parliamentary leader during the reign of James I, would reflect similar sentiments:

> Time must needs bring about some alternations. . . . Therefore have those commonwealths been ever the most durable and perpetual which have often reformed and recomposed themselves according to their first institution and ordinance; for by this means they repair the breaches and counter-work the ordinary and natural effects of time.

Quoted by Henry B. Higgins, "The Rigid Constitution," *Political Science Quarterly* 20 (March 1905), p. 203. Higgins did not cite the specific source of this quotation.

52. Machiavelli, *The Prince and The Discourses*, p. 400.

53. John Locke, *Two Treatises of Government* (New York: New American Library, 1965; reprint of Cambridge University Press, 1963), pp. 119, 124.

54. Richard Hooker, *Of the Laws of Ecclesiastical Polity* (New York: Dutton, Everyman's Library, 1909), vol. 1, pp. 219, 224.

55. Ibid., p. 220.

56. Ibid., p. 326.

57. Ibid., p. 328.

58. Ibid., p. 331.

59. Ibid., p. 339.

60. Ibid., p. 188.

61. Catherine D. Bowen, *The Lion and the Throne* (Boston: Little, Brown, 1957), pp. 393–411.

62. See "An Offer to the King of a Digest to be Made of the Laws of England," *The Works of Francis Bacon*, ed. James Spedding, Robert L. Ellis, and Douglas D. Heath (New York: Garrett Press, 1968; reprint of 1874 ed.), pp. 358–65. The letter is dated March 20, 1620.

63. Paul H. Kocher, "Francis Bacon on the Science of Jurisprudence," *Essential Articles for the Study of Francis Bacon*, ed. Brian Vickers (Hamden, CT: Archon, 1968), p. 177, quoting Sir Edward Coke, *The Reports*, ed. J. Thomas and J. Frazer (London, 1826), vol. 2, pt. 4, p. v.

64. Ibid., p. 179, quoting Bacon, *Civil Code*, ed. Scott, vol. 13, p. 67.

65. Francis Bacon, "Of Innovation," *The Essays or Counsels, Civil and Moral of Francis Bacon*, ed. Samuel H. Reynolds (Oxford: Clarendon Press, 1890), p. 171.

66. Ibid., p. 173.

67. Hamburger, "The Constitution's Accommodation of Social Change," p. 249.

68. Matthew Hale, *The History of the Common Law of England*, ed. Charles M. Gray (Chicago: University of Chicago Press, 1971), p. 40.

69. Matthew Hale, "Considerations Touching the Amendment or Alteration of Lawes," *A Collection of Tracts Relative to the Laws of England From Manuscripts*, ed.

Francis Hargrave (Dublin: Printed for E. Lynch et al., 1787), p. 253. Here, and in quotations following, modern spellings have been used to make Hale's meaning clear.

   70. Ibid., p. 254.
   71. Ibid., p. 255.
   72. Ibid.
   73. Ibid., p. 256.
   74. Ibid., p. 257.
   75. Ibid., p. 258.
   76. Ibid., p. 262.
   77. Ibid., p. 263.
   78. Ibid., p. 264.
   79. Ibid., p. 265.
   80. Ibid., p. 266.
   81. Ibid., p. 268.
   82. Ibid., p. 269.
   83. Ibid., p. 270.
   84. Ibid.
   85. Ibid., p. 272.
   86. Ibid.
   87. Ibid., p. 273.
   88. Ibid., p. 274.
   89. Cahn, "An American Contribution," pp. 6–7.
   90. Locke, *Two Treatises on Government*, p. 418.
   91. Ibid., p. 420.
   92. Mason and Baker, *Free Government in the Making*, p. 4.
   93. Thomas Hobbes, *Leviathan*, ed. M. Oakeshott (New York: Collier Books, 1962).
   94. Locke, *Two Treatises on Government*, p. 462.
   95. Ibid., p. 466.
   96. Edward C. Beatty, *William Penn as Social Philosopher* (New York: Octagon Books of Farrar, Strauss and Giroux, 1975), p. 61.
   97. Ibid., p. 29.
   98. Francis N. Thorpe, *The Federal and State Constitutions, Colonial Charters and Other Organic Laws of the States, Territories, and Colonies Now or Heretofore Forming the United States of America* (Washington, DC: Government Printing Office, 1909), vol. 5, pp. 3053–54.
   99. Ibid., p. 3052.
   100. Ibid., pp. 3059, 3063, 3068, 3076.
   101. Ibid., pp. 3079–80.
   102. U.S. Constitution, Article V.
   103. Bernard Bailyn, *The Ideological Origins of the American Revolution* (Cambridge, MA: Belknap Press of Harvard University Press, 1967), pp. 35–37.
   104. John Trenchard and Thomas Gordon, *Cato's Letters: Essays on Liberty, Civil and Religious, and Other Important Subjects* (New York: Da Capo Press, 1971), vol. 1, 121–22.
   105. Ibid., vol. 2, p. 65.
   106. Ibid., vol. 3, p. 154.

107. Ibid., vol. 2, pp. 217–18.

108. Ibid., vol. 3, p. 159.

109. Ibid., pp. 162–63.

110. Melvin Richter, *The Political Theory of Montesquieu* (New York: Cambridge University Press, 1977), pp. 63–64.

111. Baron de Montesquieu, *The Spirit of the Laws*, trans. T. Nugent (New York: Hafner Press, 1949), vol. 1, p. 6.

112. Ibid., p. 2. For comments on the relationship between law and society in Montesquieu's writings, see Hamburger, "The Constitution's Accommodation of Social Change," p. 252.

113. Montesquieu, *The Spirit of the Laws*, vol. 1, p. 6.

114. Ibid., vol. 2, p. 164.

115. Ibid., vol. 1, p. 119.

116. Ibid., vol. 2, p. 157.

117. Jean-Jacques Rousseau, *The Social Contract and Discourse on the Origin of Inequality*, ed. Lester G. Crocker (New York: Simon & Schuster, 1967), p. 95.

118. Ibid., p. 97.

119. Ibid., p. 107.

120. See the discussion of Jefferson in Chapter 4 of this book.

121. McDonald, "A Founding Father's Library," p. 9.

122. See Russell Kirk, "Edmund Burke and the Constitution," *The Intercollegiate Review* 21 (Winter 1985–86), pp. 3–11.

123. David Hume, *Hume's Moral and Political Philosophy*, ed. H. D. Aiken (New York: Hafner Press, 1948), p. 311.

124. Ibid., pp. 356–59.

125. Ibid., pp. 364–65.

126. Ibid., pp. 113–14.

127. Ibid., p. 121.

128. Douglass Adair, " 'Experience Must be Our Only Guide,' History, Democratic Theory, and the United States Constitution," in Douglass Adair, *Fame and the Founding Fathers*, ed. Trevor Colbourn (New York: W. W. Norton, 1974), pp. 107–23.

129. Hume, *Hume's Moral and Political Philosophy*, p. 373.

130. Ibid.

131. Ibid., p. 374.

132. See Martin Diamond, "The Revolution of Sober Expectations," *America's Continuing Revolution* (Garden City, NY: Anchor Books, 1970), pp. 23–40.

133. Edmund Burke, *Reflections on the Revolution in France* (Garden City, NY: Anchor Books, 1973), p. 33.

134. Ibid., p. 265.

135. Edward S. Corwin, *The "Higher Law" Background of American Constitutional Law* (Ithaca, NY: Cornell University Press, 1965).

Chapter 2

The Creation and Justification
of Article V

The previous chapter establishes that problems of constitutional change and stability have been a perennial staple of political thought. There is, of course, a more focused origin of the provision that became Article V of the Constitution. This genesis can be divided into four parts: prior state charters and constitutions; the revolutionary sentiment that had been articulated in the conflict with Great Britain; experience under the Articles of Confederation; and, finally and more particularly, the deliberations at the Constitutional Convention, which met in Philadelphia in the summer of 1787. The philosophy behind the amending process may in turn be conveniently summarized by a look at the arguments raised during the Federalist/Anti-Federalist debates over the Constitution, and, especially, at Publius's argument in defense of the new Constitution in *The Federalist Papers*.

COLONIAL CHARTERS

Just as denizens of Great Britain who had no formal written constitution turned to the Magna Carta and the English Bill of Rights for a defense of their liberties, so too many of the colonists came to look to their ancient charters for a defense of their rights. Such charters, preludes to later state constitutions, became increasingly important as conflict developed with the mother country over the issue of parliamentary sovereignty.[1] As grants that had been given by the Crown (then more powerful than Parliament, which had gained power in the interim) or the Crown's agents, the charters allowed the colonists to claim their rights as British subjects without having to recognize the claim of parliamentary sovereignty that the British government sought to attach to such rights.[2] Chapter 1 demonstrated that some of the charters originally granted by William Penn appear to have been the first such charters or constitutions that specifically provided for amendment, with due protections, however, for certain rights thought to be fundamental.

THE DECLARATION OF INDEPENDENCE

While the colonists thought of charters as inviolable, it was clear that the Crown did not always take such a high view of such documents.[3] Moreover, the American Revolution prompted most of the former colonies to rewrite their fundamental charters, placing their authority to do so on the idea of a social contract and on the more general right of revolution that was so forcefully articulated in the Declaration of Independence. There Jefferson and his revolutionary colleagues affirmed the Lockean view that governments are founded on popular consent and are instituted to secure fundamental human rights. They further asserted:

Whenever any Form of Government becomes destructive of these Ends, it is the Right of the People to alter or to abolish it, and to institute new Government, laying its Foundation on such Principles, and organizing its Powers in such Form, as to them shall seem most likely to effect their Safety and Happiness.

The revolutionary right asserted was, to be sure, a qualified right. Thus, Jefferson noted, "Governments long established should not be changed for light and transient Causes," and he sought to justify the actions of his compatriots as the result of "a long Train of Abuses and Usurpations" pursued with the design of placing the colonists "under absolute Despotism." Moreover, scholars have convincingly argued that the goals of the American revolutionaries were relatively modest ones, more consistent with earlier conceptions of revolution as a process of orderly change[4] than with ideas of radical social transformation later identified with the French and Russian revolutionaries.[5]

EARLY STATE CONSTITUTIONS

Jefferson's justification was sufficient for most states to initiate the writing of new constitutions at the outset of the Revolutionary War. Initially, many of these documents restated the right of revolution, often in their declaration of rights, without actually providing a specific mechanism to effect constitutional change. Thus, for example, the Maryland Declaration of Rights of 1776 proclaimed: "Whenever the ends of government are perverted and public liberty manifestly endangered and all other means of redress are ineffectual, the people ought to reform the old or establish a new government."[6] Similarly, the Massachusetts Declaration of Rights provided:

Government is instituted for the common good, for the protection, safety, prosperity and happiness of the people, and not for the profit, honor or private interest of any one man, family, or class of men, therefore the people alone have an incontestable, unalienable, and indefeasible right to institute government, and to reform, alter or totally change the same when their protection, safety, prosperity and happiness require it.[7]

While the principles thus asserted were in accord with natural rights philosophy, not only did they potentially undercut the authority of existing governments, but they also did little to distinguish fundamental constitutional change from ordinary legal change.[8]

Compounding this problem was the fact that some early state constitutions (many of which, it should be recalled, were written during the exigencies of war[9]) had no firmer grounding than the will of the legislature that happened to adopt them, a complaint Jefferson would make of the Virginia state constitution, but which was surely not unique to it.[10] Stimulated by criticisms such as Jefferson's, however, there appears to have been a definite movement toward a mode of state constitutional adoption that more clearly distinguished such constitutions from other laws. In the states of New Hampshire, Delaware, Georgia, New York, and Vermont, the legislature was given special authority by the people to frame a constitution without further action being needed; other states provided for subsequent submission of such a document to the people. Still others set up a special body to write a constitution that would then be approved by the people.[11] As constitutions came to be distinguished from ordinary legislation, so too was it natural to create specific mechanisms for constitutional change.

Although there were still five states with no formal amending process by the time of the U.S. Constitutional Convention of 1787, three basic methods of constitutional amendment had emerged in the others. Four states provided for amendment by some type of legislative action; three called for amendment by constitutional convention; and two states provided for a council of censors to meet periodically to revise the constitution.[12] Those who wrote the U.S. Constitution thus had a variety of mechanisms from which to choose in writing Article V and some experience from which to draw in choosing which mechanisms seemed most appropriate.

THE ARTICLES OF CONFEDERATION

Still further lessons could be drawn from the Articles of Confederation that had been adopted by the Continental Congress in 1777 but not ratified by the last state until 1781. American historians are more likely to remember the flaws of this first loose confederation than achievements like the Northwest Ordinance of 1787, but the Articles of Confederation undoubtedly gave the young nation a valuable chance to experiment and to learn some lessons that could be applied in Philadelphia in 1787.[13]

The central flaw in the Articles of Confederation is generally acknowledged to have been its excessive adherence to the doctrine of state sovereignty, which was insisted on by Governor Thomas Burke of North Carolina and other delegates to the Continental Congress[14] and which was stated early in Article II of the document: "Each state retains its sovereignty, freedom, and independence, and every Power, Jurisdiction and right, which is not by this confederation expressly delegated to the United States, in Congress assembled."[15] Article IX further specified that most key matters under the article could not be undertaken by Congress, the only real branch of government in the new system, without the vote of nine of the states, each of which cast a single vote in that unicameral body.[16] It is not surprising, then, that the amending process would be even more difficult. Stated in Article XIII of the document, this process involved the approval of the legislature itself and of the states.

And the Articles of this confederation shall be inviolably observed by every state, and the union shall be perpetual; nor shall any alteration at any time hereafter be made in any of them; unless such alteration be agreed to in a congress of the United States, and be afterwards confirmed by the legislatures of every state.[17]

It should not be surprising that this obstacle proved too wooden for any amendments despite widespread agreement that the Articles had proven defective. At least one delegate at the Constitutional Convention thus observed that "it is to this unanimous consent, the depressed situation of the Union is undoubtedly owing."[18] The consequence was that the "perpetual" Articles of Confederation were amended, not as the Articles had specified, but by other means. When delegates gathered in Philadelphia in 1787, they came with some congressional approval, albeit not as members of Congress.[19] Moreover, when they submitted their handiwork to the states, they chose to seek approval from special conventions rather than from existing state legislatures. They provided, moreover, that the new Constitution would go into effect when ratified by nine or more states rather than requiring unanimity.[20]

THE CONSTITUTIONAL CONVENTION OF 1787

There were some illumining comments, albeit not extensive discussions, about the amending process at the U.S. Constitutional Convention. The first plan to be discussed at any length at the Convention was the Virginia Plan, which was introduced on May 29. Significantly, although it was originally introduced as an attempt to see that the Articles of Confederation were "so corrected & enlarged as to accomplish the objects proposed by their institution,"[21] the Virginia Plan was really a fresh start, as was soon recognized by a resolution providing "that a national government ought to

be established consisting of a supreme Legislature, Judiciary, and Executive."[22] The Virginia Plan's initial provision regarding amendments was
relatively brief, more in the way of a statement of principle than as an
outline of a specific mechanism: "Resd. that provision ought to be made
for the amendment of the Articles of Union whensoever it shall seem necessary, and that the assent of the National Legislature ought not to be
required thereto."[23] When this resolution was debated (only to be post-
poned) on June 5, Charles Pinckney of South Carolina was recorded as
doubting "the propriety or necessity of it,"[24] while Elbridge Gerry of Massachusetts approved, with a view both to state experience and toward the
desirability of peaceful change over revolutionary alteration.

The novelty & difficulty of the experiment requires periodical revision. The prospect
of such a revision would also give intermediate stability to the Govt. Nothing had
yet happened in the States where this provision existed to proves [*sic*] its
impropriety.[25]

When the amending provision was discussed before the committee of the
Whole on June 11, there were "several members" who were still uncon-
vinced either of the necessity of an amending provision or of "the propriety
of making the consent of the Natl. Legisl. unnecessary."[26] In arguments
apparently supported by Edmund Randolph (the delegate who, as state
governor, had introduced the Virginia Plan), George Mason, also of Virginia, attempted to argue for both points, again painting amendments as a
desirable alternative to revolution.

The plan now to be formed will certainly be defective, as the Confederation has
been found on trial to be. Amendments therefore will be necessary, and it will be
better to provide for them, in an easy, regular and Constitutional way than to trust
to chance and violence. It would be improper to require the consent of the Natl.
Legislature, because they may abuse their power, and refuse their consent on that
very account. The opportunity for such an abuse, may be the fault of the Constitution
calling for amendmt.[27]

The result of these arguments was the approval of an amending provision
without dissent, albeit postponing the provision that would have exempted
amendments from congressional approval.

On June 15, William Paterson introduced the New Jersey Plan before the
Constitutional Convention. Although it had itself been significantly influenced by decisions already reached at the Convention, the New Jersey Plan
was much more along the order of a revision of the Articles than an entirely
new plan. Consistent with the congressional resolution by which the convention had been called into being, the New Jersey Plan began with a
proposal "that the articles of Confederation ought to be so revised, corrected
& enlarged, as to render the federal Constitution adequate to the exigencies

of Government, & the preservation of the Union."[28] Moreover, John Lansing of New York contrasted the two plans by noting that "the one now offered is on the basis of amending the federal government, and the other to be reported as a national government, on propositions which exclude the propriety of amendment."[29] Significantly, the New Jersey Plan did not contain an amending provision—whether because its authors considered one to be unnecessary or because it expected the provisions of the Articles of Confederation to remain in place, this author is uncertain. Apparently, the majority of delegates thought the New Jersey Plan did not go far enough. Although certain of its provisions (most notably the request for equal state suffrage in Congress) would resurface, on June 19 the Convention resumed its discussion of the Virginia Plan in preference to that of New Jersey.

Ten days later James Madison contributed to an understanding of the Founders' view of amendments, albeit as part of his discussion of the troubling issue of how states would be represented in the new Congress. Opposing the solution, eventually adopted, that would give states an equal vote in the Senate and thus create a government *"partly federal and partly national,"*[30] Madison said on June 29 that it was risky to form a government with such "inconsistent principles."

The difficulty of getting its defects amended are great and sometimes insurmountable. The Virginia state government was the first which was made, and though its defects are evident to every person, we cannot get it amended. The Dutch have made four several attempts to amend their system without success. The few alterations made in it were by tumult and faction, and for the worse.[31]

Madison thus recognized that, once incorporated into a constitution, provisions were often difficult to change, partly buttressing his point, however, by not mentioning that the Virginia Constitution did not have an amending mechanism such as the Virginia Plan had proposed for the national government.

The next important mention of the amending provision is in the report of the five-man Committee of Detail (composed of Edmund Randolph, James Wilson, Nathaniel Gorham, Oliver Ellsworth, and John Rutledge) that was appointed at the end of July to formulate an understanding of agreements that had been reached at the Convention so far. It is from this Committee, which issued its report on August 6, that the first real attempt appears to have been made to translate the general sentiment for an amending clause into a specific mechanism, an attempt that departed from that of the Articles of Confederation and resembles the still unused convention mechanism of Article V rather than the more traveled route through the Congress and the state legislatures.

This Constitution ought to be amended whenever such Amendment shall become necessary; and on the Application of the Legislatures of two thirds of the States in the Union, the Legislature of the United States shall call a Convention for that purpose.[32]

Over the countersuggestion of Gouverneur Morris of Pennsylvania "that the Legislature should be left at liberty to call a Convention, whenever they please," the proposal of the Committee of Detail was unanimously agreed to on August 30.[33] The amending clause essentially remained in this shape up to the closing days of the convention.

On September 10, Elbridge Gerry moved to reconsider this proposal. Apparently, he was concerned that the new process did not adequately protect state interests.

This Constitution . . . is to be paramount to the State Constitutions. It follows, hence, from this article that two thirds of the States may obtain a Convention, a majority of which can bind the Union to innovations that may subvert the State-Constitutions altogether.[34]

Alexander Hamilton seconded Gerry's motion, albeit with a different objective. Seeing "no greater evil in subjecting the people of the U.S. to the major voice than the people of a particular State," Hamilton feared that the proposed process was not easy enough, and that Congress would be a more appropriate body to suggest needed changes.

The mode proposed was not adequate. The State Legislatures will not apply for alterations but with a view to increase their own powers—The National Legislature will be the first to perceive and will be most sensible to the necessity of amendments, and ought also to be empowered, whenever two thirds of each branch should concur to call a Convention—There could be no danger in giving this power, as the people would finally decide in the case.[35]

In a question that is prophetic of modern debates on the subject, Madison commented on the vagueness of the convention clause, asking, "How was a Convention to be formed? by what rule decide? what the force of its acts?"[36] The joint effect of these three objections led to a reconsideration of this clause on a nine-to-one vote, with one state present being split.

It was then that Sherman, seconded by Gerry, moved to add a provision specifying that "the Legislature may propose amendments to the several States for their approbation, but no amendments shall be binding until consented to by the several States."[37] Apparently Sherman was calling for the same unanimity that had been required under the Articles.[38] Fortunately this retrogressive proposal was rejected, the number of states necessary for ratification being set at three-fourths after a two-thirds figure was rejected by a narrow six-to-five vote.[39]

Madison, apparently still intent on short-circuiting the possibility of an-

other convention, next proposed a substitute motion, seconded by
Hamilton:

The Legislature of the U— S— whenever two thirds of both Houses shall deem
necessary, or on the application of two thirds of the Legislatures of the several States,
shall propose amendments to this Constitution, which shall be valid to all intents
and purposes as part thereof, when the same shall have been ratified by three fourths
at least of the Legislatures of the several States, or by Conventions in three fourths
thereof, as one or the other mode of ratification may be proposed by the Legislature
of the U.S.[40]

This motion was then amended with a clause protecting slave importation
by John Rutledge of South Carolina who said he "never could agree to give
a power by which the articles relating to slaves might be altered by the
States not interested in that property and prejudiced against it."[41] This
amended article passed by a vote of nine to one again with one state divided.

The amending clause was reconsidered on September 15, just two days
before the document would be signed. Once again, Sherman expressed fear
of the amending majorities, arguing that "three fourths of the States might
be brought to do things fatal to particular States, as abolishing them altogether or depriving them of their equality in the Senate."[42] Citing the
entrenchment provision designed to protect slavery, Sherman now proposed "that no State should be affected in its internal police, or deprived
of its equality in the Senate."[43]

Surprisingly, Mason, who had earlier in the Convention argued so
strongly for the necessity of an amending process (albeit one to which
congressional assent was unnecessary), now saw the proposed mechanism
as "exceptionable & dangerous." In sentiment that reflected his growing
concern over the role of states in the new system, he explained that

as the proposing of amendments is in both the modes to depend, in the first immediately, and in the second, ultimately, on Congress, no amendments of the proper
kind would ever be obtained by the people, if the Government should become
oppressive, as he verily believed would be the case.[44]

Apparently it was this concern that prompted Morris and Gerry to alter
the amendment provision so as to "require a Convention on application of
2/3 of the Sts. [*sic*]."[45] Madison observed that Congress would be as bound
to propose amendments called for by two-thirds of the states as "to call a
Convention on the like application," but nonetheless observed that he saw

no objection however against providing for a Convention for the purpose of amendments, except only that difficulties might arise as to the form, the quorum &c.
which in Constitutional regulations ought to be as much as possible avoided.[46]

Morris and Gerry's provision was thus adopted.

A number of proposed changes followed. Sherman proposed striking out the three-fourths requirement for state and convention approval, "leaving future Conventions to act in this matter, like the present Conventions according to circumstances." This motion was rejected by a vote of seven to three to one. Gerry, probably influenced by fears that state legislatures would be routinely bypassed, next attempted to eliminate the convention method of ratification, an attempt rejected by a vote of ten to one. Sherman proceeded to propose that "no State shall without its consent be affected in its internal police, or deprived of its equal suffrage in the Senate," and was met with Madison's reply that, were the convention to consent to such "special provisos," then "every State will insist on them, for their boundaries, exports &c."[47] Sherman's motion was defeated by an eight-to-three vote; his subsequent motion, seconded by Brearley of New Jersey, to strike Article V completely, failed eight to two to one. Morris, however, proposed to add a provision "that no State, without its consent shall be deprived of its equal suffrage in the Senate,"[48] a stipulation that Madison recorded was "dictated by the circulating murmurs of the small States" and that was adopted without dissent.[49] Mason was not as successful, however, in adopting a provision "that no law in nature of a navigation act be passed before the year 1808, without the consent of 2/3 of each branch of the Legislature," this motion failing by a vote of seven to three to one.[50]

The convention had thus created the provision that is now Article V of the Constitution.

The Congress, whenever two thirds of both Houses shall deem it necessary, shall propose Amendments to this Constitution, or, on the Application of the Legislatures of two thirds of the several States, shall call a Convention for proposing Amendments, which, in either Case, shall be valid to all Intents and Purposes, as Part of this Constitution, when ratified by the Legislatures of three fourths of the several States, or by Conventions in three fourths thereof, as the one or the other Mode of Ratification may be proposed by the Congress; Provided that no Amendment which may be made prior to the Year One thousand eight hundred and eight shall in any Manner affect the first and fourth Clauses in the Ninth Section of the first Article; and that no State, without its Consent, shall be deprived of its equal Suffrage in the Senate.

This provision emerged from several distinct concerns at the Constitutional Convention. Delegates like Gerry and Mason expressed the convention's consensus that an amending process should be included and that it would provide a mechanism for constitutional as opposed to revolutionary change. The Committee of Detail proposed that such amendments be made by convention. Hamilton's faith in Congress's ability to identify key problems resulted in the inclusion of the amending mechanism which has subsequently been most utilized. Fears expressed by Madison about the workability of a convention mechanism to propose amendments were in turn overbalanced by concerns of delegates such as Mason, Gerry, Sherman, and Morris that, without a way to bypass Congress, states might be at the mercy of the legislative branch. Gerry's fear of ratifying amendments by conventions appears to have stemmed from his faith in state legislatures, a faith probably overshadowed in the Framers' minds by recognition that the Constitution was itself to be ratified by state conventions. Concerns like Gerry's about individual state interests were, however, behind the two entrenchment clauses, representatives of the slave interests (Rutledge) and of the small states (Morris proposing a provision after concerns expressed by Sherman, and possibly Brearley) wishing to give greater security to compromises arrived at by the Convention and elsewhere incorporated into the Constitution. Sherman was less successful in protecting states against imposition on their internal police powers, and Mason failed in his attempt further to restrict the passage of navigation legislation, Madison having expressed reservations about including too many such provisos.

THE ANTI-FEDERALIST CRITIQUE

It is common knowledge that there was a hard fight for constitutional ratification, pitting so-called Federalist proponents of the new document against Anti-Federalist opponents.[51] For the most part, the Federalists appeared to profit in this debate from the proposed amending mechanism in Article V. Thus, in the debates over constitutional ratification in Massachusetts, Rufus King praised "the superior excellence of the proposed Constitution in this particular," calling upon his colleagues "to propose an instance, in any other national constitution, where the people had so fair an opportunity to correct any abuse which might take place in the future administration of the government under it."[52] A colleague, Dr. Charles Jarvis, concurred, indicating that whereas other revolutions had "been written in blood, . . . we shall have in this article an adequate provision for all purposes of political reformation."[53] Similarly, in North Carolina, James Iredell pointed out that "there is a remedy in the system itself for its own fallibility, so that alterations can without difficulty be made, agreeable to the general sense of the people."[54]

In Virginia, Patrick Henry, a leading Anti-Federalist who had refused to be a delegate to the Constitutional Convention because he "smelt a rat,"[55] and who was particularly protective of states' rights, failed to concur in Federalist encomiums to the amending process, objecting both to the two-thirds and three-fourths majorities required. Speaking of the latter majority, Henry commented that "to suppose that so large a number as three fourths of the states will concur, is to suppose that they will possess genius, intelligence, and integrity, approaching to miraculous."[56] Elaborating in figures similar to those later evoked by John C. Calhoun and still later by American Progressives, Henry noted:

Four of the smallest states, that do not collectively contain one tenth part of the population of the United States, may obstruct the most salutary and necessary amendments. Nay, in these four states, six tenths of the people may reject these amendments.[57]

In such circumstances Henry noted that the liberty of the American people would be "gone forever."[58]

The difficulty of Henry's argument was, of course, that, by comparison to the mechanism in the Articles of Confederation, Article V of the proposed Constitution was quite democratic indeed. Thus, in the Massachusetts debates, Oliver Ellsworth had commented on the requirement for unanimity.

How contrary then to republican principles, how humiliating is our present situation! A single state can rise up, and put a *veto* upon the most important public measures. We have seen this actually take place. A single state has controlled the general voice of the Union: a minority, a very small minority has governed us. So far is this from being consistent with republican principles, that it is in effect the worst species of monarchy.[59]

Henry was arguing, of course, that with the expanded powers of the new national government, it would be particularly likely to abuse rights and would thus pose dangers that the Articles did not.

Arguments like those of Patrick Henry led Anti-Federalists to call for a Bill of Rights as a condition of constitutional ratification. The presence of an amending process allowed Federalists to argue that there would be no obstacle to such amendments once the Constitution was adopted, an observation that proved true after leading Federalists (particularly James Madison) lent their support to the Bill of Rights in the first Congress.[60] Being more skeptical, most Anti-Federalists wished to add the Bill of Rights beforehand; many such opponents of the new Constitution advocated calling yet another constitutional convention,[61] an idea that had been proposed even before the first Convention had adjourned.[62] Madison was a particularly vehement opponent of such an expedient, fearing that it might undo the work of the Philadelphia Convention, increase public agitation, and weaken America's position in the esteem of other nations.[63] He thus noted:

Having witnessed the difficulties and dangers experienced by the First Convention, which assembled under every propitious circumstance, I should tremble for the result of a Second, meeting in the present temper of America and under all the disadvantages I have mentioned.[64]

PUBLIUS EXPLAINS AND JUSTIFIES THE AMENDING PROCESS

The most effective justification on behalf of the Constitution and in answer to Anti-Federalist critiques was that which appeared in *The Federalist Papers*, originally a series of articles appearing in New York under the pen name of Publius and representing the collective contributions of Alexander Hamilton, James Madison, and John Jay.[65] Publius had both to justify the new Constitution against charges that it represented an illegal usurpation of power and to defend its provisions against Anti-Federalist criticisms.

Comments in *The Federalist Papers* relative to the amending process center around five basic themes. First was the above-mentioned defense of the amendment, or replacement, of the Articles of Confederation by a new charter of government. Second was the defense of the propriety and moderation of the amending process in the new Constitution. Third was a critique of periodic revisions of entire constitutions upon the request of two of three governmental branches or upon the authority of a council of revision. Fourth was a discussion of the tie between federalism and the amending process, and, implicitly at least, between the amending process and the analysis of factions. Fifth was the argument, cited earlier in this chapter, that revisions of the new Constitution—if they were to be adopted at all—could best be approved after its ratification rather than before it. In a sense, all of the last three arguments center around the second, that is, the claim that the mechanisms for amendments in Article V were in fact propitious and moderate.

Justifying the Constitutional Convention

As a prelude to defending any specific provisions of the new Constitution, Publius needed to defend the propriety of the writing and proposed method of ratifying the Constitution as a whole, for the fact that the amending provision of the Articles of Confederation had been bypassed was but one of a number of factors that could undermine the legitimacy of the new document. This defense of the new Constitution is most clearly outlined in *Federalist* Nos. 38 and 40.

In the first of these essays, Madison focused on the comparative merits of the new Constitution over the Articles of Confederation. His argument was that, while neither document was perfect, what imperfections there were in the new Constitution resulted from absence of experience rather than from lack of attention or care on the part of those who had written it. So arguing, Madison reflected that "among the numerous objections and amendments suggested by the several States, when these articles were submitted for their ratification, not one is found which alludes to the great and radical error which on actual trial has discovered itself."[66] Madison further noted that the patient, America, was clearly "sensible of her malady,"[67] but that, while those who authored the Constitution had agreed on the sickness and the cure, Anti-Federalists could only agree that the patient was ill.

Two analogies were drawn into play, both designed to show the comparative advantages of the new Constitution over the Articles.

It is not necessary that the former [the Constitution] should be perfect: it is sufficient that the latter is more imperfect. No man would refuse to give brass for silver or gold, because the latter had some alloy in it. No man would refuse to quit a shattered and tottering habitation for a firm and commodious building, because the latter had not a porch to it, or because some of the rooms might be a little larger or smaller, or the ceiling a little higher or lower than his fancy would have planned them.[68]

Here Madison followed Benjamin Franklin's lead at the Constitutional Convention.[69] No document that was the product of collective wisdom would be perfect, but the Constitution was far superior to the Articles.

In writing the Constitution, had the Framers exceeded their powers and commissions? Madison's multifaceted answer to this question in *Federalist* No. 40 is more ambiguous but perhaps no less convincing. Examining the resolution by which the Annapolis Convention and then the Congress had called the Constitutional Convention into being, Madison first distinguished the ends for which the Convention was authorized from the means specified for attaining them. Entrusted with the goal of formulating a union "*adequate to the exigencies of government and the preservation of the Union,*"[70] delegates had chosen partially to disregard the means that had been specified and to begin anew rather than simply to rewrite the Articles of Confederation. Moreover, Madison opined, after considerable, albeit not always convincing, efforts at comparison, "The great principles of the Constitution proposed by the convention may be considered less as absolutely new, than as the expression of principles which are found in the articles of Confederation."[71]

Madison did acknowledge that delegates to the Constitutional Convention had "departed from the tenor of their commission[s],"[72] first by permitting ratification by the people of the states and second by not adhering to the requirement in the Articles of Confederation for state unanimity. Focusing immediately on the latter part of this objection, Madison noted that few Anti-Federalists had made much of a point of this complaint, realizing "the absurdity of subjecting the fate of twelve States to the perverseness or corruption of a thirteenth; from the example of inflexible opposition given by a majority of one sixtieth of the people of America to a measure approved and called for by the voice of twelve States."[73]

Moving on to another argument, Madison focused on the duty of the convention delegates to seek an adequate remedy to the problems of the union. This duty was especially incumbent upon these delegates because they realized that their own role was "advisory" and "recommendatory" only since the proposed Constitution was "to be of no more consequence than the paper on which it is written, unless it be stamped with the approbation of those to whom it is addressed."[74] Now picking up on the advantage of the convention method of ratification that he had previously left dangling, Madison noted that this mechanism had been used during the Revolutionary period to write the constitutions under which most states were governed.[75] Thus, the propriety of this mechanism had already been established, and the popular approval represented by its use would presumably negate any earlier errors in convention proceedings.

Finally, Madison conceded for the sake of argument that "the convention were neither authorized by their commission, nor justified by circumstances in proposing a Constitution for their country."[76] Even then, he argued, the relevant consideration was not whether the convention was fully authorized to do what it did but whether its product was a worthy one; the focus should not be on whether the new Constitution had an immaculate conception but whether it would be better than the Articles of Confederation had been.

The Propriety and Moderation of the Amending Process

Given the many questions that surrounded the transition from the Articles of Confederation to the new Constitution, it was particularly important to show that this new document made adequate provisions for change. Madison elaborated this theme in *Federalist* No. 43 where he argued that the amending process adopted was "stamped with every mark of propriety."[77] Such a process was necessary, he argued, because "useful alterations will be suggested by experience."[78] The process is moderate in guarding both "against that extreme facility, which would render the Constitution too mutable; and that extreme difficulty, which might perpetuate its discovered faults."[79] Moreover, the process avoided possible obstructions in governmental structure by allowing both "the general and the State governments to originate the amendment of errors, as they may be pointed out by the experience on one side, or on the other."[80]

Madison's defense of the entrenchment clauses was briefer and less persuasive. As to the provision for equal state suffrage which he had so vehemently opposed, he noted that it "was probably insisted on by the States particularly attached to that equality." Commenting in similar cryptic fashion about the slave proviso, Madison noted that it "must have been admitted on the same considerations which produced the privilege defended by it."[81]

Critiques of Periodic Constitutional Revisions

While *Federalist* No. 43 argued for the propriety and moderation of the amending process, *Federalist* No. 49 directed itself to a proposal that had originated in Jefferson's reservations about the Virginia Constitution in his book, *Notes on the State of Virginia*.[82] Undoubtedly Madison agreed with many of the ideas there, including Jefferson's concerns about a constitution that had never been ratified by the people.[83] Jefferson had further feared that, as a state with no formal amending process, there would be no remedy for abuses of power other than "an appeal to the people, or in other words a rebellion."[84] Jefferson had proposed a new state constitution with a unique mechanism for change. He suggested that a convention should be called to alter the constitution upon the mandate of a two-thirds vote of the members of any two branches of government. In this way, Jefferson supposed, any one branch of government could be prevented from arrogating power to itself and thus overstepping its bounds. While Madison was doubtless sympathetic to this objective, *Federalist* No. 49 shows his clear disapproval of Jefferson's suggested means of carrying it into effect. Hence, having agreed with Jefferson that "a constitutional road to the decision of the people ought to be marked out and kept open, for certain great and extraordinary occasions," Madison went on to argue that there were "insuperable objections" to Jefferson's specific proposal.[85]

Altogether, Madison raised four objections. First, from a practical vantage point, Madison argued that Jefferson's proposal might lead to the collusion of two governmental departments against a third.[86] Second, Madison argued that frequent appeals to the people could have a destabilizing effect on government. Frequent constitutional conventions could become more important for what they came to symbolize in the public mind than for the good they might accomplish.

As every appeal to the people would carry an implication of some defect in the government, frequent appeals would, in a great measure, deprive the government of that veneration which time bestows on every thing, and without which perhaps the wisest and freest governments would not possess the requisite stability.[87]

While a "nation of philosophers" might find itself attached to a constitution by reason alone, absent such a utopia, "the most rational government will not find it a superfluous advantage to have the prejudices of the community on its side."[88]

Madison's third objection to Jefferson's proposal was similar to his second. In stressing "the danger of disturbing the public tranquillity by interesting too strongly the public passions," Madison sought to contrast the formation of existing state constitutions during a time of patriotism to occasions of possible future tumults.[89]

Raising a fourth objection to Jefferson's proposal, Madison argued that legislators, being more numerous and closer to the people, would probably have inordinate influence in calling and influencing conventions. Thus, a proposal designed to curb the excesses of arrogated power by one branch over another could contribute to this very excess allowing "the *passions*, therefore, not the *reason*" to "sit in judgment."[90]

In *Federalist* No. 50, Madison focused on reasons for rejecting a Council of Censors, like that in Pennsylvania, whereby conventions were called for "*enforcing*" rather than necessarily "*altering*" the constitution.[91] Madison saw such conventions impaled on one or another horn of a dilemma. If the periodic reviews were too far apart, he argued, the prospect of future review would be insufficient to deter governmental abuses. If, on the other hand, reviews were too frequent, each such review would be associated with the passions of the moment.

Madison sought to clinch this argument by raising five specific criticisms of the system as it had operated in Pennsylvania. Thus, he argued that: (1) members of the Council had earlier participated in the actions they were convened to judge; (2) some council members had previously served as "active and influential members of the legislative and executive branches, within the period to be reviewed, and even patrons or opponents of the very measures to be thus brought to the test of the constitution";[92] (3) the council split into factions productive of "*passion*" rather than "*reason*";[93] (4) the council misconstrued governmental powers; and (5) the Council's decisions went unheeded.[94] Madison thus concluded that the Pennsylvania experience proved "at the same time, by its researches, the existence of the disease, and by its example, the inefficacy of the remedy."[95]

One of the best known of the *Federalist Papers* is the subsequent essay, No. 51, with its frank assessment of human nature and its discussion of the need for a system of checks and balances. Rarely, however, has the discussion of this essay been tied to the arguments of the two essays that preceded it. It was, however, because of the dangers and inadequacies of the periodic revision and review mechanisms proposed by Jefferson and practiced in Pennsylvania that Madison was able to argue so convincingly in *Federalist* No. 51 for "so contriving the interior structure of government as that its several constituent parts, may, by their mutual relations, be the means of keeping each other in their proper places."[96] While the amending mechanism of Article V would stand as a last resort in this and other matters, it was clear that Madison hoped that most problems would not require so drastic a remedy. Structural prevention was to be preferred to constitutional cure.

Federalism and the Amending Process

Defense of the amending process was inevitably tied to description. Among the questions that proponents of the new Constitution faced was what kind of government it had produced. Was the new Constitution federal, like the Articles of Confederation, or was it national, like the government in England?

Madison took a middle ground in essay No. 39, now advocating a position that he had opposed at the Convention.[97] Arguing that the new system was "neither wholly *national* nor wholly *federal*," but a combination of both,[98] Madison argued that this combination was especially evident in the amending process.

In requiring more than a majority, and particularly in computing the proportion by *States*, not by *citizens*, it departs from the *national* and advances towards the *federal* character; in rendering the concurrence of less than the whole number of states sufficient, it loses again the *federal* and partakes of the *national* character.[99]

This explanation would be clearly counter to the explanation of the amending process that John C. Calhoun would later advance, as well as to a recent proposal that amendments be proposed and/or ratified by mere majority vote.[100]

Federalist No. 10, while not directly concerned with the amending process, further illuminates the nature of this procedure. In expressing his concern with the problem of factions, Madison argued that, while factions could not be eliminated, their effects could nonetheless be controlled by representative government spread out over a large land area.[101] Madison was anxious to control factions because of their association with party spirit and passion and because of the dangers they posed to personal liberties. Since a central aim of the new Constitution was to preserve such liberties, it was essential that the document, even more than ordinary legislation, contain built-in guards against factions.[102] Certainly this concern helps explain the requirements in Article V for a two-thirds vote by both houses of Congress and for ratification by three-fourths of the states.

To carry this analysis further, the Founders had every reason to fear factions occasioned by sectional splits. Indeed, at the Convention, Madison had predicted that the split between the North and the South would be a more likely source of future controversy than would the controversy between large and small states which so engaged the Philadelphia delegates.[103] Given the recognition of such controversy and the desire to tame it, the Framers were willing to permit occasional frustrations of majority will incident to this end. Martin Diamond, an astute reader of *The Federalist Papers*, made such a point by arguing that the numerical requirements in Article V were there to assure "nationally distributed majorities."[104] Pointing to the way that the requirements in Article V would allay fears of the small states about domination by their neighbors, Diamond thus noted that in "harkening back to the 'multiplicity of interests,' it was also hoped that a national distributed majority, engaged in the solemn process of constitutional amendment, would favor only necessary and useful amendments."[105]

Arguments That the Bill of Rights Could Wait

Hamilton wrote the concluding essay, No. 85, of *The Federalist Papers*. It is significant that he devoted a large part of this essay to convincing Anti-Federalists that they could wait until after the Constitution was adopted to obtain the Bill of Rights that they desired. Another scholar has noted that Hamilton thus gave less attention to the moderation of the amending process, preferring to paint it as completely efficacious for any reasonable measure the Anti-Federalists wanted.

When Madison wrote *Federalist* No. 43, he was satisfied to expound Article V and to find in it 'every mark of propriety'; but by the time Hamilton was ready to compose No. 85, which would serve as the peroration and ultimate epitome of the whole federalist case in New York, he found himself compelled to endow Article V with supreme practical importance. He took Article V out of its modest position, burnished it until it fairly shone, and displayed it to America as an incomparably easy and expeditious arrangement for the remedying of errors, compared to which an attempt to improve the instrument before it was ratified would be desperately difficult, inept, and divisive.[106]

Since this same strategy was followed more generally by Federalists in the state ratifying conventions, Hamilton's arguments deserve special scrutiny.

Hamilton began modestly. He and other advocates of the Constitution were willing to admit that it was not perfect, but they denied that it should be perfected by amendment before being ratified. Here Hamilton argued, much as Madison had in *Federalist* Nos. 49 and 50, against the likelihood "of assembling a new convention, under circumstances in any degree so favorable to a happy issue, as those in which the late convention met, deliberated, and concluded."[107] Having so discounted a new convention, Hamilton argued that "it will be far more easy to obtain subsequent than previous amendments to the Constitution."[108] His argument was based on the fact that amendments adopted prior to constitutional ratification would require approval by all of the states whereas, once the new constitution went into effect, only ten states had to give their consent. Moreover, if each state hedged the Constitution with reservations, the number of constitutional particulars would become so great that any ratification would be unlikely. By contrast, if, after ratification of the Constitution, amendments were introduced one at a time, each could be considered without the need for compromise and would become effective with the consent of ten of the states.

Opponents of the new Constitution had argued, however, "that the persons delegated to the administration of the national government will always be disinclined to yield up any portion of the authority of which they were once possessed."[109] Hamilton offered five responses to this objection. First, using language that suggests that Hamilton still hoped to avoid adoption of a bill of rights, he doubted that future amendments would find it necessary to take away governmental powers, being more likely to deal with "the organization of government" than with "the mass of its powers."[110] Second, Hamilton foresaw, much in line with the theme of *Federalist* No. 10, that the very diversity of a nation of thirteen states would bring forth from its leaders "a spirit of accommodation to the reasonable expectations of their constituents."[111] Third, in a comment highly relevant to current discussions over the convention option, Hamilton argued that, if the convention mechanism were to be utilized, Congress would have no discretion about calling such a convention, since "the words of this article are peremptory. The Congress 'shall call a convention.' Nothing in this particular is left to the discretion of that body."[112] Fourth, admitting the difficulty of rallying the number of states for "amendments which may affect local interests," he argued that there would be no such problem enacting amendments "on points which are merely relative to the general liberty or security of the people."[113] Making a virtue of the state powers he had so opposed at the Convention,[114] Hamilton sought to assuage the Anti-Federalists' states' rights fears with the argument that "we may safely rely on the disposition of the state legislatures to erect barriers against the encroachments of the national authority."[115]

Having so argued, Hamilton classified his plea for adoption of the Constitution prior to amendment as a "political truth" capable of withstanding "the test of a mathematical demonstration."[116] Presumably, Hamilton here meant to point to the universally recognized fact that the number thirteen was larger than the number ten. In any case, Hamilton went on to quote Hume to the effect that all constitutions "*inevitably*" contain mistakes that are only correctable with time.[117] Such a fact counseled moderation, argued Hamilton, for delay in ratification of the new Constitution could lead to "anarchy, civil war, a perpetual alienation of the states from each other, and perhaps the military despotism of a victorious demagogue."[118] The spectacle of constitutional deliberations in a time of peace was an extraordinary one, Hamilton wrote, and granted this arduous exertion and the consent of seven states already, the Constitution's adoption should not be further delayed. Such delay, Hamilton warned in his closing words, could lead to the dominance of those "POWERFUL INDIVIDUALS, in this and in other States," who "are enemies to a general national government in every possible shape."[119]

CONCLUSION

Publius and other defenders of the new Constitution thus argued simultaneously for the efficacy and safety of the constitutional amending process. As they envisioned and defended this proposal, it was a moderate one, embodying a judicious compromise between making the Constitution too flexible and making it too immutable. Moreover, the process recognized the complexities involved in the nature of the new Union. Use of such a process was preferable both to future wholesale revision and to delay which might further disrupt the political system. Such arguments helped to side-track a second convention and thus assured that the results of the first convention would be given a fair chance. The ratification of the Bill of Rights in 1791 must have gone far toward confirming in the popular mind the accuracy of Publius's description of the amending power as an adequate but moderate mechanism fully capable of remedying any perceived defects in the nation's new charter of government.

NOTES

1. Donald S. Lutz, *The Origins of American Constitutionalism* (Baton Rouge: Louisiana State University Press, 1988).
2. See Carl L. Becker, *The Declaration of Independence* (New York: Vintage Books, 1970), p. 103.
3. Roger J. Traynor, *The Amending System of the United States Constitution, An Historical and Legal Analysis* (Ph.D. diss., University of California, January 1927), pp. 8–9.
4. Garry Wills thus notes:

> Americans were willing to call their actions revolution precisely *because* it was an orderly and legal procedure. The first English meaning of "revolution" had been astronomical—the revolving of the heavens, an exchange of planetary positions; or the "period" (which is simply "revolution" in Greek) covered by such alterations.

Wills, *Inventing America: Jefferson's Declaration of Independence* (Garden City, NY: Doubleday, 1978), p. 51.
5. Martin Diamond, "The Revolution of Sober Expectations," in *America's Continuing Revolution* (Garden City, NY: Anchor Press, 1976), pp. 23–40. But see J. Franklin Jameson, *The American Revolution Considered as a Social Movement* (Princeton, NJ: Princeton University Press, 1967).
6. Traynor, *The Amending System*, p. 45, citing B. P. Poore, *The Federal and State Constitutions, Colonial Charters and Other Organic Laws of the United States*, vol. 1, p. 817.
7. Ibid., p. 46.
8. Walter F. Dodd, *The Revision and Amendment of State Constitutions* (Baltimore, MD: Johns Hopkins University Press, 1910), notes that the development of "independent machinery for the framing of state constitutions" proceeded in three steps:

> (1) The establishment of the distinction between the constitution and ordinary legislation, and the development of a distinct method for the formation of constitutions. (2) The development of the constitutional convention as a body distinct and separate from the regular legislature. (3) The submission of a constitution to a vote of the people, after it has been framed by a constitutional

convention. The first step is fundamental; the other two involve but the elaboration of machinery to carry out more clearly the distinction between constitutions and ordinary legislation. (pp. 21–22)

9. Ibid., p. 3.

10. Dodd points out that the constitutions of South Carolina and New Jersey had similar origins. Ibid., p. 24.

11. Ibid., pp. 24–25.

12. Traynor, *The Amending System*, pp. 61–62.

13. See Merrill Jensen, *The Articles of Confederation* (Madison: University of Wisconsin Press, 1966).

14. See Alpheus Thomas Mason and Gordon E. Baker, *Free Government in the Making: Readings in American Political Thought*, 4th ed. (New York: Oxford University Press, 1985), p. 133.

15. Winton Solberg, *The Federal Convention and the Formation of the Union of the American States* (Indianapolis: Bobbs-Merrill, 1958), p. 42.

16. Ibid., p. 49.

17. Ibid., p. 51. This provision makes an interesting contrast to the provision (Article XII) of Benjamin Franklin's proposal for confederation written on or before July 21, 1775:

> As all new Institutions may have Imperfections which only Time and Experience can discover, it is agreed, that the General Congress from time to time shall propose such Amendment of the Constitution as may be found necessary; which being approved by a Majority of the Colony Assemblies, shall be equally binding with the rest of the Articles of Confederation.

See *The Papers of Benjamin Franklin*, ed. William B. Willcox (New Haven, CT: Yale University Press, 1982), vol. 22, p. 125.

18. Max Farrand, *The Records of the Federal Convention of 1787* (New Haven, CT: Yale University Press, 1966), vol. 3, p. 120, citing Charles Pinckney.

19. On February 21, 1787, Congress thus adopted the following resolution:

> *Resolved* that in the opinion of Congress it is expedient that on the second Monday in May next a Convention of delegates who shall have been appointed by the several states be held at Philadelphia for the sole and express purpose of revising the Articles of Confederation and reporting to Congress and the several legislatures such alterations and provisions therein as shall, when agreed to in Congress and confirmed by the states render the federal constitution adequate to the exigencies of Government and the preservation of the Union. (Ibid., p. 64.)

20. See Article VII of the U.S. Constitution. For the extralegal, or illegal, aspects of the U.S. Constitutional Convention, see Richard S. Kay, "The Illegality of the Constitution," *Constitutional Commentary* 4 (Winter, 1987), pp. 57–80.

21. Farrand, *The Records of the Federal Convention*, vol. 1, p. 22.

22. Ibid., p. 30.

23. Ibid., p. 22.

24. Ibid., p. 121. The author is uncertain whether Pinckney was doubting the

necessity of an amending power or merely questioning the provision that made legislative consent to amendments unnecessary.

25. Ibid., p. 122.

26. Ibid., p. 202.

27. Ibid., p. 203.

28. Ibid., p. 242.

29. Ibid., p. 246.

30. Though later repeated by Madison in *The Federalist*, these words were uttered at the Convention by Judge Ellsworth. See Farrand, *The Records of the Federal Convention*, vol. 1, p. 474.

31. Farrand, The Records of the Federal Convention, vol. 1, p. 476. Also see p. 478.

32. Ibid., vol. 2, p. 159.

33. Ibid., p. 468.

34. Ibid., pp. 557–58.

35. Ibid., p. 558.

36. Ibid.

37. Ibid.

38. Paul J. Weber and Barbara A. Perry, *Unfounded Fears: Myths and Realities of a Constitutional Convention* (New York: Praeger, 1989), p. 35.

39. Farrand, *The Records of the Federal Convention*, vol. 2, pp. 558–59.

40. Ibid., p. 559.

41. Ibid.

42. Ibid., p. 629.

43. Ibid.

44. Ibid.

45. Ibid.

46. Ibid., p. 630.

47. Ibid.

48. Ibid., p. 631.

49. Ibid.

50. Ibid.

51. For a state-by-state account, see Michael A. Gillespie and Michael Lienesch, eds., *Ratifying the Constitution* (Lawrence: University Press of Kansas, 1989). For a helpful account of the Federalist/Anti-Federalist debates that focus less on specifically what the proponents of these views said about the amending process and more on what each had to say about the relationship between constitutions and social change, see Philip S. Hamburger, "The Constitution's Accommodation of Social Change," *Michigan Law Review* 88 (November 1989), pp. 239–327, especially pp. 265–99.

52. Jonathan Elliott, *The Debates in State Conventions on the Adoption of the Federal Constitution* (New York: Burt Franklin, 1888), vol. 2, p. 116.

53. Ibid.

54. Ibid., vol. 4, p. 177.

55. Catherine Drinker Bowen, *Miracle at Philadelphia* (Boston: Little, Brown, 1966), p. 18.

56. Elliott, *Debates*, vol. 3, p. 49.

57. Ibid., pp. 49–50.

58. Ibid., p. 50.

59. Ibid., vol. 2, p. 199. Also see Madison's specific critique of Henry on this same point, in Elliott, *Debates*, vol. 3, pp. 88–89.

60. See Jack N. Rakove, "Inspired Expedient," *Constitution* 3 (Winter 1991), pp. 19–25.

61. The best treatment of this movement is still Edward P. Smith, "The Movement Towards a Second Constitutional Convention in 1788," *Essays in the Constitutional History of the United States in the Formative Period, 1775–1789*, ed. John F. Jameson (Boston: Houghton, Mifflin, 1909), pp. 49–115.

62. See Weber and Perry, *Unfounded Fears*, pp. 37–40.

63. Madison's objections are analyzed in ibid., pp. 46–48. Also see Paul Finkelman, "James Madison and the Bill of Rights: A Reluctant Paternity," *1990 Supreme Court Review*, ed. Gerhard Casper, Dennis P. Hutchinson, and David A. Strauss (Chicago: University of Chicago Press, 1991), pp. 325–37.

64. Quoted in Weber and Perry, *Unfounded Fears*, p. 47.

65. Alexander Hamilton, James Madison, and John Jay, *The Federalist Papers*, ed. Clinton Rossiter (New York: New American Library, 1961).

66. Ibid., p. 233.

67. Ibid., p. 235.

68. Ibid., p. 237.

69. Farrand, *Records of the Federal Convention*, vol. 2, pp. 641–43.

70. Hamilton, Madison, and Jay, *The Federalist Papers*, p. 248, quoting the congressional authorizing resolution.

71. Ibid., p. 251.

72. Ibid.

73. Ibid. Madison is making a reference to Rhode Island, which had refused to send delegates to Philadelphia. The Founders sometimes uncharitably referred to this state as "Rogues Island." See John P. Roche, "The Founding Fathers: A Reform Caucus in Action," *The American Political Science Review* 55 (1961), p. 813.

74. Hamilton, Madison, and Jay, *The Federalist Papers*, p. 252.

75. For development of this unique mechanism, see Gordon S. Wood, *The Creation of the American Republic, 1776–1787* (New York: W. W. Norton, 1969), pp. 303–43. Also see Bruce Ackerman, *We the People: Foundations* (Cambridge, MA: Belknap Press, 1991), pp. 174–75. Ackerman's comments on *The Federalist* and constitutional change (pp. 165–99) are particularly illuminating.

76. Hamilton, Madison, and Jay, *The Federalist Papers*, p. 254.

77. Ibid., p. 278.

78. Ibid.

79. Ibid.

80. Ibid., pp. 278–9.

81. Ibid., p. 279.

82. For a modern edition, see Thomas Jefferson, *Notes on the State of Virginia* (New York: Harper & Row, 1964).

83. Ibid., p. 115.

84. Ibid., p. 124.

85. Hamilton, Madison, and Jay, *The Federalist Papers*, p. 314. For reflections on Madison's arguments, see Sanford Levinson, " 'Veneration' and Constitutional Change: James Madison Confronts the Possibility of Constitutional Amendment," *Texas Tech Law Review* 21 (1990), pp. 2443–61.

86. Hamilton, Madison, and Jay, *The Federalist Papers*, p. 314.
87. Ibid.
88. Ibid., p. 315.
89. Ibid.
90. Ibid., p. 317.
91. Ibid. For the best historical treatment of the Council of Censors, see Lewis A. Meador, "The Council of Censors," *The Pennsylvania Magazine of History and Biography* 22 (1898), pp. 265–300.
92. Hamilton, Madison, and Jay, *The Federalist Papers*, p. 319.
93. Ibid.
94. Ibid., pp. 319–20.
95. Ibid., p. 320.
96. Ibid.
97. Farrand, *Records of the Federal Convention*, vol. 1, p. 476.
98. Hamilton, Madison, and Jay, *The Federalist Papers*, p. 246.
99. Ibid.
100. Calhoun's views are treated in Chapter 5 of this book. For the referendum proposal, see Akil R. Amar, "Philadelphia Revisited: Amending the Constitution Outside Article V," *The University of Chicago Law Review* 55 (1988), pp. 1043–1104.
101. This view contrasted with the dominant Anti-Federalist belief that republican government was impossible in a large land area. See Herbert J. Storing, *What the Anti-Federalists Were For* (Chicago: University of Chicago Press, 1981), pp. 15–23.
102. In *Federalist* No. 78, Hamilton acknowledged "the right of the people to alter or abolish the established Constitution whenever they find it inconsistent with their happiness," but he proceeded to justify the exercise of judicial review on the basis that, "until the people have, by some solemn and authoritative act, annulled or changed the established form, it is binding upon themselves collectively, as well as individually." See Hamilton, Madison, and Jay, *The Federalist Papers*, 469–70.
103. Farrand, *Records of the Federal Convention*, vol. 1, p. 476.
104. Martin Diamond, Winston Fisk, and Herbert Garfinkel, *The Democratic Republic: An Introduction to American National Government* (Chicago: Rand McNally, 1966), p. 98.
105. Ibid.
106. Edmond Cahn, "An American Contribution," *Supreme Court and Supreme Law*, ed. Edmond Cahn (New York, 1971), p. 11.
107. Hamilton, Madison, and Jay, *The Federalist Papers*, p. 524.
108. Ibid.
109. Ibid., p. 525.
110. Ibid.
111. Ibid.
112. Ibid., p. 526.
113. Ibid.
114. Farrand, *Records of the Federal Convention*, vol. 1, pp. 304–11.
115. Hamilton, Madison, and Jay, *The Federalist Papers*, p. 526.
116. Ibid.
117. Ibid.
118. Ibid., p. 527.
119. Ibid.

Chapter 3

George Washington, the Constitutional Amending Process, and the Farewell Address

Scholars of American political thought more frequently turn to writings of Adams, Jefferson, Hamilton, and Madison than to pronouncements by the nation's first president who is more recognized for his practical statesmanship and for his role as a national symbol[1] than for his political theory.[2] Because his role as military leader during the Revolutionary War and as first president gave him a unique vantage point, and because Washington cannot as readily be identified with one or another philosophical school of thought, however, his statements on the Constitution are especially important. His Farewell Address is one of his best known speeches on the subject.

THE FAREWELL ADDRESS AND THE AMENDING PROCESS

In this address, Washington announced that he would not seek a third term, attempted to promote national unity, and tried to secure his reputation for public spiritedness and patriotism.[3] The best known parts of this speech reveal Washington's negative views on political parties,[4] his regard for the public benefits of religion and morality,[5] and his concern about entangling European alliances.[6] At least three recent commentators have also cited Washington's comments in this speech on the constitutional amending process.[7]

Three critical passages in the Farewell Address treat this process. The first is from that part of the speech extolling the Union and urging for its support. Having lauded the people for improving the Articles of Confederation, Washington cited the amending process as reason for continuing loyalty to this new government.

This Government . . . containing within itself a provision for its own amendment, has a just claim to your confidence and your support. Respect for its authority, compliance with its laws, acquiescence in its measures, are duties enjoined by the fundamental maxims of true liberty. The basis of our political systems is the right of the people to make and to alter their constitution of government. But the constitution which at any time exists till changed by an explicit and authentic act of the whole people is sacredly obligatory upon all.[8]

Washington's second mention of the amending process came amid warnings against party strife. Cautioning against "innovation" in the principles of government, Washington advised that "one method of assault may be to effect in the forms of the Constitution alterations which will impair the energy of the system, and thus to undermine what cannot be directly overthrown."[9] Washington warned against premature changes.

In all the changes to which you may be invited remember that time and habit are at least as necessary to fix the true character of governments as of other human institutions; that experience is the surest standard by which to test the real tendency of the existing constitution of a country; that facility in changes upon the credit of mere hypothesis and opinion exposes to perpetual change, from the endless variety of hypothesis and opinion.[10]

Several paragraphs later, Washington praised the system of checks and balances and warned again against encroachments by departments of government on one another.

If in the opinion of the people the distribution or modification of the constitutional powers be in any particular wrong, let it be corrected by an amendment in the way the Constitution designates. But let there be no change by usurpation; for though this in one instance may be the instrument of good, it is the customary weapon by which free governments are destroyed.[11]

WASHINGTON'S BROADER VIEWS OF THE AMENDING PROCESS

Washington's correspondence evidenced several themes that illuminate his praise of the amending process in his Farewell Address. A major theme was Washington's belief that the new Constitution, while imperfect, was a significant improvement over the Articles of Confederation. Washington had so recognized the faults of the Articles that he proved willing, albeit with great hesitation, to risk his reputation on extralegal, if not illegal means, to change it.[12] Washington served as president of the Constitutional Convention and is generally credited with having an important influence on its deliberations and ratification. At Convention's end, Washington observed in a letter to Charles Carter that: "I am not a blind admirer (for I saw the imperfections) of the Constitution to which I have assisted to give birth, but I am fully persuaded it is the best that can be obtained at *this* day and that it or disunion is before us."[13] Similarly, in a letter to Governor Randolph, Washington acknowledged:

There are some things in the new form, I will readily acknowledge, wch. [*sic*] never did, and I am persuaded never will, obtain my *cordial* approbation; but I then did conceive, and do now most firmly believe, that, in the aggregate, it is the best Constitution that can be obtained at this Epocha, and that this, or a dissolution of the Union awaits our choice, and are the only alternatives before us.[14]

So viewing the options, Washington praised the new amending process for providing greater flexibility than the mechanism in the Articles.[15] Like other proponents of the new Constitution, Washington saw the new amending process as a way of perfecting the document.[16] A modern scholar correctly identifies Washington's central analogy as that of a "constitutional door" that would be kept open to amendments.[17]

Writing to Lafayette, Washington shared the faith of his enlightened contemporaries that progress was possible and that the amending process would allow the fruits of progress to be added peacefully to the Constitution.[18]

We are not to expect perfection in this world; but mankind, in modern times, have apparently made some progress in the science of government. Should that which is now offered to the People of America, be found on experiment less perfect than it can be made, a Constitutional door is left open for its amelioration.[19]

Washington expressed similar sentiments in a letter to Bushrod Washington.

The warmest friends and the best supporters the Constitution has, do not contend that it is free from imperfections; but they found them unavoidable and are sensible, if evil is likely to arise there from, the remedy must come hereafter; for in the present moment, it is not to be obtained; and, as there is a Constitutional door open for it, I think the People (for it is with them to Judge) can as they will have the advantage of experience on their Side, decide with as much propriety on the alterations and amendments which are necessary [as] ourselves.[20]

If progress were possible, change for the sake of change was to be avoided. Writing to James McHenry, Washington echoed sentiments similar to Madison's and to those of earlier theorists like Plato, Aristotle, and St. Thomas Aquinas which were examined in the first chapter of this book.[21] Provision needed to be made "for effecting such explanations and amendments as might be really proper and generally satisfactory; without producing or at least fostering such a spirit of innovation as will overturn the whole system."[22]

Washington opposed making amendments a precondition to constitutional ratification or calling a second convention prior to ratifying the work of the first.[23] Writing to Lafayette, Washington argued that "if that acceptance shall not previously take place, men's minds will be so much agitated and soured, that the danger will be greater than ever of our becoming a disunited People."[24] Similarly, Washington wrote to John Armstrong on April 25, 1788:

That the proposed Constitution will admit of amendments is acknowledged by its warmest advocates; but to make such amendments as may be proposed by the several States the condition of its adoption would, in my opinion amount to a complete rejection of it; for upon examination of the objections, which are made by the opponents in different States and the amendments which have been proposed, it will be found that what would be a favorite object of one State, is the very thing which is strenuously opposed by another.[25]

Moreover, in a proposed address to Congress, Washington echoed Hamilton's arguments[26] that it would be easier for three-fourths of the states to amend the Constitution once ratified than to achieve the unanimity required under the Articles of Confederation before such ratification.[27]

Once the Constitution was ratified, Washington was pleased that its former opponents were ready "to co-operate" and to "content themselves with asking amendments in the manner prescribed by the Constitution."[28] In his inaugural address, he offered moderate counsel.

For I assure myself that whilst you carefully avoid every alteration which might endanger the benefits of an United and effective Government, or which ought to await the future lessons of experience; a reverence for the characteristic rights of freemen, and a regard for the public harmony, will sufficiently influence your deliberations on the question how far the former can be more impregnably fortified, or the latter be safely and advantageously promoted.[29]

Similarly, in corresponding with James Madison,[30] Washington observed in May 1789:

I see nothing exceptionable in the proposed amendments. Some of them, in my opinion, are importantly necessary, others, though in themselves (in my conception) not very essential, are necessary to quiet the fears of some respectable characters and well meaning Men. Upon the whole, therefore, not foreseeing any evil consequences that can result from their adoption, they have my wishes for a favourable reception in both houses.[31]

To the time of his Farewell Address, then, Washington expressed faith in the amending process as a peaceful means of change that would remedy perceived governmental defects, calm public misgivings, and help ensure the success and progress of the constitutional "experiment."[32]

THE WRITING OF THE FAREWELL ADDRESS

The Farewell Address appears to develop new themes, namely, fear that novel practices might subvert the true spirit of the Constitution and that innovations in constitutional structures might be adopted short of constitutional amendment. Such concerns are illuminated by examining the writing of the Farewell Address.

Washington considered retiring at the end of his first term in office in 1793, and he contacted James Madison in May 1792 to help him announce his intention. Working from a list of "thoughts & requests" that Washington submitted,[33] Madison drafted a speech which he sent to Washington on June 20.[34] After pleas from numerous friends, Washington successfully ran for reelection.[35]

During his second term, Washington once more determined to retire. Accordingly, on May 15, 1796, Washington sent Alexander Hamilton a draft of the speech he had composed with reliance on Madison's earlier draft,[36] asking Hamilton to revise or recast the speech as he thought better. Hamilton drew up an abstract of Washington's draft and wrote a new speech which he returned to Washington on July 30.[37] Less interested in revising Washington's original speech,[38] Hamilton sent this additional draft on August 10.[39] By August 25, Washington had settled on Hamilton's complete revision, which he reworked. This corrected speech, dated nine years from the signing of the Constitution, was first published in a Philadelphia newspaper and quickly copied by others.[40] The author of the most complete account of the Farewell Address summarizes:

The final manuscript of the Farewell Address, used as printer's copy, was deduced from Washington's own first draft, embodying in part Madison's draft; Hamilton's major draft and its subsequent amendments, Hamilton's other draft for incorporating, and Washington's own changes made in process to the very end before its publication.[41]

The address was clearly Washington's own.

In the last analysis he was his own editor; and the Farewell Address, in the final form for publication, was *all* in his own handwriting. It was then in content and form what *he* had chosen to make it by processes of adoption and adaptation in fulfillment of what *he* desired. By this procedure every idea became his own without equivocation.[42]

ANALYZING THE FAREWELL ADDRESS

Attention to the steps of composition of the Farewell Address helps to ascertain when various ideas were added to the speech. In his letter to Madison of May 20, 1792, Washington included the following sentiments:

That the established government being the work of our own hands, with the seeds of amendment engrafted in the Constitution, may by wisdom, good dispositions, and mutual allowances; aided by experience, bring it as near to perfection as any human institution ever approximated; and therefore, the only strife among us ought to be, who should be foremost in facilitating & finally accomplishing such great & desirable objects; by giving every possible support, & cement to the Union.[43]

Madison's and Washington's first drafts incorporated these thoughts.[44] Washington also added the words, "that the several departments of Government may be preserved in their utmost Constitutional purity, without any attempt of the one to encroach on the rights or privileges of another."[45]

In Hamilton's draft of 1796, the latter sentiments began to find fuller expression.

It is important likewise that the habits of thinking of the people should tend to produce caution in their agents in the several departments of Government, to retain each within its proper sphere and not to permit one to encroach upon another— that every attempt of the kind from whatever quarter should meet with the discountenance (reprobation) of the community, and that in every case in which a precedent of encroachment shall have been given, a corrective be sought in a careful attention to the choice (election) of public Agents.[46]

A bit later, Hamilton continued:

Let there be no change by usurpation, for thought this may be the instrument of good in one instance, it is the ordinary and natural instrument of the destruction (death) of free Government—and the influence of the precedent is always infinitely more pernicious that [sic] any thing which it may atchieve [sic] can be beneficial.[47]

In the Farewell Address, Washington expanded the warning against departmental incursions and further advised changing the Constitution by amendment rather than by mere usage. Stephen Markman believes that Washington was warning against judicial usurpation.[48] It is certainly true that John Marshall would later see broad constitutional constructions as desirable alternatives to constant textual changes or to future conventions.[49] Thus noting in *Marbury v. Madison* that the people "have an original right to establish for their future government, such principles as, in their opinion, shall most conduce to their own happiness," Marshall proceeded to say that, "the exercise of this original right is a very great exertion, nor can it,

nor ought it, to be frequently repeated."[50] Similarly, in denying the appl-
icability of the Bill of Rights to the states in *Barron v. Baltimore* (and thus
effectively limiting the role of the Supreme Court on the basis that its
judgments were so difficult to overturn), Marshall would describe the
amending process in Article V as "unwieldy and cumbrous machinery."[51]
When written, however, Washington's words almost surely were not directed to the Supreme Court. The Court was then still in its infancy, its
first Chief Justice, John Jay, having resigned to run for governor of New
York and John Marshall not assuming his position on the Court for another
five years.[52]

Washington's concern with encroachments is better traced to events in
his second administration, when the main focus was foreign policy, and
especially the Jay Treaty.[53] After the treaty had been approved by the Senate
by the bare two-thirds majority required and signed by the president, the
House attempted to stymie it through its appropriations process.[54] A commentator notes that Washington "saw the entire Constitution 'brought to
the brink of a precipice' " over this controversy,[55] and convincingly traces
Washington's words in the Farewell Address to this cause.

However, the first wish—an admonition to extinguish or, at least, moderate party
disputes—and the last—a council to maintain the constitutional delimitations of
powers—were inspired by developments in the area of foreign policy, by the bit-
terness of party differences revealed in the debate over the Jay Treaty, and by the
attempts of the House to have a part in the making of treaties.[56]

SUMMARY

Washington expressed clear views on the amending process, which illuminated more widely held sentiments of his day. His words testified to
the Founders' pride in the Constitution and its provision for peaceful change
and progress. Valuing precedents and "habits," Washington opposed pre-
cipitous change, but he accepted changes based upon experience. Always,
he thought, a constitutional door should be left open, and branches should
respect one another's prerogatives. As a former military leader, Washington
hoped that future revolutions could be written with ink rather than blood,
and, to a large extent, these wishes have come true.[57]

Contemporary scholars would undoubtedly be more divided about the
extent to which Washington's warnings against encroachments of governmental branches on one another have been heeded. Certainly, the specific
treaty-making issue that Washington desired to address does not recur often,
but perhaps because it so directly addresses constitutional issues, decisions
by the judicial branch are often criticized along these lines. It is, however,
interesting that, in all American history, only four Supreme Court decisions

have been reversed,[58] and, while the balance between state and national authority has been altered, especially in the aftermath of the Civil War, few amendments seem even indirectly relevant to the balance of power among the three branches of the national government.

NOTES

1. See Barry Schwartz, *George Washington: The Making of an American Symbol* (New York: Free Press, 1987), and Garry Wills, *Cincinnatus: George Washington and the Enlightenment* (Garden City, NY: Doubleday, 1984).

2. The author thus finds no writings by George Washington in a number of American political thought texts. See Michael B. Levy, *Political Thought in America: An Anthology* (Homewood, IL: Dorsey Press, 1982); Kenneth M. Dolbeare, *American Political Thought* (Monterey, CA: Duxbury Press, 1981); and Morton J. Frisch and Richard G. Stevens, eds., *American Political Thought: The Philosophic Dimension of American Statesmanship* (Dubuque, IA: Kendall/Hunt, 1976). There is a single letter of Washington's in the more comprehensive book by Alpheus T. Mason and Gordon E. Baker, *Free Government in the Making*, 4th ed. (New York: Oxford University Press, 1985), pp. 148–51.

For a good article on Washington's political thought, see Harold W. Bradley, "The Political Thinking of George Washington," *The Journal of Southern History* 11 (November 1945): pp. 469–86. Also see Roger Karz, "The Original Washington," *PS: Political Science and Politics* 24 (December 1991), pp. 705–6.

3. The partisan elements of Washington's Farewell Address, while clear to many contemporaries, were nonetheless concealed by the rhetoric of opposition to parties. See Jeffrey K. Tulis, *The Rhetorical Presidency* (Princeton, NJ: Princeton University Press, 1987), p. 68, and John E. Ferling, *The First of Men: A Life of George Washington* (Knoxville: The University of Tennessee Press, 1988), pp. 469–70.

4. For Washington's advice, see "The Farewell Address of September 17, 1796," *Washington's Farewell Address: The View From the 20th Century*, ed. Burton I. Kaufman (Chicago: Quadrangle Books, 1969), pp. 23–24. Washington was arguably better at giving such advice than at following it. Joseph Charles thus notes, "As parties began to form and opinion became more and more divided, people naturally consorted more with their own kind than before, but the more Washington followed this tendency, the more bitterly he denounced parties." See Charles's *The Origins of the American Party System* (Williamsburg, VA: The Institute of Early American History and Culture, 1956), p. 44. For further discussion of Washington's views of political parties with specific reference to his Farewell Address, see Richard Hofstader, *The Idea of a Party System: The Rise of Legitimate Opposition in the United States, 1780–1840* (Berkeley: University of California Press, 1972), pp. 91–102, and William N. Chambers, *Political Parties in a New Nation* (New York: Oxford University Press, 1963), pp. 6–7.

5. Washington, *Washington's Farewell Address*, p. 24.

6. Ibid., pp. 26–30. A number of interpretations of the Farewell Address, focusing almost exclusively on foreign policy concerns, are found in Kaufman's book. Also see Albert Weinbert, "Washington's 'Great Rule' in its Historical Evolution," *Historiography and Urbanization*, ed. Eric F. Goldman (Port Washington, NY: Ken-

nikat Press, 1941), pp. 109–38, and Felix Gilbert, *To the Farewell Address: Ideas of Early American Foreign Policy* (Princeton, NJ: Princeton University Press, 1961).

7. See John R. Vile, "American Views of the Constitutional Amending Process: An Intellectual History of Article V," *The American Journal of Legal History* 35 (January 1991), p. 52; George W. Nordham, "A Constitutional Door is Opened for Amendment," *Texas Bar Journal* 51 (September 1988), pp. 804–6; and Stephen J. Markman, "The Jurisprudence of Constitutional Amendments," *Still the Law of the Land?* ed. Joseph S. McNamara and Lissa Roche (Hillsdale, MI: Hillsdale College Press, 1987), p. 90.

8. Washington, *Washington's Farewell Address*, p. 21.

9. Ibid., p. 22.

10. Ibid.

11. Ibid., p. 24.

12. On this point, see Wills, *Cincinnatus*, pp. 151–72. On the more general issue, see Richard S. Kay, "The Illegality of the Constitution," *Constitutional Commentary* 4 (Winter 1987), pp. 57–80.

13. George Washington, *The Writings of George Washington*, ed. John C. Fitzpatrick (Washington, DC: U.S. Government Printing Office, 1931–44), vol. 29, p. 340. Letter is dated December 14, 1787.

14. Ibid., p. 358. Letter is dated January 8, 1788.

15. The mechanism for amendment outlined in Article XIII of the Articles required state unanimity whereas Article V of the new Constitution allows for adoption of amendments proposed by two-thirds of both houses of Congress and ratified by three-fourths of the states. See Vile, "American Views of the Constitutional Amending Process," pp. 47–48.

16. Edmond Cahn, "An American Contribution," *Supreme Court and Supreme Law*, ed. Edmond Cahn (New York: Simon & Schuster), pp. 10–12.

17. See Nordham, "A Constitutional Door is Opened for Amendment." For Washington's use of this analogy, see *The Writings of George Washington*, vol. 29, letter to Patrick Henry of September 24, 1787, p. 278; letter to Henry Knox of October 15, 1787, p. 289; letter to David Humphreys of October 20, 1787, p. 287; letter to Charles Carter of December 14, 1787, p. 340; letter to John Armstrong of April 25, 1788, p. 466; and letter to Richard Butler, April 3, 1788, p. 454.

A more prominent nineteenth-century analogy appears to have been the mechanical analogy of a safety valve. See Joseph Story, *Commentaries on the Constitution of the United States*, intro. Ronald D. Rotunda and John F. Nowak (Durham, NC: Carolina Academic Press, 1987), p. 680.

18. Bradley, "The Political Thinking of George Washington," pp. 482–83.

19. Washington, *The Writings*, vol. 29, p. 411. Letter is dated February 7, 1788.

20. Ibid., p. 311. Letter is dated November 10, 1787.

21. Alexander Hamilton, James Madison, and John Jay, *The Federalist Papers*, ed. Clinton Rossiter (New York: New American Library, 1961), p. 315. Madison's caution, and its contrast to Jefferson's greater willingness to risk constitutional and even violent change, is analyzed in John R. Vile, *Rewriting the United States Constitution: An Examination of Proposals From Reconstruction to the Present* (New York: Praeger, 1991), pp. 2–4. Also see Paul Weber, "Madison's Opposition to a Second Convention," *Polity* 20 (Spring 1989), pp. 498–517, and Adrienne Koch, *Jefferson*

and Madison: The Great Collaboration (London: Oxford University Press, 1964), pp. 62–96.

22. Washington, *The Writings*, vol. 30, p. 29, letter to James McHenry.

23. For an account of this movement, see Edward P. Smith, "The Movement Towards a Second Constitutional Convention in 1788," *Essays in the Constitutional History of the United States in the Formative Period, 1775–1789*, ed. John Franklin Jameson (Boston: Houghton, Mifflin, 1909). For Madison's views on this subject, see Weber, "Madison's Opposition to a Second Convention."

24. Washington, *The Writings*, vol. 29, p. 478. Letter is dated April 28, 1788.

25. Ibid., p. 465.

26. Hamilton, Madison, and Jay, *The Federalist Papers*, p. 524.

27. Washington, *The Writings*, vol. 30, p. 304.

28. Ibid., p. 41, letter to Charles Pettit dated August 16, 1788.

29. Ibid., p. 295. Paul Finkelman has linked this sentiment to James Madison, who helped draft this speech. See "James Madison and the Bill of Rights: A Reluctant Posterity," *1990 The Supreme Court Review*, ed. Gerhard Casper, Dennis J. Hutchinson, and David A. Strauss (Chicago: University of Chicago Press, 1991), pp. 338–39.

30. Madison was particularly influential in the drafting and adoption of the Bill of Rights. See Robert A. Rutland, *James Madison: The Founding Father* (New York: Macmillan, 1987), pp. 59–65.

31. Washington, *The Writings*, vol. 30, pp. 341–42.

32. A suggestive term Washington sometimes used to describe the whole constitutional enterprise. See Washington, *The Writings*, vol. 31, p. 66, letter to Comte de Segur of July 1, 1790.

33. Quoted from Victor H. Paltsits, *Washington's Farewell Address* (New York: New York Public Library, 1935), p. 14.

34. Ibid., p. 19.

35. Ibid., p. 24.

36. Ibid., p. 32.

37. Ibid., p. 41.

38. Ibid., p. 45.

39. Ibid.

40. A point noted by Michael Kammen, *A Machine That Would Go of Itself: The Constitution in American Culture* (New York: Alfred A. Knopf, 1987), p. 70.

41. Paltsits, *Washington's Farewell Address*, p. 53.

42. Ibid., p. 54.

43. Cited in ibid., pp. 222–23.

44. Ibid., pp. 162, 167.

45. Ibid., p. 170. Paltsits prints this document, complete with original words and emendations. Only the amended version is cited here.

46. Ibid., p. 191. Amended version with alternative words in parentheses.

47. Ibid., pp. 191–92.

48. See Markman, "The Jurisprudence of Constitutional Amendments."

49. Cahn, "An American Contribution," p. 25.

50. *Marbury v. Madison*, 5 U.S. 137, 176 (1803).

51. *Barron v. Baltimore* 7 Peters 243, 250 (1833).

52. Melvin I. Urofsky, *A March of Liberty* (New York: Alfred A. Knopf, 1988), p. 140.

53. See Forrest McDonald, *The Presidency of George Washington* (Lawrence: University Press of Kansas, 1974), pp. 159–76.

54. See Jerald A. Combs, *The Jay Treaty* (Berkeley: University of California Press, 1970), pp. 171–88. Also see Samuel F. Bemis, *Jay's Treaty* (New Haven, CT: Yale University Press, 1962).

55. Gilbert, *To the Farewell Address*, p. 120, quoting from a letter to Charles Carroll dated May 1, 1796.

56. Ibid., p. 122.

57. For a good history of amendments to the U.S. Constitution, see Alan P. Grimes, *Democracy and the Amendments to the Constitution* (Lexington, MA: Lexington Books, 1978).

58. The Eleventh Amendment reversed the Court's decision in *Chisholm v. Georgia*, 2 Dallas 419 (1893) and limited suits against the states. The Fourteenth Amendment reversed *Dred Scott v. Sandford*, 19 Howard 393 (1857) and provided that blacks could now be American citizens. The Sixteenth Amendment overturned *Pollock v. Farmers' Loan & Trust Company*, 158 U.S. 601 (1895) and constitutionalized the income tax, and the Twenty-sixth Amendment overturned *Oregon v. Mitchell*, 400 U.S. 112 (1970), lowering the voting age to eighteen in state and local elections to be consistent with national elections.

The Seventeenth Amendment provided for direct election of senators without otherwise altering the powers of that body, and the Twentieth Amendment sought to shorten the power of lame-duck representatives albeit otherwise continuing the power of Congress. The Twenty-second Amendment may have undercut the presidency in relation to the other two branches by limiting the president to two terms, but it is not clear that the amendment, which had partisan motivations, was directed to weakening this office. See Stephan W. Stathis, "The Twenty-Second Amendment: A Practical Remedy or Partisan Maneuver?" *Constitutional Commentary* 7 (Winter 1991), pp. 61–68.

Chapter 4

Thomas Jefferson and the Amending Process

THOMAS JEFFERSON AND JAMES MADISON: COMPARISON AND CONTRAST

The views represented in Publius's defense of the amending process and in Washington's expostulations of the subject are moderate and conservative ones. A much more liberal use of the constitutional amending process was, however, advocated by another prominent early American, Thomas Jefferson, who happened to be a close friend to, and Republican Party colleague of, James Madison. This tie has indeed sometimes obscured Jefferson's distinctiveness on the subject.[1] Yet another view, which has depicted Jefferson as a radical, suggests that his affinity is more with the revolutionaries and anarchists than with those who would seek changes by constitutional means.[2]

This chapter supports the view that Jefferson's opinions about constitutional change were important precisely because they were, like Madison's views, at once opposed both to doctrinaire constitutional conservatism and to extreme notions of revolution. In this, commentators are correct to link Jefferson's and Madison's opinions. At the same time, Jefferson usually expressed less caution than Madison about constitutional change, he emphasized express rather than implied consent, and he was more willing to experiment with the convention mechanism and was less wary of ongoing popular input into the Constitution. In combination with the views that have been advanced in earlier chapters of this book, Jefferson's opinions on constitutional change provide a broader spectrum of opinion against which contemporary debates about constitutional amendments can be understood and assessed.

BALANCING NATURAL RIGHTS AND MAJORITY RULE

The Declaration of Independence

Jefferson's most famous work, the Declaration of Independence, contained several themes that illuminated his views of change and set him apart from those who glorify revolutionary change for its own sake or prefer revolutionary to constitutional change. As was indicated in a previous chapter, in both his own rough draft and the version of the document approved by Congress, Jefferson recognized the existence of certain natural rights which governments are designed to secure, namely, the rights to "life, liberty, and the pursuit of happiness." Jefferson further acknowledged "the right of the people to alter or to abolish" governments that do not secure such rights and "to institute new government, laying its foundation on such principles and organizing its powers in such form as to them shall seem most likely to effect their safety and happiness."[3] Far from assuming a radical revolutionary stance like that later associated with Robespierre and Marx, Jefferson's position on revolution was basically Lockean. Jefferson thus indicated that "prudence . . . will dictate that governments long established should not be changed for light and transient causes." Moreover, Jefferson followed with a long series of indictments designed to show that the Declaration of Independence was not precipitate but came only after "a long train of abuses & usurpations" evincing a design to place the colonies "under absolute Despotism."[4]

Jefferson's View of Human Nature

Jefferson clearly tied the right of revolution to the lesser right of amendment; the people have the right either "to alter or abolish" the government. More problematical was his thinking regarding the relationship between natural rights and popular consent. How far did he believe the people could go in writing constitutions? Could they choose to establish a government that denied natural rights, or could they create a "non-republican form of government?"[5]

If by the people, Jefferson meant to refer to the majority of the people, it may be that he could not long imagine a people, at least not an enlightened people, deciding to institute a government to deny, rather than facilitate, the exercise of natural rights. Certainly, Jefferson often expressed confidence in human nature and in the popular will.[6] Whereas founders like Adams thought "self-love" to be humankind's primary motive, Jefferson "believed that the moral sense, in which all men were equal, naturally led them to seek the good of others and to live justly in society."[7]

Jefferson did recognize predatory and exploitative qualities in human nature, but he may well have underestimated such qualities, particularly in the New World setting.[8] In the charitable judgment of one Jefferson commentator, in measuring "the disposition to self-interest against natural benevolence, he found no reason therein for discouragement about improvement and progress."[9] Such attitudes were reflected in a speech of 1789 to his Albemarle neighbors, which one author calls "one of the most memorable that Jefferson ever delivered."[10]

It rests now with ourselves alone to enjoy in peace and concord the blessings of self-government, so long denied to mankind: to show by example the sufficiency of human reason for the care of human affairs and that the will of the majority, the natural law of every society, is the only sure guardian of the rights of man. Perhaps even this may sometimes err. But it's errors are honest, solitary and short-lived . . . it soon returns again to the right way.[11]

Bill for Religious Freedom

Jefferson shed further light on the relationship between natural rights and majority rule in the Bill for Establishing Religious Freedom, which he introduced into the Virginia Assembly in 1778. This bill was part of a much wider effort at legal revision and reform which demonstrated the possibilities Jefferson saw in legal change.[12] In this monument to religious liberty, Jefferson recognized that, since one assembly had no legal power to bind successors, "to declare this act to be irrevocable would be of no effect in law."[13] Jefferson nonetheless continued:

Yet we are free to declare and do declare, that the rights hereby asserted are of the natural rights of mankind, and that if any act shall be hereafter passed to repeal the present or to narrow its operations, such act will be an infringement of natural rights.[14]

Similarly, in a letter of 1824, Jefferson noted, "Nothing . . . is unchangeable but the inherent and unalienable rights of man."[15]

While Jefferson's faith in natural law and in human nature was optimistic—perhaps too much so—his overall position was fairly sophisticated, resting on a distinction between natural rights and legal rights and, in a stance quite consistent with his later advocacy of the Bill of Rights, asserting long-term interests over short-term desires. Thus, Jefferson subordinated popular decisions to claims of natural rights rather than elevating popular willfulness as such.

JEFFERSON'S PROPOSALS FOR CONSTITUTIONAL AMENDING MECHANISMS AND HIS RESPONSE TO MADISON'S CRITIQUE

If natural rights were to be protected, they would need some security from the whims of the legislatures; if governments were to rest upon the consent of the governed, constitutions would have to be alterable. This paradox and the problem of balance it implies was evident in a number of Jefferson's writings and was particularly prominent in his *Notes on the State of Virginia*.[16]

While criticizing the structure and unrepresentativeness of the government established by the revolutionary Virginia legislature, Jefferson targeted the fact "that the ordinary legislature may alter the constitution itself."[17] Jefferson based this surmise on the derivation of the constitution from an ordinary legislature and from past practice. Even if the legislature had intended to make the state constitution unalterable, Jefferson noted the contradiction inherent in the claim of one "ordinary legislature" to "establish an act *above the power of the* [that is, of another] *ordinary legislature*."[18]

One could answer that popular acquiescence in the constitution had "given it an authority superior to the laws," but Jefferson was unwilling to accept this doctrine.[19] Noting the priority of resisting the British at the time the state constitution was written, Jefferson argued that excessive attachment to the doctrine of implied consent would lead to perpetual revolutions.

On every unauthoritative exercise of power by the legislature must the people rise in rebellion, or their silence be construed into a surrender of that power to them? If so, how many rebellions should we have had already? One certainly for every session of assembly.[20]

Jefferson thus urged the people to adopt a new constitution, "placing it on a bottom which none will dispute."[21]

In an appendix to the *Notes*, Jefferson proposed a draft for such a constitution which "after correction by the Convention," should be ratified by "the people, to be assembled in their respective counties" and established by the approval of two-thirds of these units.[22] This ratification mechanism was quite similar to the amending mechanism Jefferson had proposed in his second and third drafts of a constitution for Virginia in 1776,[23] after having first suggested that the constitution could be altered or repealed only "by unanimous consent of both legislative houses."[24] Now, however, Jefferson proposed another amending device which relied chiefly on the convention mechanism:

Any two of the three branches of government concurring in opinion, each by the voice of two-thirds of their whole existing number, that a convention is necessary for altering this constitution, or correcting breaches of it, they shall be authorized to issue writs to every county for the election of . . . delegates . . . and shall be acknowledged to have equal powers with this present convention.[25]

This was, of course, the proposal that Madison critiqued in *Federalist* No. 49 and that was examined in a previous chapter.

While Jefferson never completely abandoned his idea of periodic amendment, he did modify his view of the most effective amending mechanism, at least at the state level. Jefferson expressed his revised views in a letter of October 31, 1823. He changed his ideas not because, like Madison, he feared complete and/or frequent constitutional alterations. Rather he believed that the mechanism adopted in some states, whereby all changes would be initiated by special constitutional convention, had proved "too difficult."[26] Moreover, he believed that "a greater facility of amendment is certainly requisite." Still opposing a system of legislative sovereignty, Jefferson proposed a plan whereby two or more separately elected legislatures could adopt an amendment.

As this mode may be rendered more or less easy, by requiring the approbation of fewer or more successive legislatures, according to the degree of difficulty thought sufficient, and yet safe, it is evidently the best principle which can be adopted for constitutional amendments.[27]

THE EARTH BELONGS IN USUFRUCT TO THE LIVING

Jefferson's Idea

If any idea has contributed to Jefferson's reputation as a radical,[28] it is the one he tendered to Madison in a letter dated September 6, 1789. The principle was " *'that the earth belongs in usufruct to the living'*; that the dead have neither powers nor rights over it."[29] In his letter, Jefferson applied the principle first to public debts and second to perpetual laws and constitutions. The central weakness of Jefferson's application was that it rested on an abstract mechanistic view of generational succession (much different from that of Hume as discussed in Chapter 1), which was arguably too far removed from reality to be of great usefulness. Thus, in speaking of the public debt, Jefferson supposed a generation born, maturing, and dying together. Assuming that adults of 21 would typically live another 34 years, Jefferson concluded that, at 21, people may incur debts for 34 years, at 22, for 33 years, and so on. Recognizing that generations did not in fact arrive and depart so mechanistically, Jefferson examined Buffon's mortality tables and ascertained that the majority of adults 21 years of age and older would be dead in about 19 years. This period thus became the term "beyond which neither the representatives of a nation, nor even the whole nation itself assembled, can validly extend a debt."[30] Similarly, in addressing perpetual laws, Jefferson argued that "every constitution, then, and every law, naturally expires at the end of 19. years. If it be enforced longer, it is an act of force and not of right."[31]

Jefferson opposed his active view of popular approval to the more passive stance that merely acknowledged the people's right to repeal a law or constitution, a view that, he noted, "admits the right, in proposing an equivalent." Since no government is "so perfectly contrived that the will of the majority could always be obtained fairly and without impediment," Jefferson denied that this was a true equivalent. Thus, he asserted that "a law of limited duration is much more manageable than one which needs a repeal."[32]

At this point, Jefferson expressed more concern with laws of property than with periodic calls for constitutional conventions. Thus, among the specific applications Jefferson drew were debt limitations, "the descent of land holden in tail," "appropriations of land . . . in perpetuity," "charges and privileges attached on lands," "hereditary offices, authorities and jurisdictions," "perpetual monopolies in commerce," and "a long train of *et ceteras*."[33]

Madison's Critique

Considering his analysis in *The Federalist Papers*, Madison's responses to Jefferson's proposal were predictably negative. Looking first at constitutions, Madison posed three objections—the possibility of an "interregnum" between governments; the concern that government would become "too mutable & novel to retain that share of prejudices in its favor which is a salutary aid to the most rational government"; and the fear that "pernicious factions" would "agitate the public mind more frequently and more violently than might be expedient."[34]

Madison then looked at "laws involving some stipulation, which renders them irrevocable at the will of the Legislature."[35] Here Madison distinguished the descent of unencumbered land from the descent of land that has been improved, a debt which could be discharged only "by a proportionate obedience to the will of the Authors of the improvements." "Debts," Madison pointed out, "may be incurred with a direct view to the interests of the unborn as well as of the living." Appealing to "equity" and "mutual good," Madison did agree that one generation should "see that the debts against the latter do not exceed the advances made by the former."[36]

As to laws "involving no such irrevocable quality,"[37] Madison noted that, even here, the threat of constant change would "discourage every useful effort of steady industry pursued under the sanction of existing laws and . . . give an immediate advantage to the more sagacious over the less sagacious part of the Society."[38]

Madison, whose views on this point were quite close to those of Locke and Hume as articulated in Chapter 1 of this book, proposed to give wider scope—very wide for majoritarian democratic theory—to the doctrine of implied consent than Jefferson had conceded. For Madison, consent was "to be inferred from the omission of express revocation."[39] The principle of majority rule was itself, Madison observed, a product of "compact" rather than "a law of nature."[40] Without some such doctrine,

> no person born in Society could on attaining ripe age, be bound by any acts of the majority, and either a unanimous renewal of every law would be necessary, as often as a new member should be added to the Society, or the express consent of every new member be obtained to the rule by which the majority decides for the whole.[41]

Thus, Madison refused to apply the truths "seen through the medium of Philosophy" directly to politics.[42]

Proposals for Continuing Reform and a System of Wards

If Madison's response temporarily moderated Jefferson's enthusiasm, it hardly extinguished his hope that consent, particularly at the state level, could be given more concrete embodiment than republican theory had hitherto accorded it. This theme emerged clearly almost thirty years later in Jefferson's letter of 1816 to Samuel Kerchival, rehashing his critique of the still unchanged Virginia constitution and asserting that "governments are republican only in proportion as they embody the will of their people, and execute it."[43] Here, as elsewhere, Jefferson was confident of "the spirit of our people," a spirit which he asserted "would oblige even a despot to govern us republicanly."[44] Indeed, it was because of this republican spirit, rather than "the form of our constitution," that "all things have gone well."[45]

Anticipating the argument that "it is easier to find faults than to amend them," Jefferson responded, "I do not think their amendment so difficult as is pretended."[46] The "fifteen or twenty [state] governments" of the last forty years showed to Jefferson's satisfaction that the people's work in writing constitutions had not "done half the mischief . . . that a single despot would have done in a single year."[47] Jefferson heartily reaffirmed the equal rights of all citizens to participate in government, and he offered a radical plan in proposing that counties be divided into "wards of such size as that every citizen can attend, when called on, and act in person."[48] Patterned after New England townships, Jefferson wished to give such units a large share of responsibility. In *The Federalist Papers*, Madison had suggested that frequent constitutional change might undermine governmental stability.

Perhaps as a result of reflecting on Madison's comments, however, Jefferson now hoped that by involving each citizen in government, he could "attach him by his strongest feelings to the independence of his country, and its republican constitution."[49]

In any case, Madison's earlier criticism of periodic revisions of the national constitution had little apparent influence on Jefferson's call for "periodic amendments of the [state] constitution," a call again tied to exhortations against "perpetual debt" and a less than idolatrous view of constitutions generally.[50]

Some men look at constitutions with sanctimonious reverence, and deem them like the arc [sic] of the covenant, too sacred to be touched. They ascribe to the men of the preceding age a wisdom more than human, and suppose what they did to be beyond amendment. I knew that age well; I belonged to it, and labored with it. It deserved well of its country. It was very like the present, but without the experience of the present; and forty years of experience in government is worth a century of book-reading; and this they would say for themselves were they to rise from the dead.[51]

While renouncing "frequent and untried changes in laws and constitutions," and agreeing, much as he had done in the Declaration of Independence, that "moderate imperfections had better be borne with,"[52] Jefferson argued "that laws and institutions must go hand in hand with the progress of the human mind." In Jefferson's analogy, "We might as well require a man to wear still the coat which fitted him when a boy, as civilized society to remain ever under the regimen of their barbarous ancestors."[53]

How frequently should the constitution change? Here, as in the letter to Madison and a letter of June 24, 1813, to John Eppes,[54] Jefferson turned to mortality tables and arrived at the figure of nineteen years.

Each generation is as independent as the one preceding, as that was of all which had gone before. It has then, like them, a right to choose for itself the form of government it believes most promotive of its own happiness; consequently, to accommodate to the circumstances in which it finds itself, that received from its predecessors; and it is for the peace and good of mankind that a solemn opportunity of doing this every nineteen or twenty years, should be provided by the constitution.[55]

Jefferson's advocacy of majority rule was tied to his emphasis on a system of wards, now promoted as the means by which "the voice of the whole people would be thus fairly, fully, and peaceably expressed, discussed, and decided by the common reason of the society."[56] A modern interpreter sees Jefferson's emphasis on wards as designed to address the question of "how to preserve the revolutionary spirit once the revolution had come to an end."[57] Jefferson himself defended such a mechanism for constitutional revision, however, not as a revolutionary tool but in fairly conventional fashion as a counterrevolutionary measure.

> If this avenue be shut to the call of sufferance, it will make itself heard through that of force, and we shall go on, as other nations are doing, in the endless circle of oppression, rebellion, reformation; and oppression, rebellion, reformation, again; and so on forever.[58]

Jefferson's goal was not continuing revolution, and surely not continuing violence, but continuing popular input.

JEFFERSON'S COMMENTS ON SPECIFIC REVOLUTIONS

Shays's Rebellion

Jefferson's indulgent stance on Shays's Rebellion shows that he viewed revolution with less alarm than many of the other Founders. Addressing Madison from Paris in January 1787, Jefferson expressed his hope that, however "unjustifiable" the acts in Massachusetts might be, "they will provoke no severities from their governments."[59] While monarchies governed by force, Jefferson preferred governments "wherein the will of everyone has just influence."[60] The "turbulence" of free governments was nothing compared to "the oppressions of monarchy" and might even produce good by preventing "the degeneracy of government" and nourishing "a general attention to the public affairs."[61] Jefferson continued:

> I hold it that a little rebellion now and then is a good thing, & as necessary in the political world as storms in the physical. Unsuccessful rebellions indeed generally establish the encroachments on the rights of the people which have produced them. An observation of this truth should render honest republican governors so mild in their punishment of rebellions, as not to discourage them too much. It is a medicine necessary for the sound health of government.[62]

Similarly, writing to Abigail Adams a month later, Jefferson said, "The spirit of resistance to government is so valuable on certain occasions, that I wish it to be always kept alive."[63]

By November 1787, reports of anarchy in America had swept through Europe, and Jefferson advanced an even more shocking defense. Referring to the revolutionaries' good motives and honorable conduct, Jefferson calculated:

> We have had 13. states independent 11. years. There has been one rebellion. That comes to one rebellion in a century & a half for each state. What country before ever existed a century & half without a rebellion? & what country can preserve it's

liberties if their rulers are not warned from time to time that their people preserve the spirit of resistance? Let them take arms. The remedy is to set them right as to facts, pardon & pacify them. What signify a few lives lost in a century or two? The tree of liberty must be refreshed from time to time with the blood of patriots & tyrants. It is it's natural manure.[64]

Aside from the language, Jefferson's statement is shocking because it treats individuals who fall prey to revolutionary violence as mere abstractions and because it equates revolutionary change with its constitutional counterpart. Jefferson was apparently so confident in the American people's basic moderation and so concerned about oppression from the national government that he found it unnecessary to fear revolutionary excess.

The French Revolution

While Jefferson defended Shays's Rebellion, this defense must be balanced by the consistently moderate counsel he offered to participants in the French Revolution, advice that distanced him from radical revolutionaries and may even have signaled a shift from his earlier comments.[65] Thus, Jefferson continually urged his French friends to consolidate gains before pushing on to new ones. Moreover, Jefferson advised those favoring change to "be contented with a peaceable & passive opposition."[66]

After years of turmoil and counter revolution in France, Jefferson's approach continued to be similar. Reviewing the progress of the French Revolution to the time he wrote to Lafayette in February 1814, Jefferson cautioned that France might not be ready for "a full measure of liberty" for another generation.[67] True liberty would necessarily grow in reason rather than being established by force. Acknowledging that his advice had lagged behind Lafayette's, Jefferson observed that others had not heeded Lafayette's own prudent boundaries.

They did not weigh the hazards of a transition from one form of government to another, the value of what they had already rescued from those hazards, and might hold in security if they pleased, nor the imprudence of giving up the certainty of such a degree of liberty, under a limited monarchy, for the uncertainty of a little more under the form of a republic.[68]

Jefferson attributed "all the subsequent sufferings and crimes of the French nation"[69]—including the accessions of Robespierre and Napoleon—to this error and counseled caution. The revolutionaries should "be contented with a certain portion of power, secured by formal compact with the nation, rather than grasping at more, hazard all upon uncertainty, and risk meeting the fate of their predecessor."[70]

JEFFERSON AS A PRACTICING STATESMAN

As a practicing statesman, Jefferson several times considered the desirability of another constitutional convention or of other proposed constitutional changes. His responses to such situations provide further clues to his attitude toward change and demonstrate further contrast to Madison and some of the other Founding Fathers.

Ratification of the U.S. Constitution

Jefferson was serving as minister to France during debates over the U.S. Constitution. Initially, Jefferson was lukewarm to the document, less concerned than Madison and other Federalist proponents about the dangers of a new convention and sharing Anti-Federalist fears of a government that was "too energetic." Thus, Jefferson wrote in December 1787, with no apparent regrets, that "it is probable that . . . another Convention shall be assembled to adopt the improvements generally acceptable, and omit those found disagreeable."[71] He focused more in subsequent letters on the need for a bill of rights, a matter on which he particularly pressed James Madison.[72] Jefferson wrote, "Were I in America, I would advocate it warmly till nine should have adopted, and then as warmly take the other side to convince the remaining four that they ought not to come into it till the declaration of rights is annexed to it."[73]

In a later letter, Jefferson subsequently abandoned his own approach for "the much better plan of Massachusetts,"[74] a state that had ratified the Constitution and proposed nine amendments.[75] Thus, in a letter to Madison of November 1788, Jefferson now agreed: "I should deprecate with you indeed the meeting of a new convention. I hope they will adopt the mode of amendment by Congress and the Assemblies, in which case I should not fear any dangerous innovations in the plan."[76]

By his willingness to accept the Constitution while pressing for a bill of rights, Jefferson demonstrated a spirit of compromise that placed him in the mainstream. While he was more willing than Federalist partisans to accept another convention, this was hardly extraordinary, particularly for one judging events from a distance.[77]

The Election of 1800

In the election of 1800, Jefferson, who admittedly had much more to gain, evidenced greater willingness to accept the risks of a constitutional convention (and even the possibility of armed conflict) than did his opponents. After the election was thrown into the House of Representatives by an electoral malfunction eventually remedied by the ratification of the Twelfth Amendment, Jefferson's proclaimed "revolution" faced the threat of a Federalist-instigated derailment.[78] It is well known that a number of Federalists, including Hamilton, resolved the crisis by backing Jefferson. The role of the amending mechanism is less known but may be equally significant.[79]

Jefferson indicated that a catalyst to his selection was his threat to resolve the issue by calling a special constitutional convention, presumably under the untried provision of Article V of the Constitution. In a letter to Monroe dated February 15, 1801, Jefferson explained his response to Federalist attempts to prevent an election by "putting the government into the hands of an officer":

But we thought it best to declare openly and firmly, one & all, that the day such an act passed, the middle States would arm, & that no such usurpation, even for a single day, should be submitted to. This first shook them; and they were completely alarmed at the resource for which we declared, to wit, a convention to re-organize the government, & to amend it. The word convention gives them the horrors, as in the present democratical spirit of America, they fear they should lose some of the favorite morsels of the Constitution.[80]

Writing to Dr. Joseph Priestly, Jefferson subsequently likened the government "in the event of a non-election of a President" to "a clock or watch run down" and described the convention as a means of winding it back.

A convention . . . would have been on the ground in 8. weeks, would have repaired the Constitution where it was defective, & wound it up again. This peaceable & legitimate resource, to which we are in the habit of implicit obedience, superseding all appeal to force, and being always within our reach, shows a precious principle of self-preservation in our composition.[81]

Jefferson's willingness to play what the Federalists considered to be a risky game of constitutional chicken apparently helped resolve this troubling electoral deadlock.

The Louisiana Purchase

Jefferson's actions in purchasing Louisiana in 1803 are also pertinent to his view of constitutional change.[82] Jefferson drafted an amendment incorporating this territory into the United States and specifying how it would be governed.[83] This proposed amendment was consistent with Jefferson's views favoring strict constitutional construction.[84]

The Constitution has made no provision for our holding foreign territory, still less for incorporating foreign nations into our Union. The Executive in seizing the fugitive occurrence which so much advances the good of their country, have done an act beyond the Constitution.[85]

Soon however, concern developed that talk of constitutional difficulties might enable the French to void the treaty or Senate opponents to delay or defeat it.[86]

Pursuing behind-the-scenes plans for a revised amendment, Jefferson continued to believe that amendment was preferable to broad constitutional construction.

I had rather ask an enlargement of power from the nation, where it is found necessary, than to assume it by a construction which would make our powers boundless. Our peculiar security is in possession of a written Constitution. Let us not make it a blank paper by construction.[87]

Then, in a stance Henry Adams saw as a renunciation of his republican principles, Jefferson said that he would not insist.[88] "If, however, our friends shall think differently, certainly I shall acquiesce with satisfaction; confiding, that the good sense of our country will correct the evil of construction when it shall produce ill effects."[89]

Adams directed his critique not at what Jefferson did but at his apparent willingness to forsake his principles in doing it. Madison, secretary of state during the Louisiana Purchase, remained silent about the matter of constitutional amendment.[90] A perceptive study has noted that Madison proposed more amendments when he was out of office than when he was occupying it. The explanation for Madison's stances might equally serve for Jefferson's:

It may stem from an innate superiority complex which seemed to visit Madison when he was considering matters constitutional. He *knew* that the Constitution was safe in his hands and in Jefferson's. . . . But when Madison departed from the national political scene, he became more concerned about the danger that the Constitution might fall into improper hands.[91]

In this connection, it is noteworthy that in 1824 Jefferson again opposed liberal construction of the Constitution in favor of an amendment "giving to Congress the power of internal improvement, on condition that each State's federal proportion of the moneys so expended, shall be employed within the state," as well as favoring amendment limiting the presidential term and changing the electoral college.[92]

COMMENTS FROM RETIREMENT

Additional observations from Jefferson's retirement years further illustrate his desire for continuing constitutional alteration. Writing to John Taylor in 1816, Jefferson noted that deference to European philosophers had subverted true republican principles in America, and he expressed the desire for some unspecified amendments to make American government more republican.

The functionaries of public power rarely strengthen in their disposition to abridge it, and an unorganized call for timely amendment is not likely to prevail against an organized opposition to it. We are always told that things are going on so well; why change them? *"Chi sta bene, non si muove,"* said the Italian, "let him who stands well, stand still." This is true; and I verily believe they would go on well with us under an absolute monarch, while our present character remains. . . . But it is while it remains such, we should provide against the consequences of its deterioration.[93]

Later, discussing the presidential electoral system in a letter of August 17, 1823, Jefferson again indicated that further reform was desirable, but un-likely: "But the states are now so numerous that I despair of ever seeing another amdmt to the constn, altho the innovns [*sic*] of time will certainly call and now already call for some." Jefferson observed that "another general convention can alone relieve us."[94]

Jefferson further evidenced his commitment to the convention idea in a letter to John Cartwright of June 5, 1824. John Marshall and others had attempted to establish the courts as the arbiters of state and federal respon-sibilities.[95] James Madison, generally supportive of judicial review but more ambivalent about the role of the courts, would later express the general hope that federal/state boundaries could be resolved by a constitutional amendment.[96] Jefferson, even more wary of the danger of judicial suprem-acy,[97] went farther, arguing in his letter to Cartwright that, when such conflicts could not be resolved by the "prudence" of those involved, then "a convention of the States must be called, to ascribe the doubtful power to that department which they may think best."[98] One could debate whether Jefferson's advice on this subject was closer to that of Washington's Farewell Address as discussed in Chapter 3 or of Calhoun's theory of amendment, which is treated in Chapter 5.

SUMMARY AND ANALYSIS

Like other Americans from the founding period, Jefferson believed both in the right of revolution and in the desirability of providing less violent means of change. While Jefferson's philosophy of rebellion was generally moderate, he was more likely to express sympathy for revolutionaries than were this compatriots, and, as a consequence, was more likely to blur the distinction between constitutional change and revolutionary change. For Jefferson, the American people as a whole could rarely do wrong, at least over the long term, and occasional uprisings served to keep governors alert to natural rights, the protection of which was the measure of all governments.

Jefferson admired the success of the American achievement and favored a constitution adopted by special convention and unchangeable by ordinary acts of legislation. However, he was sometimes as willing to attribute American successes to the republican character of the people as to the perfection of the Constitution. Moreover, as one who believed firmly in the benefits of experience and the possibility of real progress, Jefferson was usually more willing to consider change than were most of the other early American leaders. While many of these leaders had a cautious, if not essentially negative, view of formal constitutional change, Jefferson's views were basically positive. He advocated periodic revisions of the Constitution, and he was willing to entrust constitutional ratification—at least at the state level— directly to the people. Madison argued that the people should be assumed to agree with a constitution unless they amended it. Jefferson's republicanism, though grounded in a highly abstract model of generational succession, was stronger. He thought that continuing assent was relatively meaningless without more affirmative approval expressed at least once every generation.

Many early American leaders preferred to change the Constitution by the mechanism used in the adoption of the first twelve amendments, or they advocated broad constructions of its provisions. Jefferson, however, was more willing to follow the less-traveled convention route. While not inflexible in applying his theories, he was more concerned that liberal constitutional construction, particularly by the judicial branch, could undermine the Constitution.

Emphasizing the practical role of custom, Madison hoped to enhance governmental stability by hedging the Constitution about with an aura of veneration. He was willing to accept minor changes but, in the words of one acute observer, reluctant to contemplate "radical changes" that might risk "upsetting a system which had proven its worth."[99] Jefferson, by contrast, viewed the document more like other human creations, putting greater emphasis on active consent, on the role of reason, and on the probable benefits of progress, at least in America, over the possible risks of change.

Madison's cautious stance on formal constitutional change—frequently combined with a stress on judicially initiated adaptations of the Constitution to changing times—has dominated much of the history of the United States Constitution. There have been few successful amendments together with long periods between amendment clusters.[100] The Madisonian view recognizes that obedience to law is in large part shaped by ties of sentiment, and it warns that constitutional changes may have unintended consequences. Overall, the general acceptance of Madison's views has been salutary, contributing to the stability of and respect for the Constitution, though arguably distancing the people from a sense of ongoing participation in the makeup of government.

Jefferson's views on governmental change suffer from greater abstractness than Madison's but are helpful in understanding the amending experience in many states, where the adoption of amendments and the drafting of new constitutions have been relatively frequent.[101] Jefferson's views also help explain periods of upheaval in American constitutional history, such as those immediately after the Civil War and during the Progressive Era.[102] More-over, Jefferson's opinions indicate that those who call for more frequent and profound changes in the Constitution are a well-established element in the American tradition. His views affirm that there are times when the Constitution must change, sometimes significantly if it is to survive. Jefferson's philosophy is a reminder that a government formed by individuals and professing to rest upon the consent of the governed must be at once sensitive to alterations proposed by the people and wary of changes not formally sanctioned by the majority.

NOTES

1. For an interpretation that sees the work of the two men as an ongoing conversation, see Adrienne Koch, *Jefferson and Madison: The Great Collaboration* (New York: Alfred A. Knopf, 1950).

2. See Richard K. Matthews, *The Radical Politics of Thomas Jefferson* (Lawrence: University Press of Kansas, 1984).

3. Wilton U. Solberg, ed., *The Federal Convention and the Formation of the Union of the American States* (Indianapolis: Bobbs-Merrill, 1958), p. 34.

4. Ibid.

5. Question posed by Hannah Arendt, *On Revolution* (New York: Viking, 1965), p. 237.

6. Gilbert Chinard, *Thomas Jefferson: The Apostle of Americanism* (Ann Arbor: University of Michigan Press, 1957), pp. 203, 429. Also see Thomas Jefferson, *The Writings of Thomas Jefferson*, ed. Albert Bergh (Washington, DC: The Thomas Jefferson Memorial Association Monticello Edition, 1904), vol. 6, p. 57; vol. 7, p. 253.

7. Merrill D. Peterson, *Adams and Jefferson: A Revolutionary Dialogue* (New York: Oxford University Press, 1976), p. 21. William Parks, *The Influence of Scottish Sentimentalist Ethical Theory on Thomas Jefferson's Philosophy of Human Nature* (Ph.D. diss., Department of History, College of William and Mary, 1975), pp. 204–13, argued that Madison's views of human nature fell somewhere between the Jeffersonian and Hamiltonian beliefs. Also see Shannon C. Stimpson, *The American Revolution in the Law* (Princeton, NJ: Princeton University Press, 1990), p. 97.

8. C. Randolph Benson, *Thomas Jefferson as Social Scientist* (Rutherford, NJ: Fairleigh Dickinson University Press, 1971), p. 85.

9. Adrienne Koch, *The Philosophy of Thomas Jefferson* (Chicago: Quadrangle Books, 1964), p. 119.

10. Noble E. Cunningham, *The Pursuit of Reason: The Life of Thomas Jefferson* (Baton Rouge: Louisiana State University Press, 1987), p. 133.

11. Ibid., pp. 133–134.

12. Ibid., pp. 52–63.

13. Thomas Jefferson, *The Works of Thomas Jefferson*, ed. Paul Leicester Ford (New York: G. P. Putnam's Sons, Knickerbocker Press, 1905), vol. 2, p. 441.

14. Ibid.

15. Jefferson, *The Writings of Thomas Jefferson*, vol. 16, p. 48.

16. Thomas Jefferson, *Notes on the State of Virginia* (New York: Harper & Row, 1964).

17. Ibid., p. 115.

18. Ibid., p. 118. For a fascinating criticism of Jefferson's views on the subject, see Noah Webster, "Government," *American Magazine* 1 (1787–8), pp. 137–45. The article is signed Giles Hickory.

19. Jefferson, *Notes on the State of Virginia*, p. 118.

20. Ibid., pp. 118–19. Also see pp. 123–25. For a letter showing that Jefferson maintained this view in later years, see his letter of April 19, 1824, to John Pleasants, in Jefferson, *The Writings of Thomas Jefferson*, vol. 16, pp. 26–30.

21. Ibid., p. 119. For development of the convention mechanism in America, which Jefferson was advocating, see Gordon S. Wood, *The Creation of the American Republic, 1776–1787* (New York: W. W. Norton, 1969), pp. 306–43.

22. Jefferson, *The Works of Thomas Jefferson*, vol. 2, p. 158.

23. Thomas Jefferson, *The Papers of Thomas Jefferson*, ed. Julian Boyd (Princeton, NJ: Princeton University Press, 1950), vol. 1, pp. 354, 364.

24. Ibid., p. 345.

25. Jefferson, *Notes on the State of Virginia*, pp. 204–5.

26. Thomas Jefferson, *The Writings of Thomas Jefferson*, ed. H. A. Washington (New York: H. W. Derby, 1861), vol. 7, p. 323.

27. Ibid.

28. Matthews, *The Radical Politics of Thomas Jefferson*, pp. 19–20.

29. Jefferson, *The Works of Thomas Jefferson*, vol. 6, pp. 3–4.

30. Ibid., p. 6.

31. Ibid., p. 9. Noah Webster took a similar position in an article in his *American Magazine* entitled "On Bills of Rights" (December 1787), p. 14, where he asserted, "The very attempt to make *perpetual* constitutions, is the assumption of a right to control the opinion of future generations; and to legislate for those over whom we have as little authority as we have over a nation in Asia." Contrary to Jefferson, however, Webster concluded that legislative assemblies were sovereign and that bills of rights were useless. See Gordon S. Wood, *The Creation of the American Republic, 1776–1787* (New York: W. W. Norton, 1969), pp. 372–83, for further analysis of Webster's views.

32. Jefferson, *The Works of Thomas Jefferson*, vol. 6., p. 9.

33. Ibid., p. 10.

34. James Madison, *The Writings of James Madison*, ed. Gaillard Hunt (New York: G. P. Putnam's Sons, Knickerbocker Press, 1904), vol. 5, pp. 438–39.

35. Ibid., p. 438.

36. Ibid., p. 439.

37. Ibid., p. 438.

38. Ibid., p. 440.

39. Ibid.

40. Ibid.

41. Ibid.

42. Ibid., p. 441.

43. Jefferson, *The Works of Thomas Jefferson*, vol. 12, p. 4.

44. Ibid., p. 6.

45. Ibid.

46. Ibid.

47. Ibid., p. 7.

48. Ibid., p. 8.

49. Ibid., p. 9. For further elaboration of ward responsibilities, see Jefferson's letter to John Cartwright of June 5, 1824, in Jefferson, *The Writings of Thomas Jefferson*, ed. Albert Bergh, vol. 16, p. 46. A parallel to the ideas of Jean-Jacques Rousseau in *The Social Contract*, trans. Willmore Kendall (Chicago: Henry Regnery Company, 1954), pp. 142–46, should be apparent.

50. Jefferson, *The Works of Thomas Jefferson*, vol. 12, p. 10.

51. Ibid., p. 11.

52. Ibid.

53. Ibid., p. 12. An almost identical analogy had been used by Matthew Hale. See his "Considerations Touching the Amendment or Alteration of Lawes," *A Collection of Tracts Relative to the Law of England*, ed. Francis Hargrave (Dublin: Printed for E. Lynch et al., 1787), p. 269. Hale's views are discussed in greater length in Chapter 1 of this book.

54. See Jefferson, *The Writings of Thomas Jefferson*, ed. Albert Bergh, vol. 15, p. 271.

55. Jefferson, *The Works of Thomas Jefferson*, vol. 12, p. 13.

56. Ibid., p. 14.

57. Arendt, *On Revolution*, p. 235.

58. Jefferson, *The Works of Thomas Jefferson*, vol. 12, p. 14. For similar sentiments, see Jefferson, *The Writings of Thomas Jefferson*, ed. Albert Bergh, vol. 16, p. 15.

59. Jefferson, *The Works of Thomas Jefferson*, vol. 5, pp. 254–55.

60. Ibid., p. 255.

61. Ibid., pp. 255–56.

62. Ibid., p. 256.

63. Ibid., p. 263.

64. Ibid., p. 362.

65. Arendt, *On Revolution*, p. 236.

66. Jefferson, *The Works of Thomas Jefferson*, vol. 5, p. 393.

67. Ibid., vol. 11, p. 455.

68. Ibid., p. 456.

69. Ibid.

70. Ibid., p. 457.

71. Thomas Jefferson, *The Papers of Thomas Jefferson*, ed. Julian Boyd (Princeton, NJ: Princeton University Press, 1983), vol. 12, p. 426.

72. Alpheus T. Mason and Donald Grier Stephenson, Jr., *American Constitutional Law*, 8th ed. (Englewood Cliffs, Prentice-Hall, 1987), pp. 452–55.

73. Jefferson, *The Papers of Thomas Jefferson*, vol. 12, p. 558, letter to William Smith, February 2, 1788. Also see letter to James Madison, February 6, 1788, p. 569; and letter to Alexander Donald, February 7, 1788, p. 571.

74. Jefferson, *The Works of Thomas Jefferson*, vol. 5, p. 457.

75. Forrest McDonald, *The Formation of the American Republic, 1776–1790* (Baltimore, MD: Penguin Books, 1965), p. 221.

76. Jefferson, *The Papers of Thomas Jefferson*, vol. 14, p. 188.

77. See Edward P. Smith, "The Movement Towards a Second Constitutional

Convention in 1788," *Essays in the Constitutional History of the United States in the Formative Period, 1775–1789*, ed. John F. Jameson (Boston: Houghlin, Miflin, 1909), pp. 46–115.

78. Alan P. Grimes, *Democracy and the Amendments to the Constitution* (Lexington, MA: D. C. Heath, 1978), pp. 19–25.

79. Cahn, "An American Contribution," pp. 24–25. Also see Cunningham, *The Pursuit of Reason*, pp. 235–36.

80. Jefferson, *The Works of Thomas Jefferson*, vol. 9, p. 179. Also see letter to James Madison, ibid., p. 192.

81. Ibid., vol. 11, pp. 218–19.

82. Jefferson's stance on the embargo points in a similar direction. See Garrett W. Sheldon's very helpful book, *The Political Philosophy of Thomas Jefferson* (Baltimore, MD: Johns Hopkins University Press, 1991), pp. 99–102.

83. For a text of this and his subsequent proposal, see Jefferson, *The Works of Thomas Jefferson*, vol. 10, pp. 3ff.

84. Cunningham, *The Pursuit of Reason*, p. 167.

85. Jefferson, *The Works of Thomas Jefferson*, vol. 10, p. 7.

86. Cunningman, *The Pursuit of Reason*, p. 266.

87. Jefferson, *The Works of Thomas Jefferson*, vol. 10, pp. 10–11.

88. Henry Adams, *The Formative Years*, ed. Herbert Agar (London: Collins), vol. 1, pp. 185–86.

89. Jefferson, *The Works of Thomas Jefferson*, vol. 10, p. 11.

90. Albert E. Smith, *James Madison: Builder* (New York: Wilson–Erickson, 1937), p. 246.

91. Donald O. Dewey, *The Sage of Montpelier: Madison's Thought, 1817–36* (Ph.D. diss., University of Chicago, 1960), p. 85.

92. Jefferson, *The Writings of Thomas Jefferson*, ed. Albert Bergh, vol. 16, pp. 14–15.

93. Jefferson, *The Works of Thomas Jefferson*, vol. 11, p. 532.

94. Ibid., vol. 12, p. 303.

95. For thought on the tie between *Marbury v. Madison* and Jefferson's willingness to evoke the convention mechanism, see Cahn, "An American Contribution," pp. 24–25.

96. See Dewey, *The Sage of Montpelier*, citing letter to Jonathan Roberts, February 29, 1828. Leonard W. Levy, in *Original Intent and the Framers' Constitution* (New York: Collier Macmillian, 1988), p. 25, emphasizes Madison's reliance on judicial interpretation.

97. Levy, *Original Intent*, pp. 359–60.

98. Jefferson, *The Writings of Thomas Jefferson*, ed. Albert Bergh, vol. 16, p. 47.

99. Dewey, *The Sage of Montpelier*, p. 14.

100. Grimes, *Democracy and the Amendments*, pp. 157–58. Edward T. Silva, "State Cohorts and Amendment Clusters in the Process of Federal Constitutional Amendment in the United States, 1869–1931," *Law and Society Review* 4 (1970), pp. 451–52.

101. Elmer E. Cornwell, Jr., "The American Constitutional Tradition: Its Impact and Development," *The Constitutional Convention as an Amending Device*, ed. Kermit

L. Hall, Harold M. Hyman, and Leon V. Sigal (Washington, DC: The American Historical Association and the American Political Science Association, 1981), pp. 9–13. Also see Z. Melissa Lawrence, "Constitution Revision by Amendment—A Louisiana Tradition," *Louisiana Law Review* 51 (March 1991), pp. 849–60.

102. Grimes, *Democracy and the Amendments*, pp. 157–58.

Chapter 5

John C. Calhoun: The Amending Process and the Theory of Concurrent Majorities

THE EARLY AND MID-NINETEENTH-CENTURY BACKGROUND—JOSEPH STORY AND ALEXIS DE TOCQUEVILLE

Opinion in early and mid-nineteenth-century America appears to have been generally positive about the Article V amending process. Citing Article V in his *Commentaries on the Constitution of the United States*, U.S. Supreme Court Justice and Harvard Professor Joseph Story[1] alluded to the "utility and importance"[2] of the process in an argument similar to that of Publius in *The Federalist Papers*.[3]

It is wise, therefore, in every government, and especially in a republic, to provide means for altering, and improving the fabric of government, as time and experience, or the new phases of human affairs, may render proper, in order to promote the happiness and safety of the people. The great principle to be sought is to make the changes practicable, but not too easy; to secure due deliberation, and caution; and to follow experience, rather than to open a way for experiments, suggested by mere speculation or theory.[4]

Like Madison, Story argued that the amending process guarded against "the besetting sin of republics," namely, "a restlessness of temperament, and a spirit of discontent at slight evils."[5] By the same token, the amending process would serve, in a mechanical analogy repeated by many subsequent constitutional commentators, as "the safety valve to let off all temporary effervescences and excitements; and the real effective instrument to control and adjust the movements of the machinery, when out of order, or in danger of self-destruction."[6] Story argued that the adoption of twelve amendments had demonstrated the sufficiency of Article V, and he favorably contrasted such peaceful change with the "convulsions" associated with change in other governments.[7]

The French observer Alexis de Tocqueville, while not as liberal with his praise, also indicated the way that the amending process had come to be understood as an important part of the American system of checks and balances. Noting that the U.S. Constitution was "the primary law" and "the fount of all authority," he observed that this Constitution could only "be changed by the will of the people, in accordance with established forms in anticipated eventualities."[8] American judges were duty-bound to "obey the Constitution rather than all the laws."[9] This power did not jeopardize democracy, however, because "the nation always can, by changing the Constitution, reduce the judges to obedience."[10] When the courts negate the application of a law, "either the people change the Constitution or the legislature repeals the law."[11] Rarely had the relationship between judicial review and the amending process, first evident with the adoption of the Eleventh Amendment, been stated more clearly, concisely, and logically.[12]

CALHOUN'S BACKGROUND

John C. Calhoun exhibited a far more complex, but no less fascinating, view of the amending process. Certainly, among Americans, Calhoun is generally regarded by scholars not only as a prominent nineteenth-century statesman but also as one of the most original and logical political thinkers.[13] Initially a strong nationalist who professed little concern "for refined arguments on the constitution,"[14] Calhoun increasingly became the acknowledged spokesman for those Southerners who turned to the Constitution for support of their peculiar institution and the way of life that it fostered.[15] In the process, Calhoun both praised the amending process and saw it as something to fear, making his extensive reflections among the most interesting to be penned by an American thinker.

CALHOUN'S GENERAL THEORY OF GOVERNMENT

Calhoun's most theoretical work was his *Disquisition on Government*,[16] wherein he outlined his view of human nature, challenged then-dominant conceptions of the state of nature, defended freedom as a prize to be won by superior races rather than as a right to be shared by all, and developed his view of concurrent majorities.[17] In this book, Calhoun argued that, while man was a social being, his feelings were so constituted that "his direct or individual affections are stronger than his sympathetic or social feelings."[18] Such self-orientation leads to societal conflict which necessitates government to keep it in check. Being administered by individuals who are themselves self-oriented, however, government has a tendency toward injustice which must be held in check by a constitution: "*Constitution* stands to *government* as *government* stands to *society*; and as the end for which society is ordained would be defeated without government, so that for which government is ordained would, in a great measure, be defeated without constitution."[19] The task of constitution making is a difficult one requiring that government be strong enough to protect both against internal and external dangers while preventing those who administer government from abusing power and using it to their own advantage.

While "indispensable and primary" to constitutional government, the suffrage is far from "sufficient" to this end since it merely assures control to the majority of voters over those whom they elect, changing "the seat of authority without counteracting, in the least, the tendency of the government to oppression and abuse of its powers."[20] Moreover, it is difficult to "equalize the action of the government" among the numerous interests into which society is divided,[21] and, when interests combine to form a majority party, they will use government to advance their ends, distributing benefits to their friends and taxing their opponents, even to the point of impoverishing them.

Against such a majority, Calhoun insisted that a written constitution was, by itself, an insufficient barrier, since those in control will necessarily favor liberal constructions of such a document by which their own powers can be furthered. Similarly, while dividing the powers of government might lead to "greater caution and deliberation," all decisions would eventually fall under the sway of the numerical majority exercising the suffrage.[22]

As opposed to the rule of the numerical majority, Calhoun proposed that a mechanism—the concurrent majority—be instituted whereby "each division or interest" operating "through its appropriate organ" would have "either a concurrent voice in making and executing the laws or a veto on their execution."[23] While an ideal system would represent each interest, a system taking "a few great and prominent interests only . . . would still, in a great measure if not altogether, fulfill the end intended by a constitution."[24] Calhoun referred to the concurrent majority as a "negative power—the power of preventing or arresting the action of the government."[25]

In his *Discourse on the Constitution and Government of the United States*, Calhoun linked his theory of concurrent majorities to the principle of state sovereignty.[26] He argued that the Constitution of 1787 represented a compact among individual states rather than creating a social bond among a truly united people.[27] By Calhoun's analysis, little had changed in the transition from the government under the Articles of Confederation to that of the new Constitution.[28] States had individually ratified the new Constitution and could, only as states, amend it. As continuing geographical entities, or interests, individual states had the right to nullify acts sanctioned by the numerical majority. If this failed, states would have to decide whether to continue under the federal constitution or secede.

The act of secession would imply, of course, that problems were beyond constitutional remedy, but the Founders had provided a constitutional amending process to provide such remedies. Calhoun's recognition of the pivotal role for the amending process led him to heap lavish praise upon it as an embodiment of his theory of concurrent majorities and to recommend its use on a number of important occasions. A review of Calhoun's reflections on the amending process, however, shows that his praise sometimes proved unwarranted in light of the implicit difficulties he himself raised as to its use in protecting minorities.

CALHOUN'S PRAISE FOR THE AMENDING PROCESS

Calhoun's greatest praise for the amending process is found in the *Discourse*, where he said:

It is, when properly understood, the *vis medicatrix* of the system;—its great repairing, healing, and conservative power;—intended to remedy its disorders, in whatever cause or causes originating; whether in the original errors or defects of the constitution itself,—or the operation of time and change of circumstances, or in conflict between its parts,—including those between the co-ordinate governments. By it alone, can the equilibrium of the various powers and divisions of the system be preserved; as by it alone, can the stronger be preserved from encroaching on, and finally absorbing the weaker.[29]

This passage also marks Calhoun's most extensive discussion of the amending process in which he respectively examined its necessity, nature, safety, and sufficiency.

Calhoun's argument for the necessity of the amending process followed earlier justifications by the Founding Fathers. Calhoun observed:

[They] were not so vain as to suppose that they had made a perfect instrument; nor so ignorant as not to see, however perfect it might be, that derangements and disorders, resulting from time, circumstances, and the conflicting elements of the system itself, would make amendments necessary.[30]

Calhoun noted that, without a process being specified, changes would have required the states' unanimous consent.

Such a view was consistent with Calhoun's emphasis on the federal nature of American government and of the amending process. Calhoun stressed that amendments were "the acts of the several States, voting as States,—each counting one,—and not the act of the government."[31] Earlier in the *Discourse*, Calhoun, drawing upon the provision in Article VII by which the Constitution had been ratified and the provision in Article V for amendment, had argued that both showed "conclusively, that the people of the several States still retain that supreme ultimate power, called sovereignty."[32]

Against Publius's argument in *Federalist* No. 39 that the amending process was "neither wholly *national* nor wholly *federal*,"[33] Calhoun argued that it was solely federal.[34]

Calhoun praised the safety of the amending process as guarding against "too much facility as too much difficulty, in amending it."[35] Explaining the requirements in Article V as a compromise at the Constitutional Convention between simple majority rule and unanimity,[36] Calhoun said:

It is difficult to conceive a case, where so large a portion as *three fourths* of the States would undertake to insert a power, by way of amendment, which, instead of improving and perfecting the constitution, would deprive the remaining *fourth* of any right, essentially belonging to them as members of the Union, or clearly intended to oppress them.[37]

Similarly, he contended that Article V furnished "sufficient protection against the combination of a few States to prevent the rest from making such amendments as may become necessary to preserve or perfect it."[38]

As to the sufficiency of the amending process, Calhoun argued that it was second only to the power of the states in creating the Union: "Within its appropriate sphere,—that of *amending* the constitution,—all others are subject to its control, and may be modified, changed or altered at its pleasure."[39] Calhoun thus proceeded to praise the amending process as the *"vis medicatrix"* of the constitutional system.[40]

Calhoun saw in the amending mechanism an embodiment of the principle of concurrent majorities. Calhoun developed this point earlier in the *Discourse* where, in analyzing the contemporary application of Article V, he observed that, at the proposal stage, the eleven smallest states with a population of 1,638,521 could defeat an amendment desired by the other members with a population of 14,549,082, while the twenty smallest states with a population of 3,526,811 could compel Congress to call a convention against the wishes of the most populous ten with a population of 12,660,793.[41] At the ratification stage, Calhoun concluded, eight states with a population of 776,969 could defeat a proposal desired by twenty-two with a population of 15,410,635, while the less populous twenty-three states with a population of 7,254,400 could ratify an amendment against the wishes of the seven most populous with a total of 8,933,204.[42] Moreover, even the smallest state could prevent an alteration in the provision granting equal suffrage in the Senate.[43]

CALHOUN AND DORR'S REBELLION

Calhoun's praise of the amending process in the *Discourse* was consistent with his comments in a letter to William Smith in which he answered a number of questions that Smith had directed to him and other potential

presidential nominees regarding Dorr's Rebellion,[44] and the appropriate
response to it.[45] This rebellion, which must have done much to confirm in
the popular mind the necessity for a regularized amending process, had
developed in Rhode Island. This state, which had simply reaffirmed its
colonial charter at the time of the American Revolution, found itself without
a formal mechanism for constitution change and, in a recurring situation
not remedied until the reapportionment cases of the 1960s,[46] with a malap-
portioned legislature little inclined to provide for the kinds of democratic
reforms that had swept through most of the other states beginning in the
1820s.[47] In his letter to Smith, Calhoun continued to support the amending
process as the lawful way to bring about governmental change.

One of Smith's questions concerned the right of a majority of citizens of
a state to seek change through means other than those provided in the state's
constitution or sanctioned by the state government.[48] While not completely
closing the door on the idea that there might be some extreme occasions
where individual revolutionary actions might be permissible, Calhoun indicated that all legal means of effecting change must first be exhausted.
Calhoun argued logically that the right of a majority to effect change was
necessarily either a natural right or a conventional right and, since the former
rights applied only in the state of nature, the right to effect constitutional
change must be conventional, "belonging to the body politic, and subject
to be regulated by it."[49] In a more questionable assertion, Calhoun argued
that even in states providing no formal mechanism for constitutional change,
majority alterations in the constitution required the consent of the
government.

Calhoun agreed that "the people are the source of all power; and that
their authority is paramount over all."[50] Where governments are in place,
however, he argued that they, rather than any abstract numerical majorities,
articulated the popular will. When people act apart from governmental
forms, as they may rightfully do "only where government has failed in the
great objects for which it was ordained," they commit a revolutionary act
on the basis of natural rights and "as a natural right, it is the right of
individuals, and not that of majorities."[51] Calhoun thus agreed with Daniel
Webster's arguments on behalf of the charter government in *Luther v. Borden;*[52] were the general government to recognize as a legal right the authority
of a majority of such individuals acting apart from governmental forms,
the result would be "anarchy and violence."

It would be the death-blow of constitutional democracy, to admit the right of the
numerical majority, to alter or abolish constitutions at pleasure,—regardless of the
consent of the Government, or the forms prescribed for their amendment. It would
be to admit, that it had the right to set aside, at pleasure, that which was intended
to restrain it,—and which would make it just no restraint at all.[53]

Calhoun observed that, in writing the federal Constitution, the Founders knew that methods for peaceful change were desirable alternatives to "violence and revolution"; they also knew that systemic stability required guards against "hasty and thoughtless innovations."[54] While the ruling majority might attempt to use the amending process to forestall all needed changes, Calhoun praised the Founders for opening doors

for the free and full operation of all the moral elements in favor of change; not doubting that, if reason be left free to combat error, all the amendments which time and experience might show to be necessary, would, in the end, be made; and that the system, under their salutary influence, would go on indefinitely, purifying and perfecting itself.[55]

CONSTITUTIONAL AMENDMENT AND NULLIFICATION

Having praised the amending process, it is not surprising that recourse to it would occupy an important place in Calhoun's theory. This pivotal role of the amending process is illustrated by the fact that Calhoun's most lavish praise for it came during his defense of his cherished doctrine of nullification in the *Discourse*.

According to this doctrine, states had the power to challenge the constitutionality of a law by "interposing for the purpose of arresting, within their respective limits, an act of the federal government in violation of the constitution; and thereby of preventing the delegated from encroaching on the reserved powers."[56] Opponents justifiably feared that the federal government might thereby be prostrated at the feet of the states, causing "dangerous derangements and disorders in the system."[57] Calhoun responded that any apparent inconveniences could be remedied by the amending process, but, as he described the amending process, it appeared to give more weight to those challenging the national government than to those who were trying to uphold its power.

In Calhoun's scheme, when met by the action of a nullifying state, the federal government's duty was to forego use of a disputed power until such time as an amendment could be adopted to settle the question. Obviously the interposing states, typically being in a minority, could not be expected to adopt amendments themselves.[58] Moreover, Calhoun asserted both that "the party who claims the right to exercise a power, is bound to make it good, against the party denying the right" and, that, in cases of conflict between delegated and reserved powers, "the presumption is in favor of the latter, and against the former."[59] To allow the exercise of delegated powers until an amendment was adopted would work "a revolution in the character of the system" by transforming the federal system into a consolidated one.[60]

Calhoun had developed a similar analysis in a letter to General Hamilton on August 28, 1832, where, in outlining his controversial views of nullification and secession, Calhoun had portrayed the chief function of the amending process as that of preserving *"the equilibrium"* between the delegated powers of the general government and the reserved powers of the states.[61] Whereas interposition was designed to protect the states against intrusions of the delegated powers, the amending process was formulated to protect the general government against encroachments by the states: "In virtue of the provisions which it contains, the resistance of a State to a power cannot finally prevail, unless she be sustained by one fourth of the co-States."[62] By such analysis, the amending process was the very "pivot of the system" since "by diminishing or increasing the number of States necessary to amend the Constitution, the equilibrium between the reserved and the delegated rights may be preserved or destroyed at pleasure."[63]

Calhoun had to acknowledge, as an objection to his scheme, that one-fourth of the states might "change the Constitution, and thus take away powers which have been unanimously granted by all the States."[64] To this fear, Calhoun responded both that state encroachments on the federal government were less likely than encroachments by the latter against the former and, more circuitously,

It is, then, more hostile to the nature and genius of our system to assume powers not delegated, than to resume those that are; and less hostile that a State, sustained by one fourth of her co-States, should prevent the exercise of power really intended to be granted, than that the General Government should assume the exercise of powers not intended to be delegated.[65]

Usurpation of power by the federal government "would be against the fundamental principle of our system—the original right of the States to self-government"; claims of state power, by contrast, would be "in the spirit of the Constitution itself."[66]

What would happen in cases where the majority of states asserting the exercise of a power adopted an amendment granting them the disputed authority? Even here, Calhoun proved unwilling to concede state sovereignty. His position on this point was more developed in the *Discourse* than in his letter to Hamilton and other more obviously political writings which seemed purposely ambiguous on this point.[67] He argued that the state must decide whether a given amendment came "fairly within the scope of the amending power."[68] Should an amendment transcend such scope, a state might, by Calhoun's analysis, secede.[69] Just as under Article VII a state had to decide whether to join the Union, so now it might withdraw either "if a power should be inserted by the amending power, which would radically change the character of the constitution, or the nature of the system; or if the former should fail to fulfill the ends for which it was established."[70]

CALHOUN'S ADVOCACY AND FEAR OF
SPECIFIC AMENDMENTS

As a politician engaged in day-to-day politics, Calhoun sometimes advocated the exercise of the power he had so praised and analyzed. Calhoun's most publicized and criticized effort centered around the Nullification Crisis during which, in the "Address to the People of the United States Prepared for the Convention of the People of South Carolina," he called for the reconvening of "the body, to whose authority and wisdom we are indebted for the Constitution."[71] Calhoun favored a convention, believing that this mechanism, rather than the more-traveled route of congressional proposal and state ratification, was uniquely suited to "great emergencies."[72]

Consistent with this view, Calhoun had in the aforementioned letter to General Hamilton distinguished those occasions involving "a single power, and that in its nature easily adjusted," when the tried method of amendment should be used, from a more serious "derangement of the system . . . embracing many points difficult to adjust."[73] In the latter case, he argued:

The States ought to be convened in a general Convention—the most august of all assemblies—representing the united sovereignty of the confederated States, and having power and authority to correct every error, and to repair every dilapidation or injury, whether caused by time or accident, or the conflicting movements of the bodies which compose the system.[74]

While he was not completely clear on the subject, it appears from this quotation that Calhoun did not anticipate that such a convention would have to submit its work to the states for ratification.[75] In this and other particulars, Calhoun's proposed constitutional convention mechanism seemed to anticipate a body whose power "was much broader than that actually set forth in the exact language of the amending article."[76] In the process, Calhoun may well have undermined the protection for minority rights that he so vaunted.

Outside South Carolina, Calhoun's call for a convention largely fell upon deaf ears, and, in other ways to be discussed below, Calhoun's hopes for the amending process were not realized. Indeed, despite his expressed faith in the safety of the amending process, Calhoun indicated concern in a speech authorized for the Southern delegates to Congress to their constituents, dated February 2, 1849, that the amending process might not be adequate to protect the South's peculiar institution against the addition of new free states who might use the amending process to emancipate the slaves.[77]

Calhoun thought that constitutional and institutional guarantees might guard against such a possibility. Thus, in his last major speech to the Senate, his "Speech on the Slavery Question," dated March 4, 1850, Calhoun raised his hope for "an amendment, which will restore to the South, in substance,

the power she possessed of protecting herself, before the equilibrium between the sections was destroyed by the action of the Government."[78]
Calhoun described his specific proposal more fully in the *Discourse*, where
he called for a "change which shall so modify the constitution, as to give
to the weaker section, in some one form or another, a negative on the action
of the government."[79] Going far beyond his earlier advocacy of proposals
for changing the manner of electing the president,[80] Calhoun now called
for the creation of a dual executive, in which the two great national interests
could be represented by giving each a veto over congressional legislation.[81]

As with his interposition scheme, however, Calhoun faced the problem
of how to get the states of the majority section to agree to any diminution
or sharing of their electoral control. Once again, Calhoun had to appeal to
considerations of what he considered to be logic and fairness which would
prove to be inadequate. The responsibility for ratifying such an amendment
would rest with those least disposed to use it.

> The responsibility . . . rests on the States composing the stronger section. Those of
> the weaker are in a minority, both of the States and of population; and, of conse-
> quence, in every department of the government. They, then, cannot be responsible
> for an act which requires the concurrence of two thirds of both houses of Congress,
> or two thirds of the States to originate, and three fourths of the latter to
> consummate.[82]

In respect to protecting the two major interests, at least, the federal Constitution was not, in Calhoun's judgment, as well constituted as South
Carolina's where the state's two dominant interests—the upper country and
the lower country—were equally represented in the legislature and where
both houses of two successive legislatures had to approve amendments by
a two-thirds vote.[83]

CONCLUSIONS

Calhoun's theory of concurrent majorities has been subjected to a great
deal of justifiable criticism. Certainly, for all its professed concern for minorities, Calhoun's theory neither offered a system to identify which minorities were to be considered important nor offered protection to minorities
within the geographical areas for which he advocated representation. His
system was designed as a sure means of perpetuating slavery, not perceiving
that the slave interest he so desperately tried to protect was morally repug-
nant in principle[84] and arguably moribund as a semifeudal social order, in
increasing tension with the system of free labor in the North.[85]

To focus more specifically upon Calhoun's view of the constitutional
amending process is to address a tragic irony in his work. That is that while
Calhoun lavished praise on the safety and sufficiency of this process and

cited it as an example of a properly working federal mechanism and an embodiment of his cherished principle of concurrent majorities, all those points were subject to criticism, some by Calhoun's own implicit analysis.

On the issue of federalism, it is sufficient to point out that Calhoun's analysis of the amending process as a federal mechanism, while near the mark, overstated the federal character and understated the consolidated nature of the government. While Publius had called the process partly federal and partly national, Calhoun saw no ambiguity, professing to see the process as an embodiment of the former alone. Calhoun frequently linked the amending process in Article V to the ratification provision in Article VII, ultimately granting each state the same freedom to reject an amendment as it originally had to reject the Constitution itself. By such analysis, states had, in effect, given up little, if any, of their sovereignty in joining the Union, making the ratification debates appear to have been but a tempest in a teapot.

Calhoun's affinity for the amending process stemmed in large part from his recognition that, like his own theory of concurrent majorities, the amending process was not a purely majoritarian institution. Calhoun did not demonstrate, however, that the amending process—any more than his own scheme of concurrent majorities—protected all significant minorities. Indeed, by providing figures that suggested that a minority of the population might even adopt an amendment over the objections of the majority, Calhoun raised questions about whether the process even protected all majority interests. No wonder that Calhoun would fear that the institution of slavery, which he and other Southerners so cherished, might eventually be abolished (as it eventually was) through the amending process.

The desire to protect the Southern slave-holding minority was, of course, a central purpose of Calhoun's theories of nullification and secession in which the amending process played such an important part. The greatest difficulty with this part of Calhoun's analysis was that, while Calhoun could implore the majority not to act on the basis of disputed powers and argue that the majority should not act until its power had been affirmed by an amendment, by his own analysis of the self-directed character of human nature, no majority was likely so to wait. Moreover, no matter how much Calhoun would prefer that the federal government suspend all powers upon a state's interposition and appeal to the states for an amendment, no constitutional mechanism—including the dubious act of interposition—could compel such a suspension, absent a two-thirds vote in both houses of Congress and approval by three-fourths of the states. By Calhoun's own implicit analysis, the amending process was defective precisely to the extent that it could not guard against questionable constitutional interpretations approved by the majority.

Even when the federal government sought authorization for its powers, Calhoun refused to guarantee that the states would accede to it. In what one writer has called a game of "heads-I-win-and-tails-you-lose,"[86] Calhoun left open the possibility that states might secede in cases where they thought the nature of the Constitution had been radically changed or in instances where they thought it no longer continued to serve the limited ends for which it was established. The doctrine of secession was eventually answered by the Civil War. As to Calhoun's belief in implicit limits on the constitutional amending process, the Constitution's two explicit limits on the content of amendments within the text of Article V would suggest,[87] but not necessarily prove,[88] that Calhoun was mistaken on this point.

Calhoun's distinction between those routine occasions where the tried method of amendment should be used and those extraordinary occasions where a convention might prove necessary has a commonsense appeal to it, although his apparent efforts to bypass the requirements in Article V for calling such a convention and ratifying its proposals demonstrate that, once again, Calhoun faced the problem of initiating amendments desired for the protection of a minority of the states. As in the case of Calhoun's failed plan for a dual executive—a plan that would have most certainly led to government deadlock—Calhoun could show some logical desirability of this plan without being able to provide either a sufficient motive for the majority to adopt it or a constitutional requirement that it do so.

Calhoun's praise for the amending process, then, turned out to be more extravagant than his analysis warranted. Calhoun certainly advanced a strong case for following legal processes as opposed to entrusting such changes to any temporary majority. So too, by his analysis, the super majorities required by the amending process are revealed as a fairly good protection for clearly accepted interpretations of the Constitution against which one cannot rally two-thirds of both houses of Congress and three-fourths of the states. The amending process may also serve to adopt constitutional understandings that are favored by such majorities against minorities without sufficient representation in the amending process. The mechanism is far less useful in adopting new measures for the protection of minority rights not favored by the requisite majorities of Congress or the states. Similarly, there is little chance that the amending process can serve, as Calhoun wanted it to do, to overturn questionable assumptions of power supported by a majority of the states. In perhaps the ultimate irony, the very difficulty of amendment, which Calhoun so admired as a conservative force, probably turned out to be one factor that accelerated the drive for extraconstitutional interpretations with which he differed.

NOTES

1. For discussion of Story, see James McClellan, *Joseph Story and the American Constitution: A Study in Political and Legal Thought* (Norman: University of Oklahoma Press, 1971).

2. Joseph Story, *Commentaries on the Constitution of the United States*, ed. Ronald D. Rotunda and John E. Nowak (Durham, NC: Carolina Academic Press, 1987), p. 678.

3. See especially *Federalist* No. 43. This essay is discussed in greater length in Chapter 2 of this book.

4. Story, *Commentaries on the Constitution*, p. 679.

5. Ibid., pp. 679–80.

6. Ibid., p. 680. The machine analogy was frequently invoked in discussions of the Constitution. See Michael Kammen, *A Machine That Would Go of Itself: The Constitution in American Culture* (New York: Alfred A. Knopf, 1987). This writer has not found the safety valve analogy in writings prior to Story's but cannot be absolutely sure that Story originated it.

7. Ibid., p. 682.

8. Alexis de Tocqueville, *Democracy in America*, ed. J. P. Mayer (Garden City, NY: Doubleday, 1969), pp. 101–2.

9. Ibid., p. 102.

10. Ibid.

11. Ibid.

12. This amendment, which limited suits against the states, had overturned the Supreme Court's decision in *Chisholm v. Georgia*, 2 Dallas 419 (1793).

13. For discussion of prominent interpretations of Calhoun, see Richard N. Current, *John C. Calhoun* (New York: Washington Square Press, 1968), and J. William Harris, "Last of the Classical Republicans: An Interpretation of John C. Calhoun," *Civil War History* 30 (1984), pp. 255–67.

14. John C. Calhoun, *The Papers of John C. Calhoun*, ed. Robert L. Meriwether (Columbia: University of South Carolina Press, 1959), vol. 1, p. 403.

15. Jesse T. Carpenter, *The South as a Conscious Minority, 1789–1861* (Gloucester, MA: Peter Smith, 1963; reprint of 1930 edition), pp. 127–70.

16. John C. Calhoun, *A Disquisition on Government and Selections From the Discourses* (Indianapolis: Bobbs-Merrill, 1953).

17. See A. G. Beitzinger, *A History of American Political Thought* (New York: Dodd, Mead, 1972), pp. 379–87, for an outline of Calhoun's major arguments.

18. Calhoun, *A Disquisition on Government*, p. 4.

19. Ibid., pp. 7–8.

20. Ibid., pp. 11–13.

21. Ibid., p. 13.

22. Ibid., p. 27.

23. Ibid., p. 20.

24. Ibid., p. 21.

25. Ibid., p. 28.

26. Found in John C. Calhoun, *The Works of John C. Calhoun*, ed. Richard K. Cralle (New York: Russell and Russell, 1968; reprint of 1851–56 edition), vol. 1, pp. 111–406.

27. For possible origins of this view in the Virginia and Kentucky resolutions, see H. Jefferson Powell, "The Original Understanding of Original Intent," *Harvard Law Review* 98 (March 1985), pp. 927–35.

28. Calhoun, *The Works of John C. Calhoun*, vol. 1, p. 131.

29. Ibid., p. 295.

30. Ibid., p. 285.

31. Ibid., pp. 285–86.

32. Ibid., p. 138.

33. Alexander Hamilton, James Madison, and John Jay, *The Federalist Papers*, ed. Clinton Rossiter (New York: New American Library, 1961), p. 246.

34. Calhoun, *The Works of John C. Calhoun*, vol. 1, p. 158.

35. Ibid., p. 291.

36. Ibid., pp. 286–96.

37. Ibid., pp. 292–93.

38. Ibid., p. 294.

39. Ibid.

40. Ibid., p. 295.

41. Ibid., p. 172.

42. Ibid., p. 173.

43. Ibid. For parallel analysis, see Calhoun's "Speech on Veto Power," February 28, 1842, in ibid., vol. 4, pp. 74–99. For a modern citation and critique of similar patterns of analysis, see William S. Livingston, *Federalism and Constitutional Change* (Oxford: Clarendon Press, 1956), pp. 242–44.

44. For information on this crisis, see George M. Dennison, *The Dorr War: Republicanism on Trial, 1831–1861* (Lexington: University Press of Kentucky, 1976).

45. Calhoun, *The Works of John C. Calhoun*, vol. 6., pp. 209–38.

46. *Baker v. Carr*, 369 U.S. 186 (1962) and *Reynolds v. Sims*, 377 U.S. 533 (1964).

47. For debates at these conventions, see Merrill D. Peterson, *Democracy, Liberty, and Property: The State Constitutional Conventions of the 1820's* (Indianapolis: Bobbs-Merrill, 1966). For further discussion of Calhoun's opinions on Dorr's Rebellion, see John R. Vile, "John C. Calhoun on the Guarantee Clause," *South Carolina Law Review* 40 (Spring 1989), pp. 667–92.

48. Calhoun, *The Works of John C. Calhoun*, vol. 6, p. 221.

49. Ibid., p. 223.

50. Ibid., p. 226.

51. Ibid., p. 227. For a parallel idea, see Calhoun's "Speech of January 5, 1837," in ibid., vol. 2, p. 615.

52. Webster had thus argued in this case that "our American mode of government does not draw any power from tumultuous assemblages," and that, in the absence of explicit constitutional provisions specifying otherwise, "when it is necessary to ascertain the will of the people, the legislature must provide the means of ascertaining it." *Luther v. Borden*, 48 U.S. 1, 31 (1849).

53. Calhoun, *The Works of John C. Calhoun*, vol. 6, pp. 229–30.

54. Ibid., p. 236.

55. Ibid., p. 237.

56. Ibid., vol. 1, p. 279.

57. Ibid., p. 284. For a telling critique of Calhoun's view of nullification, see James Madison's letter to the *North American Review* in *The Mind of the Founder: Sources of the Political Thought of James Madison*, ed. Marvin Meyers (Indianapolis: Bobbs-Merrill, 1973), pp. 531–44.

58. Calhoun, *The Works of John C. Calhoun*, vol. 1, p. 296.

59. Ibid., p. 297.

60. Ibid., p. 299.

61. Ibid., vol. 6, p. 174.

62. Ibid., p. 175.

63. Ibid., p. 176.

64. Ibid., pp. 176–77.

65. Ibid., p. 178. Emphasis omitted.

66. Ibid.

67. See Andrew C. McLaughlin, *A Constitutional History of the United States* (New York: Appleton-Century-Crofts, 1935), p. 445.

68. Calhoun, *The Works of John C. Calhoun*, vol. 1, p. 300.

69. Ibid.

70. Ibid., p. 301.

71. Ibid., vol. 2. p. 207.

72. Ibid., p. 208.

73. Ibid., vol. 6, pp. 179–80.

74. Ibid., p. 180.

75. See William R. Pullen, *Applications of State Legislatures to Congress for the Call of a National Constitutional Convention, 1788–1867* (Master's thesis, University of North Carolina at Chapel Hill, 1948), p. 39.

76. Ibid., p. 45.

77. Calhoun, *The Works of John C. Calhoun*, vol. 6, pp. 308–9.

78. Ibid., vol. 4, p. 572.

79. Ibid., vol. 1, p. 391.

80. See Calhoun, *The Papers of John C. Calhoun*, vol. 1, p. 364, and John C. Calhoun, *Correspondence of John C. Calhoun*, ed. J. Franklin Jameson, *Annual Report of the American Historical Association for the Year 1899* (Washington, DC: Government Printing Office, 1899), vol. 2, p. 230, Letter to Samuel Gouverneur, June 10, 1825.

81. Calhoun, *The Works of John C. Calhoun*, vol. 1, p. 393.

82. Ibid., p. 396.

83. Ibid., p. 401.

84. Kenneth D. Wald, *Religion & Politics in the United States* (New York: St. Martin's Press, 1987), pp. 52–53.

85. Arthur M. Schlesinger, Jr., *The Age of Jackson* (Boston: Little, Brown, 1945).

86. Current, *John C. Calhoun*, p. 76.

87. John R. Vile, "Limitations on the Constitutional Amending Process," *Constitutional Commentary* 2 (Summer 1985), pp. 373–88.

88. Walter Murphy, "An Ordering of Constitutional Values," *Southern California Law Review* 53 (1980), pp. 703–60. This issue is treated in much greater length in Chapter 9 of this book.

Chapter 6

The Civil War Period: Sidney George Fisher Advocates Congressional Sovereignty, and John Jameson Warns against Constitutional Conventions

PROPOSED AMENDMENTS, CONVENTIONS, AND A CONFEDERATE CONSTITUTION

The Civil War has always been regarded as an important watershed in America's political history. Along with the writing of the Constitution, the Progressive Era, and the New Deal, this war and the period of reconstruction that followed is increasingly recognized as a critical moment in American legal and constitutional history as well.[1]

Just prior to the Civil War, many observers doubted whether the existing Constitution was adequate to the exigencies posed by slavery and by attempts at Southern secession. Several unsuccessful attempts to save the Union focused on the amending process. One was a complicated amendment proposed by Senator John J. Crittenden of Kentucky (and opposed by Abraham Lincoln) that attempted to compromise a host of North/South differences over the slavery issue and entrench such compromises within the Constitution.[2] Another amendment, the so-called Corwin Amendment (named after Thomas Corwin, an Ohio representative) which was particularly aimed at placating the border states and keeping them in the Union, would have protected slavery in the slave states although not in the territories.[3] As amended, it eventually specified:

No Amendment shall ever be made to the Constitution which will authorize or give to Congress power to abolish or interfere, within any State, with the domestic institutions thereof, including that of persons held to labor or service by the laws of said State.[4]

Having received prior approval from the House, this measure was passed by the necessary majorities of the Senate on March 3, 1861. President Lincoln indicated some support for constitutional changes in his first inaugural address on the next day when he commented:

This country, with its institutions, belongs to the people who instituted it. Whenever they shall grow weary of the existing Government, they can exercise their *constitutional* right of amending it or *revolutionary* right to dismember or overthrow it. While I make no recommendation of amendments, I fully recognize the rightful authority of the people over the whole subject, to be exercised in either of the modes prescribed in the instrument itself; and I should, under existing circumstances, favor rather than oppose a fair opportunity being offered the people to act upon it.[5]

In light of the action that the Southern states would soon take, it is interesting that Lincoln favored amending the Constitution by convention.

I will venture to add that to me the convention mode seems preferable, in that it allows amendments to originate with the people themselves, instead of only permitting them to take or reject propositions originated by others, not especially chosen for the purpose, and which might not be precisely such as they would wish either to accept or refuse.[6]

Lincoln went on to indicate that an amendment declaring (as did the Corwin Amendment) that "the Federal Government shall never interfere with the domestic institutions of the States, including that of persons held to service," would be acceptable to him since he believed this principle already to be "implied constitutional law."[7] Although credited with helping to hold on to some of the border states, only three states formally ratified the Corwin Amendment which became a dead issue after the Emancipation Proclamation and the Thirteenth Amendment.[8]

At a "Peace Convention" that had been held in Washington, D.C., in February 1861, ex-president John Tyler, the convention chair, announced in Jeffersonian fashion:[9]

Our ancestors, probably, committed a blunder in not having fixed upon every fifth decade for a call of a general convention to amend and reform the Constitution. On the contrary, they have made the difficulties next to insurmountable to accomplish amendments to an instrument which was perfect for five millions of people, but not so wholly so as to thirty millions.[10]

The actions of this convention resulted in a compromise similar to that proposed by Crittenden but which, like that earlier proposal, did not prove successful in Congress. The Southern states consequently held a constitutional convention (albeit one not sanctioned under authority of Article V) and drew up a new constitution, as did individual states of the new Confederacy. Perhaps because of the lingering philosophical influence of John C. Calhoun,[11] the amending mechanism of the Confederate states (never utilized during the war years) centered on a convention called at the request of three or more states, with amendments, however, to be approved by two-thirds, rather than by three-fourths, of the states.[12] This provision, complete with continuing protection for equal state representation in the Senate, read as follows:

Upon the demand of any three States, legally assembled in their several conventions, the Congress shall summon a Convention of all the States, to take into consideration such amendments to the Constitution as the said States shall concur in suggesting at the time when the said demand is made; and should any of the proposed amendments to the Constitution be agreed on by the said Convention—voting by States— and the same be ratified by the legislatures of two-thirds thereof—as the one or the other mode of ratification may be proposed by the general Convention—they shall thenceforward form a part of this Constitution. But no State shall, without its consent, be deprived of its equal representation in the Senate.[13]

Southern secession prompted Lincoln to take forceful action to preserve the Union. Largely because of these actions and the course of conflict itself, the old constitutional faith was rekindled.[14] In the meantime, however, the Constitution of 1787 had changed, not only by the coming addition of three amendments but also by new understandings and practices.

SIDNEY GEORGE FISHER'S BACKGROUND AND SIGNIFICANCE

One of the first and most comprehensive scholarly portents of change was a work published in 1862 by Sidney George Fisher, entitled *The Trial of the Constitution.*[15] Fisher (1809–71) was a Philadelphian of aristocratic leanings who married into the Ingersoll family. After graduating from Dickinson College, Fisher preferred his largely unsuccessful ventures in farming and his more widely recognized efforts at writing poems, essays, and books to practice at the Philadelphia bar to which he had been admitted. Fisher's book on the Constitution has been praised as twenty to thirty years ahead of its time, at least in certain of its themes.[16] Fisher was surely not particularly enlightened in regard to his views of blacks or other nationalities (particularly the Irish),[17] and other aspects of his thought must have seemed as narrow-minded when they were published as they do today.[18] Fisher was, however, one of the first scholars to perceive that the Constitution was capable of tremendous growth without the need for formal constitutional change. He recognized that, by seizing the moment, Lincoln had wrought an important transformation in the Constitution, and Fisher believed that Congress could do the same.

Fisher thus became the advocate of still further constitutional changes, but, in contrast to a number of earlier thinkers examined in this book, Fisher argued that such changes did not require formal constitutional amendment. It is this aspect of Fisher's thought that will be examined here. This topic is important because Fisher's views on the amending process represent a significant break with the past; because the details of Fisher's formulations are literally unique for an American thinker; because his view, novel though it was, foreshadowed many similar arguments that would be made in the future; and because the questions Fisher raised are connected to modern arguments as to whether the processes in Article V of the Constitution should or should not be regarded as exclusive.

FISHER'S ARGUMENTS ON THE AMENDING PROCESS

Sidney Fisher certainly presented a frontal assault on existing constitutional theory. In contrast to those who praised America's reliance on a written constitution, Fisher pointed to the deficiencies of such a written instrument when compared with the customs and usages by which Great Britain was governed. Fisher identified two defects in the former: "It cannot adequately provide for the future, and its meaning is necessarily uncertain."[19] If the latter observation was hardly new, the former argument marked a departure from the paeans of praise that had previously been heaped on the adequacy of Article V even by those like Calhoun who at least implicitly acknowledged its defects.

In contrast to such encomiums, Fisher argued that the process was far too difficult to be of any use. While others, among them U.S. Supreme Court Justice Joseph Story, had praised Article V as a safety valve,[20] Fisher noted that "the efficacy of a safety-valve depends on the promptness with which it can be opened and the width of its throttle. If defective in either of these, when the pressure of steam is too high the boiler will burst."[21] This is precisely the interpretation that Fisher gave to the Civil War. Rather than a safety valve, Article V had proven to be an "iron fetter."[22] In comments reminiscent of Machiavelli's skepticism about the prospects for governmental change,[23] Fisher argued that the amending process was most likely to be called into operation when its use was most dangerous.

Unless connected with real grievances, abstract questions of government do not interest the people. They are beyond the habitual range of their thought, and they cannot be induced to entertain them or act upon them at all. Therefore, in quiet times, appropriate to the consideration of the principles of government, such topics cannot be discussed with any prospect of securing such action as the Constitution requires. To put its cumbrous machinery in motion, the people must be roused, and as the most important organic changes are generally connected with the interests of sections or of classes, the people are very likely to be roused by them, to be divided into parties, to be influenced by passion.[24]

While Britain provided for change without the heavy machinery of Article V, in America "the process is so difficult that it can rarely be resorted to at all, and so dangerous, that to use it would be only something better than civil war, for it would be likely to provoke one."[25]

If the Constitution could not be amended through Article V, then there were but two alternatives: allow the Constitution to be destroyed or find another method of amendment. Fisher opted for the latter course, substituting a system of legislative sovereignty for the mechanism he found unworkable: "We must expect that changes will be made, perhaps great changes, and they ought to be made by Congress, for they cannot be made by the Fifth Article, nor can the action of Congress be resisted by the Courts." Fisher continued:

Why should they not be made by Congress if demanded by necessity, as they would be by an English Parliament? Should they be approved and ratified by the people, what is the difference, whether their consent be expressed by a Legislature or by a Convention which they have elected, or before or after the alteration is made? It would still be the wishes of the same people carried into effect. If the people should be dissatisfied, they can say so through another Congress. If they continue to be satisfied after the alteration is tried, it would be thus established as a precedent to be engrafted on the Constitution, as is the case in England.[26]

To modern ears, at least, Fisher's plan encounters the immediate obstacle of judicial review. Fisher responded by delimiting the function that judicial review should perform. Its power to annul legislation, he argued, should be limited to three instances: unintentional violations of the Constitution, control by the federal courts over those of the states, and criminal assumptions of power.[27] Excluded from judicial purview would be instances where Congress had consciously decided that previous constitutional interpretations had to be changed. These changes would, of course, be subject to the security afforded by the fact that congressmen were elected and thus under control of the voters who might force them to reverse themselves. Fisher summarized his arguments at the end of his first chapter thus:

The Constitution belongs to the people,—to the people of 1862, not to those of 1787. It must and will be modified to suit the wishes of the former, by their representatives in Congress, just as the English Constitution has been modified by Parliament, or it will be destroyed. The great danger to our Constitution arises not from its pliability, but from its rigid resistance to change. It may be thought, by some, that it would run greater risks if committed to the caprice of the multitude, or to such a Legislature as the multitude elects. But these perils must be encountered in a republic. If the people cannot preserve the Constitution, it must perish, for it cannot be preserved by the Judiciary.[28]

To this point, then, Fisher had justified his stance chiefly by an appeal to necessity, or what he sometimes called "natural laws."[29] Changes were needed. The Constitution could not provide them. If the Constitution were to be saved, some mechanism must be found to do so. Legislative action was not only the best alternative, but it had the British experience to commend it.

Perhaps the most fascinating aspect of Fisher's thought was that he did not rest with his argument from necessity, but proceeded, in apparent contradiction to his earlier critique of a system founded upon a written constitution, to argue that the method of constitutional change for which he argued was not only necessary but constitutional. To this end, Fisher proceeded to show in his second and third chapters that the American scheme of Union and the American executive were both modeled upon the British system; given such parallels, it would not be difficult to believe that the amending mechanism had a similar origin.

Fisher also appealed to the constitutional text. Like earlier proponents of expansive constitutional construction, Fisher focused on the "necessary and proper" clause. Previous proponents of expansive constitutional construction had limited such construction both by the specification that means must be adapted to constitutional ends and by the understanding that any means so adapted must not be in violation of the letter of the Constitution.[30] By contrast, Fisher described governmental powers under the "elastic" clause, borrowing Hamilton's language in *Federalist* No. 21,[31] as " 'illimitable,' 'boundless,'—on which 'no constitutional shackles can be wisely imposed.' "[32] Clearly, Fisher was willing to sanction the exercise of powers even in clear violation of the constitutional text.[33]

Fisher followed up with a more original argument to the effect that the mechanisms outlined in Article V need not be exclusive. Here Fisher played upon the difference in wording between the Articles of Confederation and the Constitution. Whereas the Articles had provided that no alteration would be made apart from the mechanism specified, Article V contained no such proviso. It thus became, for Fisher, but one possible means of constitutional change.

Does it mean that no amendments shall be made unless in the appointed manner? This cannot be the meaning for three reasons: first, it does not say so, and a matter so important would have been expressly stated. Secondly, the similar article in the Articles of Confederation does say so, and the difference proves an intention to differ, because the commission given to the Convention was to alter and amend those articles. Third, such a restriction would be inconsistent with the implied powers granted in the clauses already referred to.[34]

There are times when the mechanism in Article V is preferable to the exercise of legislative sovereignty, but Fisher was unwilling to require that it ever be used:

The Fifth Article is adapted to quiet times and peaceful discussions, and to great organic changes in the Government, which should be made always with deliberation and forethought. Should the Government overstep the limits imposed by the Constitution, under the stress of circumstances which make it impossible to call into action the machinery of the Fifth Article, such an act would be either a temporary infringement or a permanent change in the law. If the former, a resort to the process of amendment would be unnecessary; if the latter, it certainly would be desirable, in order to ratify the change in the most solemn and formal manner possible. In neither case would the act of the Government be void, for its implied powers cover such cases.[35]

Such an argument is subject to two obvious objections. In the first place, Fisher's approach appears to undermine the protections afforded the states by the amending provision which clearly embodies the federal principle.[36] To this objection, Fisher pointed to state representation in the Senate.[37] As to the fear that tyrannical majorities might "persist in unjust and oppressive measures," Fisher argued that this is a problem against which no government can guard, given agreement among the three branches to do so.[38]

There is, of course, an additional objection to Fisher's scheme, and that is that in moving from the stalemate that he so abhorred, he would open the door to rash innovations. On this point, Fisher offered a defense of his scheme that rested in large part on the British example. Thus Fisher wrote:

The conservatism that would bind the present in the fetters of the past, is as unwise, as the rash spirit of innovation that perils attained good on the wild sea of experiment. To yield slowly, to cling to the old things that have been tried,—even because they are venerable, although their use may have apparently passed away,—to distrust new things, and so to adopt them that they may harmonize with the old, has been the practice of the English people.[39]

Indeed, as Fisher's analysis proceeded in *The Trial of the Constitution*, he increasingly sounded this conservative note. Thus, in Chapter 3 (on executive power) he cautioned against adoption of "rash and sudden changes."[40] In Chapter 4 (on slavery) he noted that "nothing but necessity can justify the exertion of the ultimate sovereignty vested in the Government. It is intended, like the omnipotence of the English Parliament, for extraordinary occasions only."[41] In concluding Chapter 5 (the last chapter, on democracy) Fisher further observed:

New forms are not easily invented, even when necessary, to serve a growing and advancing people. We should therefore retain the old that have been tested by experience, as long as we can, modify them with caution to suit new conditions, and in interests so momentous as those that depend on the organic laws of Government, "Prove all things; hold fast to that which is good."[42]

Moreover, in Fisher's appendix (praising the Emancipation Proclamation), he contrasted his own proposal for constitutional change (freeing all slaves born after a given day) with contemporary proposals for another constitutional convention:

There will be no check whatever on its action, such as Congress is subjected to by its division into two houses, by the veto of the President, and by the opinion of the Judiciary. Invested thus with the omnipotence of the English Parliament, but without any of its restraining influences, internal or external, the Convention . . . might play some fantastic tricks.[43]

Fisher further noted that a convention called apart from Article V would be "a body unknown to the law, and therefore without legal authority." A convention called under the authority would, Fisher mistakenly argued, require sanction by "a popular vote" which, in existent circumstances, would open the field "to agitators and demagogues to do their work of iniquity."[44] In this manner, Fisher was able to connect himself with the moderation of the Founders and earlier defenders of Article V, while advocating a different mechanism for constitutional change.

JUDGE JOHN JAMESON

Fisher was hardly the only one to be worried about another constitutional convention. Having witnessed the Southern attempt at secession and radical assertions of sovereignty by convention participants in Kansas (the Lecompton Constitution), Illinois, and elsewhere, Judge John Jameson published the most comprehensive and influential work ever written on constitutional conventions.[45] This work would go into a number of editions and be received with special enthusiasm in the law schools of the day.[46] Jameson's basic theme was that constitutional conventions were subordinate to constitutions, or, in cases where the constitutions were silent in providing for changes, to the legislatures that called them. That is, conventions were to operate under the authority of laws and constitutions and not above them.[47] Significantly, Jameson's title page featured a quotation from Thomas Hobbes that noted, "They that go about by disobedience to do no more than reform the commonwealth shall find that they do thereby destroy it."[48] Clearly, Jameson hoped to domesticate the convention mechanism, keeping it fully subordinate to constitutional powers.

Jameson's most significant distinction in his *Treatise* was between a revolutionary convention and a constitutional convention.[49] Where there were times, including the American Revolution, when the former might be justified, a government under law must now proceed by the second route. Thus, the irregularities that marked the first kind of convention could not serve as justification for the second kind. Like others before him, Jameson knew that change was sometimes needed; his hope was to channel such changes rather than allow them to threaten existing legitimate governments.

CRITIQUE OF FISHER

There is justice in the observation that Fisher "was seeking a useful, not an absolutely honest, past."[50] Whatever parallels Fisher was able to show between the American and British systems, it surely strains credulity to believe that the Founders adopted a written constitution, renounced an hereditary monarchy, wrote provisions for the adoption of formal amendments, ratified a Bill of Rights, established a federal government, and accepted (in the course of time) a system of judicial review in a desire to replicate British institutions. Almost alone among the Founders, Hamilton had praised British institutions, and his ideas were, as a consequence, of little immediate impact on the Convention.[51] The Founders claimed to be inaugurating a new science of politics, not adopting the old. The importance of Fisher's work must rest then not with his persuasiveness that America had the system of legislative sovereignty which he urged it to exercise; it lay rather in his ability to show the advantages of such a system in advancing constitutional changes.

There were certainly reasons to believe, however, that Fisher was overly optimistic about the use of such a system in America. In the first place, Fisher did not show that Americans expressed the necessary consensus that would have promoted changes that might, for example, have prevented the Civil War, resolved the status of slavery in the territories, or settled on an alternative to slavery. On such matters, basic societal disagreements may have been a far more important obstacle to change than the difficulty of effecting changes through Article V. Absent such consensus, Americans may well have faced the spectacle of one Congress overturning constitutional actions taken by a previous one.[52] The resulting instability would have proved a serious disadvantage of his system and might well have led to the same kind of conflict.

Even more troubling for defenders of America's unique experiment with a written constitution unchangeable by ordinary legislative means was the possible threat posed by Fisher's scheme both to existing governmental structures and to civil rights and liberties. The separation of powers and limits on ordinary legislative lawmaking had been adopted in America precisely because the Founders had distrusted the whims of popular opinion, particularly fearing the "impetuous vortex" of the legislative branch.[53] The notion that the British had avoided such problems, a matter that some would undoubtedly consider disputable, would not in any case be a guarantee that Americans could avoid them. American society certainly lacked a number of traditional institutions (an established church, a hereditary monarchy, a titled aristocracy) thought to give stability to the British system.[54] Moreover, as Fisher's own prejudiced racial analyses suggested, America was a much more diverse society in which special interests might be more dominant. To Fisher's argument that constitutional forms could not ultimately prevent a conspiracy against liberty engaged in by all three branches of government, one might well respond that a system of separated powers at least makes such conspiracies difficult and provides time for rational reflection.[55]

Fisher is sometimes portrayed as a harbinger of congressional reconstruction,[56] and there are certainly parallels between the scope of the kinds of actions for which he argued and those later taken by this Congress. This Congress proved, as Lincoln had proved before it, that some constitutional limitations were more apparent than real, although the eventual adoption of three amendments suggests that, even for a Reconstruction Congress, there were limits past which it was not thought prudent to go without constitutional sanction.[57] Anyone thoughtfully surveying the actions taken by the president and Congress in the Civil War period as well as those suggested by Fisher would certainly realize that the Constitution provides powers as well as limitations and that decisive actions do not always require formal constitutional adjustments. On this issue, at least, Fisher's thoughts, while not unique, are of enduring value.

Fisher's construction of Article V was more doubtful. The fact that the legislative process is different from the amending process indicates that the adoption of laws and amendments were to proceed differently. Moreover, the presence of alternate amending routes within Article V suggests that one such route (and not the legislative mechanism) is the alternative to the other, while the presence of three branches casts doubt on Fisher's commendation of solitary legislative action. Fisher's argument that the Constitution does not specifically forbid amendment by means other than those specified in Article V has parallels in arguments that state constitutions that do not provide mechanisms for constitutional conventions may nonetheless be so amended but is otherwise unconvincing.[58] If two rival amending mechanisms are established, one constitutional and the other extraconstitutional, there is likely to be a conflict of sovereignties that could result in the very type of revolutionary conflict that the establishment of an amending mechanism was designed to prevent.[59]

INFLUENCES OF FISHER'S THOUGHTS

Fisher's thoughts on the amending process were unique enough that no subsequent thinker appears to have embraced his doctrines fully. In addition to the lasting appeal of some of Fisher's views of constitutional power, his views continue to be important both because they signal an alternative to the preexisting defenses of Article V and because some specific aspects of Fisher's thought are reflected in the writings of later thinkers.

Some scholars have noted parallels between Sidney George Fisher and Woodrow Wilson.[60] Like Wilson, Fisher was an admirer of the British system and a critic of the paralysis sometimes caused by the American scheme of separated powers.[61] Unlike Wilson, who once referred to the Supreme Court as a "constitutional convention in continuous session," however, Fisher put little emphasis on adaptation of the Constitution by the judiciary.[62] Moreover, whatever admiration he expressed for Lincoln, Fisher's views of congressional sovereignty were in further tension with Wilson's later stress on executive power.[63]

One might draw parallels between Fisher and subsequent schools of legal realism.[64] Like them, Fisher emphasized the need to adapt legal forms to the times and the power of ideas to override legal forms. Fisher's ideas are, however, somewhat too legalistic to press these parallels too far. Having first criticized the written constitution, Fisher went on to show how this same Constitution posed no obstacle to reforms such as he proposed.[65]

Perhaps the strongest ties to a specific thinker can be drawn between Fisher and Christopher Tiedeman, the prominent law professor whose ideas are treated in Chapter 7. One of Tiedeman's central arguments was that law is a result of "social forces"[66] and that laws that are not in accord with such forces will either be disobeyed or interpreted by the courts in line with popular sentiments.[67] While this emphasis on judicial construction was at odds with Fisher's own reliance on the legislature, Tiedeman, like Fisher, stressed parallels between the U.S. and British constitutions in order to buttress his points,[68] and he advocated a constitution amenable to change by interpretation rather than by use of the mechanisms in Article V.

Beyond these parallels to specific thinkers, Fisher's thoughts in 1862 reflected a more general dissatisfaction with the ability of the amending process to provide adequately for change. This sentiment would continue for almost fifty years and be repeated at subsequent intervals.[69] Shortly after publication of Fisher's book, three amendments were adopted. While such amendments could be taken as proof that the Constitution was indeed more flexible than Fisher's analysis of Article V had suggested, the unusual circumstances surrounding their adoption[70] hardly boded well for the adoption of amendments in more ordinary times. Thus, as will become evident in Chapter 8, there was a rising crescendo of voices that followed Fisher in arguing that the process in Article V was too difficult.

Again, however, such cries would be muted after the adoption of four amendments in the period from 1913 to 1920.[71] Their ratification seemed to confirm that the amending process was not as rigid as Fisher and others had believed. A subsequent period of constitutional conflict (the New Deal) was handled by changes in constitutional interpretation, confirmed—if not initiated—however, in the courts rather than in the legislature as Fisher might have preferred.[72] Again, the Constitution proved itself to be adaptable.

CONTEMPORARY APPLICATION

The wide changes in constitutional understandings that have been brought about without the aid of amendment—and particularly the changes initiated during the New Deal—have recently led to renewed thinking about the adequacy of the constitutional amending process. While some, following in the line of early strict constructionists, have dismissed new judicially recognized rights out of hand,[73] others have called for even more extensive judicial activism.[74] Between these two views, there have been at least three important writers who have attempted to explain and/or justify major changes in constitutional interpretation that have been effected without using the formal amending process.[75]

Bruce Ackerman

One such attempt is that of Bruce Ackerman of Yale.[76] Aware of the "counter majoritarian difficulty" brought about by too heavy a reliance on a nonelected judiciary,[77] Ackerman proposes that the New Deal changes represent a type of "structural amendment," which required the acceptance of all three branches of government to be effective.[78] As opposed to interpretations that argue that Court opinions on economic matters after 1937 simply represented a return to earlier constitutional interpretations, and were thus a "constitutional rediscovery," Ackerman argues that a real act of "constitutional creation" occurred when the Court sanctioned the more active role of government envisioned by Franklin Roosevelt and embodied in congressional legislation.[79] The Court performed what Ackerman identifies as "signalling" and "translation" functions,[80] both informing the public of the changes in interpretation about to take place and eventually codifying such changes into legal language. Ackerman analogizes this function to the constitutional convention mechanism, and he argues that the irregular proceedings that characterized the adoption of the Fourteenth Amendment may be regarded in a similar light, albeit with Congress, rather than the president, now asserting the key motivating role.[81] Such structural amendments, even when not embodied in the written constitutional text, have, like more formal written changes, "*earned* the right to make this extraordinary higher-lawmaking claim."[82]

Robert Lipkin

Robert Lipkin of the Widener University School of Law has made a similar argument, focusing, however, almost exclusively on the role of the judicial branch.[83] Lipkin attempts to adopt Thomas Kuhn's model of scientific change and scientific revolution to American constitutional law.[84] Lipkin thus divides constitutional law into two alternating periods of "normal adjudication," during which interpretation takes place within a given constitutional understanding or "paradigm," and periods of "revolutionary adjudication," when change is much more dramatic.[85] This latter period is initiated "when the Constitution fails to provide an obvious solution to a pressing moral or political problem," and judges then "solve the problem by appealing to constitutionally extrinsic factors."[86] Like Ackerman, Lipkin does not believe that resort to such extra Article V means is a new development. Rather, he believes that major decisions of the Marshall Court, while now retrospectively viewed as inevitable, themselves initiated revolutions whose legitimacy is today accepted without cavil and without a true understanding of their extraordinary character.

Akil Reed Amar

Less as a means of justifying past constitutional revolutions than of opening up the door to new ones, Yale University professor Akil Reed Amar argues that constitutional changes can be effected by a return to "first principles," namely the right of the people, or the majority of the people, to initiate changes apart from Article V.[87] Amar favors proposing and/or ratifying constitutional amendments by national referenda. Like Fisher, Amar argues that Article V is "nonexclusive."[88] Unlike Fisher, Amar does believe that Article V limits *"ordinary government* entities."[89] His arguments for a variant of popular sovereignty applied to the amending process are developed from the precedent of the Convention of 1787, which he believes, in contrast to many others, to have been a "constitutional," though admittedly irregular, gathering.[90] In arguing for the constitutionality of national referenda, Amar also draws upon a potpourri of arguments derived from "Article VII, the Preamble, and the First, Ninth, and Tenth Amendments."[91]

Convention Advocates

In addition to those who would argue for recognition of nontraditional means of constitutional change, there have been numerous attempts to resuscitate the convention mechanism in Article V. Altogether, there have been more than forty proposals for rewriting the Constitution from Reconstruction to the present, and many advocates of these plans have advocated that their plans be effected by the Article V convention mechanism.[92] Such hopes have often encountered opposition—like that of Fisher's and Jameson's—to the safety of such a mechanism and its possible susceptibility to the claims of special interests.[93] Despite some fairly close attempts to call such conventions,[94] and despite some recent convincing arguments for the safety and propriety of such mechanisms,[95] to date the fears and ambiguities surrounding such a convention process have been sufficient to head off any changes effected in this fashion.

CONCLUSION

Proposals for conventions and the analysis of scholars like Ackerman, Lipkin, and Amar suggest, however, that the concerns Fisher raised about the adequacy of the regularized amending process and that Jameson posed about the convention process are still present. The fact that modern commentators are more likely to turn to the courts as an instrument of constitutional change—Lipkin being perhaps the most prominent example—suggests that the difference between Fisher and a number of contemporaries has less to do with ends than with means. Moreover, however much one might quarrel with the theories of constitutional change that rely on mechanisms other than those specifically outlined in Article V, it is difficult to examine constitutional practice over the last two centuries without either some formulation such as Ackerman's or Lipkin's or without a belief that the constitutional system is severely out of balance. This author, at least, is not convinced that any modern theory advanced to date is adequate both as a descriptive and prescriptive account of constitutional change,[96] but contemporary attempts to formulate mechanisms for change outside of Article V certainly show the continuing relevance, if not the direct application, of Fisher's work.

NOTES

1. For prominent analyses of the legal effects of the Civil War, see Harold M. Hyman, *A More Perfect Union: The Impact of the Civil War and Reconstruction on the Constitution* (New York: Alfred A. Knopf, 1972), and Harold M. Hyman and William M. Wiecek, *Equal Justice Under Law: Constitutional Development, 1835–1875* (New York: Harper & Row, 1982).

2. This amendment would have made the national government responsible for the return of fugitive slaves, entrenched the three-fifths clause and the fugitive slave clauses by making them unamendable, and prohibited amendments giving Congress power to abolish slavery. See resolutions 832 and 833 in Herman Ames, *The Proposed Amendments to the Constitution of the United States During the First Century of Its History* (New York: Burt Franklin, 1970; reprint of 1896 edition), p. 357.

3. See R. Alton Lee, "The Corwin Amendment in the Secession Crisis," *The Ohio Historical Quarterly* 70 (January 1961), pp. 1–26, and Stephen Keogh, "Formal & Informal Constitutional Lawmaking in the United States in the Winter of 1860–1861," *The Journal of Legal History* 8 (December 1987), pp. 275–99.

4. Lee, "The Corwin Amendment," p. 22.

5. James D. Richardson, *A Compilation of the Messages and Papers of the Presidents, 1789–1908* (n.p.: Bureau of National Literature and Art, 1908), vol. 6, p. 10.

6. Ibid.

7. Ibid., pp. 10–11.

8. Lee, "The Corwin Amendment," p. 25.

9. Jefferson had, of course, advocated revising the Constitution every generation. See Chapter 4 of this book for details.

10. L. E. Chittendon, *Report of the Debates and Proceedings of the Peace Convention Held at Washington, D.C., February, 1861* (New York: Da Capo Press, 1971; reprint of D. Appleton & Company, 1864).

11. This tie has been previously noted by Lee, "The Corwin Amendment," pp. 118–19.

12. Delegates apparently chose this smaller majority in hopes of increasing the flexibility of the new Constitution. See ibid., p. 119.

13. Charles Robert Lee, Jr., *The Confederate Constitutions* (Chapel Hill: University of North Carolina Press, 1963), p. 196. On p. 70, Lee notes that this document replaced a provisional confederate constitution that enabled Congress to alter the Constitution by a two-thirds vote.

14. Harold M. Hyman, "Reconstruction and Political-Constitutional Institutions: The Popular Expression," *New Frontiers of American Reconstruction*, ed. Harold M. Hyman (Urbana: University of Illinois Press, 1966), pp. 1–39.

15. Sidney George Fisher, *The Trial of the Constitution* (New York: Da Capo Press, 1972; reprint of J. B. Lippincott & Co., 1862). Fisher also commented on the amending process in "Duties on Exports," *North American Review* 101 (July 1865); pp. 147–62, where he argued that Congress could tax exports—as long as it did so without discriminating against a particular state or section—in the absence of a constitutional amendment specifically empowering it to do so. Fisher made this argument despite the fact that Article I, Section 9, was written "with the understanding that it prohibited the tax." See ibid., p. 156.

16. Phillip S. Paludan, *A Covenant With Death: The Constitution, Law, and Equality in the Civil War Era* (Urbana: University of Illinois Press, 1975), p. 202.

17. Thus, Fisher received the accolades of the writer on white supremacy, Joseph Arthur Comte De Gobineau. See Sidney G. Fisher, *A Philadelphia Perspective: The Diary of Sidney George Fisher Covering the Years 1834–1871* (Philadelphia: Historical Society of Pennsylvania, 1967), p. 555. For Fisher's views on the Irish, see Fisher, *The Trial of the Constitution* pp. 337–39.

18. William H. Riker, "Sidney George Fisher and the Separation of Powers During the Civil War," *Journal of the History of Ideas* 15 (June 1954), pp. 401–2.

19. Fisher, *The Trial of the Constitution*, p. 20. Writing shortly after the Civil War, Walter Bagehot noted:

> The "constitution" cannot be altered by any authorities within the constitution, but only by authorities without it. Every alteration of it, however urgent or however trifling, must be sanctioned by a complicated proportion of States or legislatures. The consequence is that the most obvious evils cannot be quickly remedied; that the most absurd fictions must be framed to evade the plain sense of mischievous clauses; that a clumsy working and curious technicality marks the politics of a rough-and-ready people.

Bagehot, *The English Constitution* (Garden City, NY: Doubleday, n.d.). The second edition of this work was published in 1872.

20. Joseph Story, *Commentaries on the Constitution of the United States*, intro. by

Ronald D. Rotunda and John E. Nowak (Durham, NC: Carolina Academic Press, 1987), p. 680.

21. Fisher, *The Trial of the Constitution*, p. 26.

22. Ibid., p. 33.

23. See Niccolo Machiavelli, *The Prince and the Discourses*, intro. Max Lerner (New York: Modern Library, 1950), pp. 170–71. Reference is to *The Discourses*. For reflections on constitutional change and stability by philosophers prior to the adoption of the formal amending process, see Chapter 1 of this book.

24. Fisher, *The Trial of the Constitution*, pp. 33–34.

25. Ibid., p. 36.

26. Ibid., p. 55.

27. Ibid., pp. 79–80.

28. Ibid., pp. 96–97.

29. Ibid., p. 64.

30. Thus, Chief Justice John Marshall wrote: "Let the end be legitimate, let it be within the scope of the constitution, and all means which are appropriate, which are plainly adapted to that end, which are not prohibited, but consist with the letter and spirit of the constitution, are constitutional." See *McCulloch v. Maryland*, 17 U.S. 316, 421 (1819).

31. The subject of Hamilton's essay was the necessity for sufficient "energy" in the national government for dealing with national defense. See Alexander Hamilton, James Madison, and John Jay, *The Federalist Papers*, ed. Clinton Rossiter (New York: New American Library, 1961), pp. 152–57.

32. Fisher, *The Trial of the Constitution*, p. 142.

33. Thus, Fisher argued that the Court should acquiesce in a case where Congress declared that the president should hold office for life. Ibid., pp. 80–85.

34. Ibid., p. 144.

35. Ibid., pp. 144–45.

36. See William S. Livingston, *Federalism and Constitutional Change* (Oxford: Clarendon Press, 1951), and Martin Diamond, Winston M. Fisk, and Herbert Garfinkel, *The Democratic Republic* (Chicago: Rand McNally, 1966), pp. 97–99.

37. Fisher, *The Trial of the Constitution*, p. 149. For a similar argument directed toward federal regulation of state and local wages, see *Garcia v. San Antonio Metropolitan Transit Authority*, 469 U.S. 528 (1985) overturning *National League of Cities v. Usery*, 426 U.S. 833 (1976).

38. Fisher, *The Trial of the Constitution*, p. 151.

39. Ibid., p. 239.

40. Ibid., p. 267.

41. Ibid., p. 314.

42. Ibid., p. 360.

43. Ibid., p. 387.

44. Ibid., p. 389. Under Article V, amendments proposed by a convention would be ratified—like any other proposals—by state legislative approval or by special conventions called in each state. See U.S. Constitution, Article V.

It has been argued that Madison and some of his contemporaries may have joined convention ratification to convention proposal and legislative ratification to legislative proposal; Fisher may have made a similar mistake. For Madison's views, see Philip L. Martin, "Madison's Precedent of Legislative Ratification for Constitutional

Amendments," *Proceedings of the American Philosophical Society* 109 (February 1965), pp. 47–52.

45. Jameson thus noted that "the desolating war of secession . . . could hardly have been inaugurated but for the use made by the revolting faction of that institution." See John A. Jameson, *A Treatise on Constitutional Conventions: Their History, Powers, and Modes of Proceeding*, 4th ed. (New York: Da Capo Press, 1972; reprint of Callaghan and Company, 1887), p. 2. For concerns about state conventions that had proclaimed their sovereignty, see ibid., p. iii.

46. Kermit Hall, "The Monster That Almost Ate Washington: Historical Reflections on Calling a Second Constitutional Convention" (paper prepared for annual meeting of the Southern Political Science Convention, Savannah, Georgia, November 1, 1984). For a more critical view of this work, see Roger S. Hoar, *Constitutional Conventions: Their Nature, Powers, and Limitations* (Boston: Little, Brown, 1919), p. vii.

47. For a later classic on conventions with a somewhat different approach, see Walter F. Dodd, *The Revision and Amendment of State Constitutions* (Baltimore, MD: Johns Hopkins University Studies in Historical and Political Science, 1910).

48. Jameson, *A Treatise on Constitutional Conventions*, p. i.

49. Ibid., pp. 6–15. Jameson distinguished both from the "spontaneous convention" (or "public meeting") and the "legislative convention" (or "general assembly").

50. Paludan, *A Covenant With Death*, p. 194.

51. Clinton Rossiter, *The Grand Convention* (New York: Macmillan, 1966), pp. 181, 252–53, 311. For opinions on the comparison between the American and British constitutions from the mid-eighteenth century through the mid-twentieth century, see Michael Kammen, *A Machine That Would Go of Itself: The Constitution in American Culture* (New York: Alfred A. Knopf, 1987), pp. 156–84.

52. Walter Dellinger has effectively argued that certainty is especially desirable when it comes to the status of constitutional amendments. See his "The Legitimacy of Constitutional Change: Rethinking the Amending Process," *Harvard Law Review* 97 (December 1983), pp. 380–432.

53. Quoted from *The Federalist* No. 48, in Hamilton, Madison, and Jay, *The Federalist Papers*, p. 309.

54. See Louis Hartz, *The Liberal Tradition in America* (New York: Harcourt, Brace & World, 1955).

55. Fisher, *The Trial of the Constitution*, p. 151.

56. For some evidence of Fisher's influence on Pennsylvania Congressman William D. Kelley, see Hyman, "Introduction," to Fisher, *The Trial of the Constitution*, pp. xxv–xxvii. Fisher himself noted:

> I think it not improbable that the reasoning & new views contained in the *Trial of the Constitution* may have had some effect, for I know that the book was known to & read by a number of the most prominent members, and the questions which it discusses are intimately connected with the measures debated & adopted.

See Fisher, *A Philadelphia Perspective*, pp. 51–52.

57. Alfred H. Kelly, "Comment on Harold M. Hyman's Paper," *New Frontiers*, ed. Harold M. Hyman, pp. 51–52.

58. See Jameson, *A Treatise on Constitutional Law*, pp. 601–2, and Dodd, *The Revision and Amendment of State Constitutions*, p. 44.

William MacDonald would later advance an argument similar to Fisher's by arguing that Congress could call a constitutional convention on its own. See *A New Constitution for a New America* (New York: B. W. Huebsch, 1921), p. 227.

59. Such occurred in the notorious case of *Luther v. Borden*, where state revolutionaries had proceeded to attempt changes in the absence of a state constitutional provision giving them authority to do so. See 48 U.S. 1 (1849).

60. Hyman, "Reconstruction and Political-Constitutional Institutions," *New Frontiers*, ed. Harold M. Hyman, p. 32; Riker, "Sidney George Fisher," pp. 398–99. Hyman notes, however, in "Introduction," *The Trial of the Constitution* (ed. Harold M. Hyman, pp. xxvi–xxxi), that Wilson himself thought his own approach to the Constitution was a new one.

61. For other examples of such criticisms of American government, see Riker, "Sidney George Fisher," pp. 398–99, 411.

62. Quoted in J. W. Peltason, Corwin and Peltason's *Understanding the Constitution*, 12th ed. (San Diego: Harcourt Brace Jovanovich, 1991), p. 157. For Wilson's views of the courts and constitutional change, see Chapter 8 of this book.

63. For this emphasis, see James W. Ceaser, *Presidential Selection: Theory and Development* (Princeton, NJ: Princeton University Press, 1979), pp. 172–73. Also see Jeffrey K. Tulis, *The Rhetorical Presidency* (Princeton, NJ: Princeton University Press, 1987), pp. 118–32.

64. Hyman, "Introduction," *The Trial of the Constitution*, ed. Harold M. Hyman. Footnote at p. xxviii hints at this when he ties Fisher to "the Populist–Progressive–New Deal half-century."

65. Paludan, *A Covenant With Death*, p. 193.

66. Christopher Tiedeman, *The Unwritten Constitution of the United States* (New York: G. P. Putnam's Sons, 1890), p. 2.

67. Ibid., pp. 43–45.

68. Ibid., pp. 16–45.

69. These arguments are treated in Chapter 8 of this book.

70. See Joseph James, *The Ratification of the Fourteenth Amendment* (Macon, GA: Mercer University Press, 1984).

71. Alan P. Grimes, *Democracy and the Amendments to the Constitution* (Lexington, MA: Lexington Books, 1978), pp. 65–100.

72. Bruce Ackerman, "The Storrs Lectures: Discovering the Constitution," *The Yale Law Journal* 93 (May 1984), pp. 1051 and following.

73. See, for example, Stephen Markman, "The Jurisprudence of Constitutional Amendments," *Still the Law of the Land*, ed. Joseph S. McNamara and Lisse Roche (Hillsdale, MI: Hillsdale College Press, 1987), pp. 79–96, and Thomas Brennan, "Return to Philadelphia," *Cooley Law Review* 1 (1982), pp. 31–43.

74. Arthur S. Miller, *Toward Increased Judicial Activism: The Political Role of the Supreme Court* (Westport, CT: Greenwood Press, 1982). For a much more balanced treatment of this subject, see Stephen C. Halpern and Charles M. Lamb, eds., *Supreme Court Activism and Restraint* (Lexington, MA: Lexington Books, 1982).

75. Sanford Levinson, "A Multiple Choice Test: How Many Times Has the United States Constitution Been Amended? (a) 14; (b) 26; (c) 420 ± 100; (d) all of

the above" (paper delivered at American Political Science Association in 1990 and scheduled for publication in a forthcoming issue of *Constitutional Commentary*), p. 34.

76. Ackerman, "The Storrs Lectures." Also see Bruce Ackerman, "Constitutional Politics/Constitutional Law," *Yale Law Journal* 99 (December 1989), pp. 453–547, and Bruce Ackerman, *We the People: Foundations* (Cambridge, MA: Belknap Press, 1991).

77. Ackerman borrows this terminology from Alexander Bickel, *The Least Dangerous Branch* (Indianapolis: Bobbs-Merrill, 1962), p. 16. For the tie between such "amendments" and the electorate, which is, however, somewhat critical of Ackerman's argument, see James G. Pope, "Republican Moments: The Role of Direct Popular Power in the American Constitutional Order," *University of Pennsylvania Law Review* 139 (December 1990), pp. 286–368. For further critique of Ackerman, see Lawrence G. Sager, "The Incorrigible Constitution," *New York University Law Review* 65 (October 1990), pp. 924–35.

78. Ackerman, "The Storrs Lectures," p. 1051.

79. Ibid., p. 1055.

80. Ibid., p. 1054.

81. Ibid., p. 1069.

82. Ibid., p. 1070.

83. Robert J. Lipkin, "The Anatomy of Constitutional Revolutions," *Nebraska Law Review* 68 (1989), pp. 701–806.

84. Thomas Kuhn, *The Structure of Scientific Revolutions*, 2nd ed. (Chicago: University of Chicago Press, 1970).

85. Lipkin, "The Anatomy of Constitutional Revolutions," 736–39.

86. Ibid., p. 746.

87. Akil Reed Amar, "Philadelphia Revisited: Amending the Constitution Outside Article V," *University of Chicago Law Review* 44 (Fall 1988), p. 1050. This work is analyzed at much greater length in John R. Vile, "Legally Amending the United States Constitution: The Exclusivity of Article V's Mechanisms," *Cumberland Law Review* 21 (1990–1991), pp. 271–308. Also see David R. Dow, "When Words Mean What We Believe They Say: The Case of Article V," *Iowa Law Review* 76 (October 1990), pp. 1–66.

88. Amar, "Philadelphia Revisited," p. 1054.

89. Ibid., p. 1055.

90. See especially Richard S. Kay, "The Illegality of the Constitution," *Constitutional Commentary* 4 (Winter 1987), pp. 57–80.

91. Amar, "Philadelphia Revisited," pp. 1046–47.

92. For a survey and analysis of such plans, see John R. Vile, *Rewriting the Constitution: An Examination of Proposals From Reconstruction to the Present* (New York: Praeger, 1991).

93. For contemporary expressions of concern, see Thomas H. Kean, "A Constitutional Convention Would Threaten Rights We Have Cherished for 200 Years," *Detroit College Law Review 1987–91* 4 (Winter 1986), pp. 1087–91; Richard Rovere, "Affairs of State," *The New Yorker* (March 19, 1979), pp. 136–43; and Gerald Gunther, "Constitutional Brinkmanship: Stumbling Toward a Convention," *American Bar Association Journal* 65 (July 1979), pp. 1046–49.

94. The nation appears to have twice come but two states shy of the necessary number to call such a convention, once on the issue of state legislative reappor-

tionment and more recently in regard to a balanced budget amendment. See Grover Rees III, "The Amendment Process and Limited Constitutional Conventions," *Benchmark* 2 (1986), pp. 65–68. But see William T. Barker, "A Status Report on the 'Balanced Budget' Constitutional Convention," *John Marshall Law Review* 20 (1986), pp. 29–96, for doubts as to the validity of many of the applications for the latter convention. For a piece that takes the opposite extreme, arguing that Congress is already obligated to call a convention, see Bruce M. Van Sickle and Lynn M. Boughey, "A Lawful and Peaceful Revolution: Article V and Congress' Present Duty to Call a Convention for Proposing Amendments," *Hamline Law Review* 14 (Fall 1990), pp. 1–115.

95. Paul J. Weber and Barbara A. Perry, *Unfounded Fears: Myths and Realities of a Constitutional Convention* (New York: Praeger, 1989), and Russell L. Caplan, *Constitutional Brinkmanship: Amending the Constitution by National Convention* (New York: Oxford University Press, 1988).

96. An author has recently suggested that it is simply impossible to formulate such a grand theory of the Constitution reconciling all its competing goals. See Dow, "When Words Mean What We Believe They Say: The Case of Article V," p. 66. For similar sentiments, see Laurence H. Tribe and Michael C. Dorf, *On Reading the Constitution* (Cambridge, MA: Harvard University Press, 1991), pp. 28–29.

Chapter 7

Christopher Tiedeman, Constitutional Interpretation, and the Amending Process

By this point in this book, it should be apparent that certain constitutional understandings can be formally changed by amendment or be changed less formally, albeit often no less effectively, by presidential and congressional practices and judicial interpretations. Given the Court's special authority "to say what the law is,"[1] its role has been a particularly important one. The more expansive role the courts take in interpreting and adapting the Constitution to new exigencies, the less need there is for constitutional amendment, except perhaps as a way of reversing overly broad judicial opinions. Contrariwise, the less the courts adapt the Constitution to changing times, the greater may be the need for amendment. It is this recognition that is implicitly behind the modern debates over a jurisprudence of original intent,[2] and over the respective merits of judicial activism and judicial restraint.[3] However contemporary such debates may be, the issues about which they revolve are old ones.

CHRISTOPHER TIEDEMAN'S BACKGROUND AND SIGNIFICANCE

This debate is illuminated by looking at a scholar of the last century whose views were particularly influential and who was especially cognizant of the tie between judicial interpretation and constitutional amendment. Christopher Tiedeman (1857–1904) was such a man. Born in Charleston, South Carolina, Tiedeman received an undergraduate degree at the College of Charleston, pursued further studies in Germany, and earned his law degree at Columbia University. Tiedeman subsequently taught at the University of Missouri, at New York University, and at the University of

Buffalo where he served briefly as dean of the law school.[4] Tiedeman ranked with Thomas M. Cooley and John F. Dillon among expositors who sought to read laissez-faire economic theories into the Constitution, and he wrote authoritative and widely read treatises on a number of subjects,[5] perhaps the most famous of which was his *Treatise on the Limitations of the Police Powers in the United States* (1886), later reissued as *State and Federal Control of Persons and Property*.[6] Even more relevant to theories of constitutional interpretation and amendment was *The Unwritten Constitution of the United States*,[7] first presented as a paper to the Missouri Bar Association in commemoration of the centennial of the U.S. Constitution.[8] Reflection on this work is particularly timely with the recent passage of its one hundredth anniversary and with the publication of a recent law review article that recognizes the relevance of Tiedeman's writings to contemporary issues involving constitutional amendment and constitutional interpretation.[9]

THE ARGUMENT OF LIMITATIONS OF THE POLICE POWERS

In his *Treatise on the Limitations of the Police Powers*, Tiedeman began by observing that the private rights of individuals originated not in municipal law, but "belong to man in a state of nature; they are natural rights, rights recognized and existing in the law of reason."[10] While governments do not create such rights, they have the responsibility of protecting them according to the principle of *"sic utere tuo, ut alienum non loedas,"*[11] a principle translated as "so use your own as not to injure another."[12] Classifying all violations of this standard as disregard for "the principles of abstract justice,"[13] Tiedeman applied this principle throughout his book to state exercises of police power, sometimes coming to innovative conclusions.[14]

There was, of course, a distinction to be drawn between that which was contrary to abstract justice and that which was illegal, and, in making this distinction, Tiedeman initially appeared to retreat from judicial activism. After citing a number of authorities, beginning with Justice Chase's opinion in *Calder v. Bull*,[15] asserting the right of judges to void legislation contravening natural justice absent specific constitutional language giving them power to do so,[16] Tiedeman said that it was "an established principle of American law that the courts . . . cannot nullify and avoid a law, simply because it conflicts with the judicial notions of natural right or morality, or abstract justice."[17] While laws that violated accepted fundamental principles "will prove ineffectual and will become a dead letter," since "no law can be enforced, particularly in a country governed directly by popular will, which does not receive the moral and active support of a large majority of the people,"[18] such concerns should be directed to legislators rather than to judges.[19]

Thus ostensibly renouncing direct judicial interference on behalf of abstract notions of justice, Tiedeman proceeded to nullify the impact of this argument by contending that "fundamental principles of natural rights and justice" were still important "in determining the exact scope and extent of the constitutional limitations."[20] Tiedeman said: "Wherever by reasonable construction the constitutional limitation can be made to avoid an unrighteous exercise of police power, that construction will be upheld, notwithstanding the strict letter of the constitution does not prohibit the exercise of such a power."[21] Continuing with analysis of the broad scope of the due process clause, Tiedeman argued:

In searching for constitutional restrictions upon police power, not only may resort be had to those plain, exact and explicit provisions of the constitution, but those general clauses, which have acquired the name of "glittering generalities," may also be appealed to as containing the germ of constitutional limitation, at least in those cases in which there is clearly unjustifiable violation of private right.[22]

Recognizing that he has given with one hand what he first took with the other, Tiedeman admitted that his argument was at once "novel" and "liable to give rise to dangerous encroachments by the judiciary upon the sphere and powers of the legislature."[23] Perhaps by way of justification, however, Tiedeman argued that judicial willingness to use the due process clause to void legislation that exceeded proper legislative power should be balanced by a willingness to accept such powers where, despite the letter of the Constitution, "the framers of the constitution could not possibly have intended to deprive the government of so salutary a power."[24] Tiedeman returned to these themes in Chapter 16, a chapter that is incorporated and refined in his work, *The Unwritten Constitution*.

THE ARGUMENT OF THE UNWRITTEN CONSTITUTION: FIRST HALF

Tiedeman began *The Unwritten Constitution* by arguing that law was not the command of the sovereign but rather "the aggregation of all the social forces, both material and spiritual, which go to make up our civilization."[25] The sovereign enforces laws that have grown up spontaneously from among the people, but laws that do not reflect popular morality are destined to fail.

The stream can never rise higher than its source, nor can it be expected that legal rules, which are but a reflection of the moral habits of a people, can effect their moral elevation; least of all, the moral elevation of a people living under a government "of the people, for the people, and by the people."[26]

The failure of laws to reflect "the prevalent sense of right" will be reflected in disobedience, and judicial evasion:[27]

When the law is brought before the courts for enforcement, its practical operation will be made by interpretation and construction to conform to the prevalent sense of right, as far as this is possible without nullifying the letter of the law.[28]

How are principles of law formulated? Tiedeman assigned a special role to elites: "Even in the land of democratic rule and of universal suffrage, only a few persons really mould and fashion public opinion."[29] Laws develop not in a smooth and uneventful fashion, but only "after a vigorous contest between opposing forces."[30] After such a contest, "private interests" seek to rely upon the new rule and thus encourage the kind of legal "fixity and certainty" evident in the rule of stare decisis.[31] Thus, "cases have frequently occurred when the variance between the law and the prevalent sense of right was so distressing that the courts have been justified by public sentiment in abrogating an established rule."[32] While judges usually seek cover under legal fictions when overturning precedents, sometimes the public preference for legal fixity is so overbalanced by its opposition to legislation that courts may proceed to abrogate existing precedents even in the absence of such fictions.

Describing a constitution as "the definition of the order and structure of a body politic," in his second chapter Tiedeman likened a constitution and constitutional law to "the anatomy and physiology of the body politic."[33] Like other laws, constitutions are "imbedded in the national character and are developed in accordance with the national growth."[34] The American Constitution deserved praise not for "the political acumen of the convention which promulgated it" but for "the complete harmony of its principles with the political evolution of the nation."[35] In Tiedeman's view, these principles were largely British principles, modified to suit a "new environment."[36] As "the resultant of all the social and other forces, which went to make up the civilization of the people," constitutional law "follows and registers all material changes in public opinion, as unerringly as the needle follows the magnetic meridian."[37]

This conception was at odds with the notion that formal amendment was the only legitimate way to effect constitutional change. If the Constitution were complete, or even if it were, like corresponding state constitutions, much more detailed than it was, resort to formal amendments might be frequent. As a mere skeletal outline of governmental functions containing "only a declaration of the fundamental and most general principles of constitutional law," however, "the real, living constitutional law," what Tiedeman called "the flesh and blood of the Constitution," was "unwritten."[38] It was "not to be found in the instrument promulgated by a constitutional convention, but in the decisions of the courts and acts of the legislature, which are published and enacted in the enforcement of the written Constitution."[39] This unwritten constitution was just as "flexible" as the British one.[40]

For if by judicial interpretation, in obedience to the stress of public opinion or private interests, the express limitations of the written Constitution are made to mean one thing at one time, and at another time an altogether different thing, there is very little restraint imposed by these written limitations. The only obstacle in the way of an untrammelled popular will is the bald letter of the Constitution; and even that does not chain the popular will in times of great excitement and extreme necessity.[41]

In Tiedeman's view, Jefferson's charge that Marshall "engaged in making a constitution for the government" was true but hardly unique, a finding he sought to demonstrate in his next several chapters.[42]

In reviewing the electoral college in Chapter 3 of his book, Tiedeman concluded that, despite the Founders' attempts to distance presidential selection from the people, subsequent changes had negated the deliberative function of the electors. While the "written constitutional rule" was still preserved to the extent that election remained indirect and minority candidates were sometimes chosen,[43] the black letter of the constitution did not give a true picture of how the system operated.

In Chapter 4 Tiedeman applied this same type of analysis to the matter of presidential reeligibility. While the Constitution did not establish a two-term limit, public opinion mandated it. Moreover, this limit was "as binding as any written limitation, and even more binding than some of the plainest directions of the written Constitution" and would remain as long as popular sentiment supported it.[44]

In Chapter 5 Tiedeman reviewed judicial treatments of the contract clause. If the Founders' intentions had been followed, the application of the clause would have been limited to debts and not extended to situations like those involved in the *Dartmouth College* case. When that decision brought problems of its own, the Court issued the *Charles River Bridge Company* case, and other decisions had followed by which the Court by "the aid of technicalities and refinements of verbal meanings"[45] brought the contract clause in line with public desires.[46] Shifting judicial interpretations come not merely from differing circumstances but from changes in public opinion.[47]

THE ARGUMENT OF THE UNWRITTEN CONSTITUTION: SECOND HALF

In Chapter 6 of *The Unwritten Constitution*, Tiedeman at once extended and deepened his analysis by writing about natural law and its role in American constitutional history. His analysis appears to be directly counter to his words in his *Treatise on the Limitations of the Police Powers*. Now tracing the development of natural law conceptions to the Roman *jus naturale* rather than to any hypothetical state of nature when mankind lived in a golden age, Tiedeman offered one of the most scathing critiques of the doctrine of natural rights by an American since the writings of another South Carolinian, John C. Calhoun.[48]

The doctrine reaches the extreme limits of absurdity in the social contract, in the claim that all governmental authority, and hence the binding force of law, is derived from the agreement or consent of the governed; and that all men are possessed of certain natural rights, rights enjoyed by them in a state of nature, and which no government can rightfully infringe or take away.[49]

Repudiating such a view, Tiedeman nonetheless argued that "popular notions of rights, however wrong they may be from a scientific standpoint, do become incorporated into, and exert an influence upon, the development of the actual law."[50]

   Such rights were clearly not "absolute" or "inalienable," but grew with the moral sentiment of a people.[51] In Tiedeman's day, such rights were best embodied in the principle that one has "a right to do any thing that does not involve a trespass or injury to others"; Tiedeman cited Spencer's *Social Statics*.[52] Law must thus, not surprisingly, be limited by the legal maxim that so dominated the *Limitations of the Police Powers*, and that Tiedeman now traced back to the Magna Carta—*sic utere tuo, ut alienum non loedas*."[53]

   Recognizing that this principle was a product of laissez-faire philosophy in no way derogated from its importance. Neither should the fact that the "glittering generalities" of natural rights were originally formulated for other purposes prevent modern judges from using them to halt the advance of doctrines of paternalistic government advocated by Socialists and Communists.[54] In the contemporary struggle between "labor and capital,"[55] when conservatives stood in "constant fear" of "the absolutism of a democratic majority," Tiedeman applauded:

The disposition of the courts to seize hold of these general declarations of rights as an authority for them to lay their interdict upon all legislative acts which interfere with the individual's natural rights, even though these acts do not violate any specific or special provision of the Constitution. These general provisions furnish sufficient authority for judicial interference.[56]

   In Chapter 7, Tiedeman applied his views to the construction of the Constitution in wartime, with particular focus on the *Merryman* and *Milligan* cases.[57] Whatever case law might proclaim upon the termination of a war, the true constitutional rule was that which had been established by "the prevalent sense of right" during war itself.[58] In America, this sense of right had sanctioned the use of extraordinary powers which some might even claim to be in contravention of the Constitution itself.

   In Chapter 8, Tiedeman discussed citizenship, focusing on the *Slaughterhouse* cases[59] which he praised, in effect, for the very reasons that many others have criticized them.[60] Tiedeman argued that both a "literal interpretation"[61] of the Fourteenth Amendment and "the intention of the political leaders"[62] who adopted it clearly indicated that they "intended to place the negro, in his daily life, completely under the control of the National Government,"[63] and that the amendment

would give to the United States Supreme Court the power at any time to inquire into the effect of State legislation on the fundamental privileges and immunities of the citizen, which, before the adoption of the amendment, were exclusively within the control and protection of the State governments.[64]

Tiedeman could still commend the Supreme Court for limiting the scope of this amendment in the *Slaughterhouse* cases.

Feeling assured that the people in their cooler moments would not have sanctioned the far-reaching effects of their action; that they lost sight of the general effect in their eager pursuit of a special end, the court dared to withstand the popular will as expressed in the letter of this amendment; and, by giving it a narrow and close construction, to cut off its injurious consequences.[65]

Such cases were instances of appealing over the will of the people who formulated the amendment on behalf of the people who had now had a chance to consider its far-reaching consequences.

Alarmed at the peril in which the people stood, and deeply impressed with the necessity of providing a remedy, the Supreme Court of the United States averted the evil consequences by keeping the operation of the amendment within the limits which they felt assured would have been imposed by the people, if their judgment had not been blinded with passion.[66]

In discussing the idea of state sovereignty in Chapter 9, Tiedeman returned to some of the themes that he had advanced in his chapter on natural rights. Another issue left vague by the Constitutional Convention, Tiedeman preferred to "bring to light the real scientific facts of the situation" in preference to perusing old debates about the location of sovereignty in the federal system.[67] Pointing to the twin Southern claims that government rested upon the consent of the governed and that the government was a league of states, Tiedeman began by pointing to the alleged fallacy of the first principle: "While that doctrine is true in the sense that all governments rest upon the acquiescence in their decrees of the great mass of the people whom they rule, it is not true that the power is derived from the consent of the governed.[68] Tiedeman proceeded to point to the large number of women and children who were disenfranchised and to compare their numbers to the small number of men who ruled over them.

But still the proposition remains true, that the exercise of political power by the few does not rest upon the consent of the subject and silent majority, but upon the possession by the few of the superior strength, both moral and material. And the commands of these few constitute the law, whatever may be their inherent viciousness or inequity.[69]

According to "the plain facts of political science,"[70] "all governments are either monarchies or oligarchies."[71] Most laws are not even made by the current generation but are acquiesced in by those who "have acquired the habit of voluntarily obeying them, and [who] desire their enforcement against others, in order to prevent injury to themselves."[72] Laws will, of course, cease to be enforced "as soon as public opinion, under the operation of the social forces, undergoes a change,"[73] and, in this sense at least, "all government authority rests upon the commands, not of a dead generation, but of a living generation."[74] The authority of such laws "rests upon the present will of those who possess the political power."[75]

Tiedeman proceeded to criticize the second Southern principle of state sovereignty. When this doctrine was applied to "popular government," to "a government which, whatever its form, is founded upon a recognition of the repose of the ultimate political power of some part of the people, . . . confusion results."[76] In such a case, one must look not "to the written words of the Constitution, or to the opinions and intentions of those who helped to frame the Constitution,"[77] but to the opinions of those individuals who can now enforce their demands. Whatever "abstract moral" claims one may make, the legitimacy of "legal claims" will be decided by those with political power.[78] Victory translated the former claims into the latter, and Northern arms thus sealed the issue of state sovereignty.

Tiedeman's arguments in Chapter 10 paralleled those of a chapter in *Limitations on the Police Power*, so they may be assumed to be especially important. Tiedeman's subject was enumerated powers, but, unlike contemporaries who cited the Tenth Amendment as a means of limiting federal powers, Tiedeman's central objective was to argue for the existence of implied powers, "without which the permanency of the Federal Government would have been seriously endangered."[79] Illustrating constitutional usage by reference to the Louisiana Purchase and the *Legal Tender* cases, he argued that these cases demonstrated the "tendency to strain and force the literal meaning of the written Constitution, in order to bring it into conformity with that unwritten constitution, which is the real constitution"[80] and adherence to which is modified only by "the popular reverence for the written word."[81] Arguing that no "stable and enduring government" could be limited to the exercise of express powers,[82] Tiedeman expounded a novel interpretation of the Tenth Amendment whereby the national government would be permitted to exercise powers prohibited to the states but neither prohibited or delegated to it. Tiedeman depicted his interpretation as consistent with "the true grammatical meaning,"[83] albeit not the "intention" of the Framers, intentions that "are not at all binding upon the present generation, except so far as they have been embodied in the written word."[84] Tiedeman elaborated: "But the intentions of our ancestors cannot be permitted to control the present activity of the government, where they have not been embodied in the habits of thought of the people . . . or in the written word of the Constitution."[85] Current interpretations must be made by "the present possessors of political power."[86]

In Chapter 11, Tiedeman continued to focus on constitutional construction, arguing that interpretations based on the letter of the law were characteristic of law in its early, rather than its more advanced, stages. While words are often mechanically conceived as "vehicles of thought," they do not serve this function apart from context.[87] Moreover, words have varying "shades of meaning" that require "liberal or logical interpretation" which ascertains all facts, connected with and influencing, their formulation.[88] Thus, the cardinal rule for constitutional interpretation states that "the intention of the lawgiver, when the law was enacted, must prevail."[89]

The trouble is that this rule cannot explain existing law. Yes, legislative intentions are effected when they find "lodgement in the written word."[90] In such cases "the prevalent sense of right usually requires a strict observance of the written word."[91] When it is possible to find more than one meaning, or when necessity appears to require it, however, the courts enforce "that shade which best reflects the prevalent sense of right,"[92] and this is indeed their duty.

Citing Marshall's dictum in the *Dartmouth College* decision that a case may come within the ambit of words even though the Founders had given such a case no consideration,[93] Tiedeman argued that the power that gave words such authority was nothing but "the present will of the people."[94] Attempts to escape the role of public opinion by distinguishing constitutional construction from constitutional interpretation were failures: "Construction . . . is nothing more than that logical interpretation, whereby the real meaning of the living lawgiver, *i.e.*, the present possessors of political power, is ascertained."[95] Again, Tiedeman pointed to the social contract doctrine by which law was seen as emanating from "our ancestors" as a source of confusion, obscuring the role of "the present will of the people as the living source of law."[96]

THE UNWRITTEN CONSTITUTION: CONCLUSION

Of what value, then, was a Constitution? In his twelfth and final chapter, Tiedeman acknowledged that attentive readers might conclude "that the superiority of written over purely unwritten constitutions had been dissipated altogether."[97] Tiedeman disagreed, pointing to two groups within society. There were those seeking "consolidation or centralization" and those contributing to "disintegration"; those willing to "sacrifice personal liberty" only on behalf of "public safety," and those willing to do so on the wider grounds of "public welfare"; those seeking to restrain officials and those desiring to restrain the people; those manifesting a "democratic" spirit and those whose spirit was "aristocratic."[98] Compromises between these two groups were embodied in the U.S. Constitution, and both had attempted to sustain these compromises by agreeing to make amendments of this document difficult. Both sides further put obstacles in the way of the passage of legislation by dividing governmental powers and providing that members of different branches would be elected at different times. To these innovations was added the power of the courts to settle upon the constitutionality of laws in cases between litigants—albeit not, Tiedeman believed, to bind coordinate branches of government.[99] Moreover, judicial power may be checked by the congressional power to add new members to the Court.

The Founders' innovations had guarded well against "official tyranny," except when it was "demanded by a popular majority."[100] Here there were problems.

The direct and constant responsibility of almost all classes or officials to public opinion, through frequent popular elections, goes very far towards nullifying any superior merit which the written constitution possesses over an unwritten constitution.[101]

This problem was partly alleviated by a system of unelected judges who served during good behavior, enabling them "to serve as a check upon the popular will in the interest of the minority."[102] Tiedeman continued:

It enables a small body of distinguished men, whose life-long career is calculated to produce in them an exalted love of justice and an intelligent appreciation of the conflicting rights of individuals, and the life-tenure of whose offices serves to withdraw them from all fear of popular disapproval; it enables these independent, rightminded men, in accordance with the highest law, to plant themselves upon the provisions of the written Constitution, and deny to popular legislation the binding force of law, whenever such legislation infringes a constitutional provision. This is the real value of the written Constitution. It legalizes, and therefore makes possible and successful, the opposition to the popular will.[103]

Judges could hardly be "a complete barrier to the popular will,"[104] but they could serve to delay its implementation, standing, in James Russell Lowell's words, as an obstacle "in the way of the people's whim, not of their will."[105] The judiciary thus preserved "popular government," while simultaneously protecting "from the evils of hasty and passionate legislation."[106] The result was thus "popular government without democratic absolutism."[107]

PHILOSOPHICAL ANALYSIS

From a philosophical standpoint, Tiedeman's work, while not unique (Calhoun and a number of antebellum Southerners come most readily to mind) surely represented a major break with the philosophy of the American Founding Fathers.[108] While they asserted that all legitimate governments were based on consent and thus commended republican government above all others, Tiedeman argued that, however the "acquiescence" of the people might be needed, elites formed and enforced opinions by superior force, and all governments were but varieties of rule by the one or the few. Tiedeman thereby left little room for distinguishing regimes that claimed to be democratic from those that were tyrannical. By his scheme, no single principle or set of principles of government would appear to have priority over others. It is thus difficult to imagine that a government in which Tiedeman's principles had been accepted would have felt the necessity of widening suffrage, providing for the direct election of senators, or otherwise democratizing the system in the fashion in which it has since been changed. Rather than understanding denials of the franchise to be failures to live up to the implications of principles articulated in the founding period, Tiedeman rather used such denials to claim that such principles had never been true.

While Tiedeman thus sought the protection of minority property rights against meddlesome state police powers, he denied the traditional understanding of natural rights articulated in the Declaration of Independence and in other founding documents. His sketchy critique centered around his view that there had been no state of nature where man's life had been idyllic and his laws perfect. Undermining Tiedeman's critique was the fact that most natural rights theorists—particularly Hobbes and Locke—had not described the state of nature as idyllic.[109] Even those, like Locke, who had recognized the existence of some basic laws of reason in the state of nature had acknowledged both that they were not "established, settled, [and] known" and that they could not be adequately and impartially enforced in such a state.[110] Perhaps more critically, for most natural rights theorists the state of nature was arguably more important as a hypothetical construct designed to illustrate basic aspects of human nature than as a historical reality that must be accepted.[111] Far more important than the descriptions of the state of nature were the conclusions that the natural rights theorists had drawn about human nature. Among the most important of these conclusions, all of which were articulated in the Declaration of Independence, were: In their common humanity, men were equal; consent was superior to force as a basis for government; reason could show the value of government and laws based on such consent; government was designed for the purpose of securing certain human goods, designated as "rights"; and people had the right to replace unjust governments with new ones.[112]

Apparently thinking that by attacking the notion that there had been a historical state of nature he had thereby discredited natural rights theory in toto, Tiedeman slighted analysis and criticism of the Founders' conclusions and of their view of the nature of man and the purposes of government. Moreover, by taking public opinion into account, Tiedeman was able to reap the benefits, as it were, of existing natural rights theory, without having to argue for it. By upholding a view on the basis that it was currently part of public opinion, however, Tiedeman left his most basic principles subject to future shifts in such opinion, as his analysis of the *Slaughterhouse* cases clearly demonstrated.[113]

CONSTITUTIONAL ANALYSIS

Most of *The Unwritten Constitution* was, of course, built on constitutional rather than on moral or philosophical theory. From this constitutional standpoint, Tiedeman's work may be examined from one of two perspectives, namely either from the standpoint of how well it described the way constitutional interpretation was carried out or from the view of how well it would serve as a prescription for the way that it should be.[114]

Tiedeman's Description of Constitutional Interpretation

Judged by the first standard, it is difficult to dispute a number of examples Tiedeman cited.[115] Largely under the pressure of party politics and democratic ideals, the electoral college did, for example, develop quite differently than those who formulated it anticipated.[116] Interpretation of the contract clause can as easily be traced to changing conceptions of property rights as to simple differences in the facts of each case. The *Slaughterhouse* cases, whatever else they reflected, showed the Supreme Court's desire to limit the scope of earlier constitutional changes in light of the waning of contemporary concerns over racial issues and increased concerns about federalism. Similarly, the Court has been more willing to affirm constitutional limits after wartime than during times of actual conflict. On these points, Tiedeman's work anticipated many of the themes later advanced by those designated legal realists.[117]

One of Tiedeman's greatest strengths was his ability to recognize the way that law and its development were influenced by extraconstitutional sources and values. However one might want to qualify nuances of his arguments, it is difficult to fault many of the ties he drew between the development of American constitutionalism and legal precedents in Britain and in the colonies. Tiedeman recognized that legal systems cannot simply be transported from one nation to another. There is also wisdom in Tiedeman's recognition that judges were, like legislators, influenced by popular sentiment and that law is limited by notions of common morality.

At the same time, Tiedeman arguably underestimated both the role of historical contingencies and the role that the Founders and authors of subsequent amendments play in choosing which strand of their tradition to emphasize. Thus it appears to have made a difference that delegates to the Constitutional Convention began with the Virginia Plan rather than attempting simply to revise the Articles of Confederation; similarly, it made a difference that Shays's Rebellion occurred at the time when states were deciding whether to send delegates to the Convention rather than the year before or the year after. It is doubtful that the forces that had led to the rise of Nazism and militarism had been obliterated by the end of World War II in Germany or Japan or that authoritarian views have been stamped out in Eastern Europe or the Soviet Union, and yet new constitutions and other developments appear to have been relatively successful in pointing these nations in a more humane and democratic direction. Similarly, one could conclude with some of the Black Panthers of the 1960s that violence is "as American as apple pie" and yet hope to establish the legal and governmental systems upon sounder principles.[118] To show that there are precedents for a particular action is not therefore to show either that such action is desirable or inevitable.

Tiedeman asserted that laws and their interpretation arose from all social forces that went to make up a civilization. Like assertions that all behavior is determined by what preceded it, such a claim is impossible to refute. No matter how bizarre a law or an interpretation of a law may seem, it will probably be possible to point to some antecedent or some motive for it.[119] Thus accounting for any law or interpretation, such a principle will do little to account specifically for any of them.

Tiedeman's view that law and its interpretation were a reflection of prevailing sentiment is subject to similar criticism. Tiedeman's use of the term "prevailing" was ambiguous, referring not simply to "the sense of the majority, but rather the sense that *prevails* in a contest among different groups."[120] The ambiguity leads in circles. Tiedeman asserted, for example, that the unwritten two-term limit on the president would persist until a different sentiment prevailed, but what proof could be offered in support of such a proposition other than adherence to or departure from such a rule? Could one, moreover, assert the same about a rule embodied in the written Constitution—such as the current Twenty-second Amendment—as about one not so embodied?

This ambiguity is even more pronounced when it is recognized that one aspect of popular sentiment to which Tiedeman pointed was the demand for adherence to precedent. While Tiedeman identified the desire for stability as one aspect of this adherence, the very fact that he believed he must argue against the wisdom of the Founders and certain natural rights principles they espoused suggests that James Madison was correct in thinking that there is a strong element of popular opinion that respects clearly stated

constitutional provisions and long-standing interpretations of law both because they are old and wise and because they are perceived to reflect the
intentions of the Founders.[121] To the extent that readers accept Tiedeman's
arguments on behalf of contemporary beliefs, such respect for past opinions
may be eroded. The persistence of such reverence suggests, however, not
only that there is no clear line between the will of the present and that of
the past (thus indicating that the doctrine of implied consent embodies an
elemental truth)but also that written constitutional provisions and the institutions they establish may exert an influence on their thinking and on
institutional arrangements about which contemporaries are not even aware.

Tiedeman identified constitutional law as that law that related to governmental form and structure, and his recognition that the Constitution had
helped guard against abuses on the part of governors was perhaps a partial
recognition that the Constitution had served at least one of its key purposes.
It appears, however, that in stressing the way that law was shaped by public
opinion, Tiedeman failed adequately to appreciate how public opinion was
in turn shaped by laws and constitutions and legal ideals. While Tiedeman
mocked the idea that government rested upon consent or that government
should protect natural rights, these very ideas provided much of the impetus
for subsequent extensions of the franchise to women and eighteen-year-
olds and for legislation that has recognized blacks and women as white
men's equals. The difficulty of the constitutional amending process to which
Tiedeman pointed might further account for many of the constitutional
evasions and creative interpretations that he documented, while his advice
to judges would be useless without a system in which judges were given
such a prominent role as occupants of one of three coequal branches of
government. However much the electoral college has been modified, it,
rather than a system of direct election, still influences the way that presidential candidates campaign and the way they are subsequently chosen, and
the progress of civil rights since 1954 would suggest that laws and cases
can sometimes influence and shape popular morality and not simply reflect
it.

Tiedeman's Prescription for Constitutional Interpretation

Without necessarily specifying how frequently this would be, Tiedeman
accepted adherence to the constitutional letter when its meaning was unambiguous. Tiedeman denied, however, that respect for the Framers' intentions should prevail absent such clear language. In such cases, Tiedeman
encouraged judges to read contemporary views into the "glittering generalities" of the Constitution. Tiedeman preferred to sanction laissez faire
principles then current. Despite apparent claims of more universal validity

in *Limitations of the Police Powers*, by Tiedeman's analysis in *The Unwritten Constitution*, such principles were neither inalienable nor universal; they were simply products of the time, effective only insofar as they were sustained by enlightened contemporary opinion.

To the extent that Tiedeman meant not only to describe what the courts had been doing but further to commend a course for them to follow, one might ask upon what basis courts should prefer contemporary standards to earlier ones? In answer, Tiedeman could, of course, assert—as for all practical purposes he did—that might makes right,[122] and that courts should accept contemporary opinions because they had no choice. His last chapter defending constitutions seems, however, to contradict this notion. Moreover, if there were no choice, no arguments or advice Tiedeman could offer would avail in any case. If he believed judges did have a choice, then Tiedeman needed to offer some reason for believing that contemporary opinion was more enlightened, or progressive, or moral, or reasonable than that of the past.

Even in such a case, Tiedeman would have had to show what particular competence judges had to ascertain such standards as opposed to legislators who might be presumed to be in even closer touch with public opinion or to Founders who might be superior in wisdom or public spiritedness to both. As to the competence of courts, Tiedeman did suggest that, being unelected, judges might serve as a hedge against popular whims on behalf of popular will, but one wonders why legislators with a view to their own long-term interests might not do likewise. More critically, the very fact that judges serve unelected life terms might make them subject to abuses not as easily remedied as those committed by legislators.[123]

Tiedeman's reliance upon the due process clause and other "glittering generalities" suggested that he envisioned the judicial role to be important. However he might refer to the protection of the "popular" will, Tiedeman's disparaging comments on democracy as well as his analysis of the contemporary situation also indicated that protecting the people as a whole was not as important as protecting the enlightened will of the elite classes. Tiedeman clearly regarded the courts as a bastion of the capitalist class in its conflict with laborers. By acknowledging that the courts' only real basis for enforcing a set of claims more conducive to the interests of the former than the latter, however, was reliance upon such "glittering generalities" as the due process clause, Tiedeman disclosed the fragility of the judicial role he and a number of his contemporaries had marked out for the courts in *Limitations of the Police Powers* and elsewhere.[124] It was this fragility, hidden for a time by the triumph of "substantive due process" in early twentieth-century jurisprudence, that eventually showed itself in the so-called "switch in time that saved nine" and in subsequent cases[125] and that did so much to discredit constitutional analyses like Tiedeman's.

IMPLICATIONS FOR MODERN
CONSTITUTIONAL INTERPRETATION

While Tiedeman used the idea of an organic constitution in pursuit of what are today considered to be fairly conservative goals, most subsequent advocates of this concept have had a more liberal agenda that was also eventually upheld by the U.S. Supreme Court.[126] It is interesting that, just as the Court's initial espousal of substantive due process and freedom of contract was never incorporated into the Constitution by the Article V amending process, so too the judicial revolution symbolized by the Supreme Court's turnabout of 1937 was never formalized by the adoption of constitutional amendments. Apparently focusing on the difficulty of adopting such amendments,[127] President Franklin D. Roosevelt deliberately chose to attempt to enlarge the Supreme Court hoping to appoint personnel to the Court who would change its judgments.[128] While losing the Court-packing skirmish, Roosevelt arguably won the wider war. He undoubtedly paid a price for his victory, however, undercutting public faith in his intentions and leaving his programs without the "democratic imprimatur" that amendments would have served.[129] This left key planks of his New Deal programs subject to continuing partisan controversy.[130]

As the Warren Court of the 1950s and 1960s further extended the range of civil rights and liberties to the applause of contemporary liberals, many must surely have been confirmed in their belief that the Supreme Court, rather than the amending process, was the true locus of change.[131] While liberals have hardly been the only heirs of Tiedeman's latitudinarian doctrine of judicial interpretation,[132] they have certainly led the way, sometimes on the basis of broad extraconstitutional principles.[133] and other times on the basis of public opinion,[134] for broad readings of such provisions as the prohibition against cruel and unusual punishments, the search and seizure clause, freedom of speech, and the even more elusive right of privacy. While public opinion has undoubtedly accepted many of these constitutional readings, on occasion judicial views of contemporary opinion have proven premature and/or inaccurate.[135] On other occasions, their views, like Tiedeman's at the time he was writing, now dominate but will not necessarily prove permanent.

In the very least, this reconsideration of Tiedeman's analysis might suggest that, when broad constitutional principles are not translated into unambiguous constitutional language, the constitutional interpretation of any given constitutional provision is, like a game of baseball, not over until it is over.[136] Perhaps in this respect, at least, Tiedeman's analysis indicates that those seeking relative permanency for their ideas should look, at least when this is possible, not to the courts but to the formulating of constitutional structures and to the very process of constitutional amendment that Tiedeman denigrated.[137]

NOTES

1. The language is that of Chief Justice John Marshall in *Marbury v. Madison*, 5 U.S. 137 (1803).

2. Elder Witt, *A Different Justice: Reagan and the Supreme Court* (Washington, DC: Congressional Quarterly, 1986), pp. 135–39.

3. For a good survey of this issue, see Stephen C. Halpern and Charles M. Lamb, *Supreme Court Activism and Restraint* (Lexington, MA: D. C. Heath, 1982). Also see Christopher Wolfe, *Judicial Activism: Bulwark of Freedom or Precarious Security?* (Pacific Grove, CA: Brooks/Cole, 1991).

4. See Clyde E. Jacobs, *Law Writers and the Courts: The Influence of Thomas M. Cooley, Christopher G. Tiedeman and John F. Dillon Upon American Constitutional Law* (Berkeley: University of California Press, 1954), pp. 58–63.

5. Lionel M. Summers reports, "By 1897 texts of his [Tiedeman's] were used in thirty-six law schools." See "Tiedeman, Christopher Gustavus," *Dictionary of American Biography*, ed. D. Malone (New York: Charles Scribner's Sons, 1964), vol. 9, p. 531. Summers also includes a more complete list of Tiedeman's works than does this book.

6. In this book, reference is to Christopher Tiedeman, *A Treatise on the Limitations of the Police Powers in the United States* (New York: Da Capo Press, 1971; reprint of F. H. Thomas Law Book Co., 1886). For other Tiedeman classics, see *An Elementary Treatise on the American Law of Real Property*, 2nd ed. (St. Louis: F. H. Thomas Law Book Co., 1892) and *A Treatise on the Law of Commercial Paper* (St. Louis: F. H. Thomas Law Book Co., 1889).

7. Christopher Tiedeman, *The Unwritten Constitution of the United States* (New York: C. P. Putnam's Sons, 1890).

8. Louise A. Halper, "Christopher G. Tiedeman, 'Laissez-Faire Constitutionalism' and the Dilemmas of Small-Scale Property in the Gilded Age," *Ohio State Law Journal* 51 (1990), p. 1349.

9. David N. Mayer, "The Jurisprudence of Christopher G. Tiedeman: A Study in the Failure of Laissez-Faire Constitutionalism," *Missouri Law Review* 55 (Winter 1990), pp. 93–161. Mayer's article is particularly useful in tracing the origins of Tiedeman's ideas and in tying Tiedeman's thoughts to recent questions involving unenumerated rights.

10. Tiedeman, *Limitations of the Police Powers*, p. 1.

11. Ibid., p. 2.

12. Translation provided in Richard M. Pious, "Introduction," in Tiedeman's *The Unwritten Constitution* (Farmingdale, NY: Dabor Social Science Publications, 1978), p. i. Since the pages to this introduction are unnumbered, lowercase Roman numeral citations are provided in this and subsequent references.

13. Tiedeman, *Limitations of the Public Powers*, pp. 4–5.

14. Mayer, "The Jurisprudence of Christopher G. Tiedeman," thus observes that Tiedeman "urged innovation, even radical innovation, in the law" (p. 130). Also see Thomas C. Grey, "Introduction," in Christopher Tiedeman, *The Unwritten Constitution of the United States* (Buffalo, NY: William S. Hein, 1974; reprint), p. iv. Louise A. Halper, "Christopher G. Tiedeman," notes that by 1900 Tiedeman placed less emphasis on the protection of property than on the survival of small businesses

against giant corporations and that he even advocated nationalization of major in-
dustries during this later period (p. 136).

15. 3 Dallas 386 (1798). For a contemporary justification of Chase's position see
Suzanna Sherry, "The Founder's Unwritten Constitution," *University of Chicago
Law Review* 54 (Fall 1987), pp. 1127–77. Also see Thomas C. Grey, "Origins of
the Unwritten Constitution: Fundamental Law in American Revolutionary
Thought," *Stanford Law Review* 30 (May 1978), pp. 843–93.

16. Tiedeman, *Limitations of the Police Power*, p. 7.

17. Ibid., p. 8.

18. Ibid., p. 10.

19. Ibid.

20. Ibid.

21. Ibid., p. 11.

22. Ibid., pp. 11–12.

23. Ibid., p. 12.

24. Tiedeman, *The Unwritten Constitution*, p. 2.

25. Ibid. Mayer, "The Jurisprudence of Christopher G. Tiedeman," traces this
view of the law to Tiedeman's German teacher, Rudolf von Jhering (1818–1892)
(p. 105).

26. Tiedeman, *The Unwritten Constitution*, pp. 6–7.

27. Ibid., p. 8.

28. Ibid.

29. Ibid., p. 9.

30. Ibid., p. 12.

31. Ibid.

32. Ibid., p. 13.

33. Ibid., p. 16.

34. Ibid.

35. Ibid., p. 21.

36. Ibid.

37. Ibid., pp. 40–41.

38. Ibid., p. 43.

39. Ibid.

40. Ibid. For other works with this same emphasis, see Herbert Horwill, *The
Usages of the American Constitution* (Oxford: Oxford University Press, 1925), and
Michael Foley, *The Silence of Constitutions: Gaps, 'Abeyances' and Political Temperament
in the Maintenance of Government* (London: Routledge, 1989). Also see Sanford Levinson, *Constitutional Faith* (Princeton, NJ: Princeton University Press, 1988), pp. 9–
53.

41. Tiedeman, *The Unwritten Constitution*, pp. 43–44.

42. Ibid., p. 44.

43. Ibid., p. 49.

44. Ibid., p. 53.

45. Ibid., p. 59.

46. It is interesting to see that Tiedeman's analysis came well before *Home
Building & Loan Assoc. v. Blaisdell*, 290 U.S. 398 (1934), which appears further to
confirm his point.

47. Tiedeman, *The Unwritten Constitution*, p. 66.

48. See, for example, Calhoun's speech on the Oregon Bill, delivered in the Senate, June 27, 1848, in John C. Calhoun, *The Works of John C. Calhoun,* ed. Richard K. Cralle (New York: Russell and Russell, 1968; reprint of 1851–56 editions), vol. 4, pp. 507–12. For further analysis, see Chapter 5 of this book. Being educated in Charleston, Tiedeman almost certainly would have been familiar with Calhoun's works.

49. Tiedeman, *The Unwritten Constitution,* pp. 70–71.

50. Ibid., p. 72.

51. Ibid., p. 76.

52. Ibid. This was, of course, the work that Oliver Wendell Holmes, Jr., referred to in his dissenting opinion in *Lochner v. New York,* where he noted, "The Fourteenth Amendment does not enact Mr. Herbert Spencer's Social Statics." 198 U.S. 45 (1905), p. 75.

53. Tiedeman, *The Unwritten Constitution,* p. 76.

54. Ibid., p. 80.

55. Ibid., p. 79.

56. Ibid., p. 81.

57. *Ex Parte Merryman,* 17 Fed. Case No. 9487 (1861) and *Ex Parte Milligan,* 4 Wallace 2 (1886).

58. Tiedeman, *The Unwritten Constitution,* p. 89.

59. 16 Wallace 36 (1873). For contemporary analysis of this case, see Ronald M. Labbe, "New Light on the Slaughterhouse Monopoly Act of 1869," *Louisiana's Legal Heritage,* ed. Edward F. Haas (Pensacola, FL: Perdido Bay Press, 1983), pp. 143–62.

60. For a view not altogether different from Tiedeman's, however, see M. E. Bradford, " 'Changed Only a Little': The Reconstruction Amendments and the Nomocratic Constitution of 1787," *Wake Forest Law Review* 24 (1989), pp. 573–98.

61. Tiedeman, *The Unwritten Constitution,* p. 99.

62. Ibid., p. 100.

63. Ibid., p. 99.

64. Ibid.

65. Ibid., pp. 102–3.

66. Ibid., p. 108.

67. Ibid., p. 111. Although his conclusions are quite different, Tiedeman's emphasis on the role of scientific fact is similar to that of John C. Calhoun in *A Disquisition on Government,* (Indianapolis: Bobbs-Merrill, 1953).

68. Tiedeman, *The Unwritten Constitution,* p. 116.

69. Ibid., p. 118.

70. Ibid., p. 120.

71. Ibid., p. 121.

72. Ibid.

73. Ibid.

74. Ibid., p. 122.

75. Ibid.

76. Ibid., p. 123.

77. Ibid., p. 125.

78. Ibid., p. 126.

79. Ibid., p. 132.

80. Ibid., p. 136.
81. Ibid.
82. Ibid., p. 137.
83. Ibid., p. 140.
84. Ibid., p. 141.
85. Ibid., p. 144.
86. Ibid.
87. Ibid., p. 146.
88. Ibid., p. 147.
89. Ibid., p. 148.
90. Ibid.
91. Ibid., pp. 149–50.
92. Ibid., p. 149.
93. See *Dartmouth College v. Woodward*, 17 U.S. 518 (1819).
94. Tiedeman, *The Unwritten Constitution*, p. 153.
95. Ibid.
96. Ibid., p. 154.
97. Ibid., p. 155.
98. Ibid., pp. 156–57.
99. Ibid., p. 161.
100. Ibid., p. 162.
101. Ibid.
102. Ibid., p. 163.
103. Ibid., pp. 163–64.
104. Ibid., p. 164.
105. Ibid.
106. Ibid., p. 165.
107. Ibid.
108. Tiedeman's work is subtitled *A Philosophical Inquiry into the Foundations of American Constitutional Law*.
109. It was, after all, Thomas Hobbes who described the life of man in the state of nature as "solitary, poor, nasty, brutish and short." See Hobbes, *Leviathan*, ed. Michael Oakeshott (New York: Collier Books, 1962), p. 100.
110. John Locke, *Two Treatises of Government*, ed. Peter Laslett (New York: New American Library, 1963), p. 396.
111. See Brian R. Nelson, *Western Political Thought: From Socrates to the Age of Ideology* (Englewood Cliffs, NJ: Prentice-Hall, 1982), pp. 138–39.
112. For such points, see Carl L. Becker, *The Declaration of Independence* (New York: Vintage Books, 1970). There were, of course, influences on the Founding Fathers other than social contract thinking. See, for example, Morton White, *The Philosophy of the American Revolution* (New York: Oxford University Press, 1978); Gordon Wood, *The Creation of the American Republic, 1776–1787* (New York: W. W. Norton, 1976); Bernard Bailyn, *The Ideological Origins of the American Revolution* (Cambridge, MA: Belknap Press, 1967); and Forrest McDonald, *Novus Ordo Seclorum* (Lawrence: University Press of Kansas, 1985).
113. Grey, "Introduction," in Tiedeman, *The Unwritten Constitution*, pp. vi–vii.
114. For a recent article blunting this distinction on the basis that "it will only be plausible to argue that actual practice has no prescriptive force if there is a

conclusive moral argument against actual practice,'' see Robert J. Lipkin, "The Anatomy of Constitutional Revolutions," *Nebraska Law Review* 68 (1989), p. 783.

For the way that Tiedeman's and other prescriptions for constitutional change grew out of descriptions of past changes, see Thomas H. Peebles, "A Call to High Debate: The Organic Constitution in its Formative Era, 1890–1920," *University of Colorado Law Review* 52 (Fall 1980), pp. 51, 56.

115. For a contemporary discussion of social influences on judicial decision making, see Louis Fisher, "Social Influences on Constitutional Law," *Journal of Political Science* 15 (Spring 1987), pp. 7–19. For a study that focuses more particularly on political influences on the amending process, see Clement Vose, *Constitutional Change: Amendment Politics and Supreme Court Litigation Since 1900* (Lexington, MA: D. C. Heath, 1972).

116. At least some recognition of this change is, however, recorded in the Twelfth Amendment to the U.S. Constitution.

117. The tie to legal realists and advocates of sociological jurisprudence has been noted by Grey, "Introduction," in Tiedeman, *The Unwritten Constitution*, p. vi. There are also some interesting parallels between Tiedeman's arguments and those of Bruce Ackerman, "The Storrs Lectures: Discovering the Constitution," *Yale Law Journal* 93 (May 1984), p. 1013. Also see Ackerman's "Constitutional Politics/Constitutional Law," *The Yale Law Journal* 99 (December 1989), pp. 453–547.

118. Thus at least two contemporary writers have made much of the distinction between constitutional aspirations and mere historical facts. See Sotirios A. Barber, *On What the Constitution Means* (Baltimore, MD: Johns Hopkins University Press, 1984), pp. 32–34, and Gary J. Jacobson, *The Supreme Court and the Decline of Constitutional Aspiration* (Totowa, NJ: Rowman & Littlefield, 1986). But also see Mark A. Grabner, "Our (Im)perfect Constitution," *Review of Politics* 51 (Winter 1989), pp. 86–106.

119. On this point, Tiedeman's reasoning bears great resemblance to the arguments of Social Darwinists of his day and is subject to many of the same criticisms. For one of the more enlightened critiques, see William James, "Great Men and their Environment," *The Will to Believe and Other Essays in Popular Philosophy* ([New York]: Dover Publications, 1956; reprint of 1897 edition), pp. 216–54.

120. Pious, "Introduction," in Tiedeman, *The Unwritten Constitution*, pp. ii–iii. Tiedeman's language further suggests a connection to Social Darwinism. For analysis of this movement, see Richard Hofstader, *Social Darwinism in American Thought* (Boston: Beacon Press, 1955).

121. James Madison recognized this aspect of public opinion, treated in Chapter 2 of this book, in *Federalist* Nos. 49 and 50.

122. Pious, "Introduction," connects Tiedeman's espousal of this principle to the influence of Social Darwinism.

123. This is the well-known "counter-majoritarian difficulty." See Alexander Bickel, *The Least Dangerous Branch* (Indianapolis: Bobbs-Merrill, 1962), 16. What makes this argument particularly telling against Tiedeman is his argument in the *Treatise on the Limitations of the Police Powers*, where he recognized that concerns about fundamental principles were best addressed to legislators.

124. Pious, "Introduction," notes:

> Rarely has the total arbitrary nature of the constitutional system constructed in the post–Civil War period (and lasting into the 1930s) been described with

such candor by one of its chief architects and defenders. Tiedeman himself makes it clear that the system rested neither on the consent of the governed nor on the intentions of the constitutional framers. Its laws were based neither on the will of the majority nor on principles of social utility. Public opinion was to be manipulated and shaped by an elite for its own purposes. The elite's notions of right and wrong were to prevail.

125. *National Labor Relations Board v. Jones & Laughlin Steel Corporation*, 301 U.S. 1 (1937).

126. Peebles, "A Call to High Debate," pp. 74–83.

127. William E. Leuchtenburg, "The Origins of Franklin D. Roosevelt's 'Court-Packing' Plan," *The Supreme Court Review*, ed. Philip B. Kurland (Chicago: University of Chicago Press, 1966), pp. 347–400.

128. David E. Kyvig, "The Road Not Taken: FDR, the Supreme Court, and Constitutional Amendment," *Political Science Quarterly* 104 (Fall 1989), pp. 463–81.

129. Ibid., p. 464.

130. Ibid., p. 481, thus notes that "recent advocates of limited government downplay or deny federal responsibility for social welfare" and that, "in the absence of a constitutional directive to follow a different course, a public with a short, selective historical memory finds no reason to demand otherwise."

131. For a recent book that questions this belief, however, see Gerald N. Rosenberg, *The Hollow Hope: Can Courts Bring About Social Change?* (Chicago: University of Chicago Press, 1991).

132. See, however, Stuart Taylor, Jr., "The 'Judicial Activists' Are Always on the Other Side," *The New York Times*, July 3, 1988, p. E5, for indications of contemporary activism among conservative justices on the Supreme Court.

133. See, for example, Justice William Brennan's reliance upon the concept of "human dignity" in "The Constitution of the United States: Contemporary Ratification," *South Texas Law Review* 27 (Fall 1986), pp. 433–45.

134. See Justice Thurgood Marshall's opinion on the constitutionality of the death penalty, in which he appealed in part to considerations of contemporary public opinion in *Furman v. Georgia*, 408 U.S. 238 (1972), pp. 332, 360–69.

135. See Justice Marshall's opinion in *Gregg v. Georgia*, 428 U.S. 153 (1976), p. 232. In light of the enactment of death penalty statutes in thirty-five states, Marshall put even more emphasis on the opinions of an "informed citizenry" than in his previous decision. Marshall's stance is treated at greater length in John R. Vile, "Constitutional Interpretation and Constitutional Amendment: Alternate Means of Constitutional Change," *Research in Law and Policy Studies*, Vol. 3, ed. Stuart Nagel (Greenwich, CT: JAI Press, 1992). For complaints from U.S. Supreme Court justices that the majority was amending the Constitution, see John R. Vile, "The Supreme Court and the Amending Process," *Georgia Political Science Association Journal* 8 (Fall 1980); pp. 33–66.

136. Yogi Berra is credited with the statement "It ain't over till it's over." See Ralph Graves, "The 'Pope' Who is Revising Our Bible of Sayings," *Smithsonian* 22 (August 1991), p. 70.

137. A central problem with this approach is, of course, the continuing difficulty of the amending process, a discussion which is treated more extensively in Chapter 8 of this book.

Chapter 8

The Progressive Era and Continuing Doubts about the Adequacy of the Amending Process

Aside from John Marshall's cryptic statements about the cumbersome nature of the amending process[1] and complaints by Anti-Federalist defenders of the even more difficult process under the Articles of Confederation, most American commentators on the amending process to the time of Sidney George Fisher appear to have been favorably impressed with this mechanism,[2] which they frequently praised as an adequate "safety-valve," or as an alternative to revolution. Nevertheless, no amendments were adopted between the ratification of the Twelfth Amendment in 1804 and adoption of the Thirteenth Amendment in 1865. While two other amendments quickly followed, they were ratified in such circumstances as to confirm the difficulty of the amending process in more normal conditions,[3] and no further amendments were ratified until 1913. Given this history, it may not be surprising that the difficulty of the amending process became a frequent subject of discussion from the 1800s up to about the 1920s, with progressive representatives particularly associated with efforts to make this process easier.[4] Much of this impetus for change appears to have come either from British observers or from those who were proponents of such a parliamentary system.

LORD BRYCE

If anyone contributed to the perception that the American constitutional amending process might be in need of repair, it was undoubtedly Lord Bryce whose study, *The American Commonwealth*, is still regarded as a classic.[5] Bryce was apparently the one to introduce a distinction that would mark discussions of the subject for the next twenty-five years, namely the distinction between "rigid" and "flexible" constitutions, a distinction which, however impartial it might first appear, seemed almost invariably to denote the superiority of the latter type of constitution to the former.[6] Who, after all, wants to be known as being rigid or as being governed by a document that is so regarded?[7]

This distinction appears to have been more fully formulated in an essay published in 1905 than in Bryce's book, the first edition of which preceded it by seventeen years. But, in his book too, Bryce used the distinction[8] and noted that the few occasions on which the Constitution had been amended were attributed "not solely to the excellence of the original instrument, but also to the difficulties which surround the process of change."[9] Bryce further indicated that the failure to utilize constitutional mechanisms for change had enabled controversies over constitutional interpretation to pass "from the law courts to the battle-field."[10] Bryce did balance this judgment by pointing out that Americans feared that "the habit of mending would turn into the habit of tinkering,"[11] and by pointing to the value that Americans placed on "solidity and security" in their "fundamental law."[12] When, in his 1905 essay, Bryce concluded that "the Constitution which it is the most difficult to change is that of the United States,"[13] however, many readers must surely have wondered if America had not pushed the idea of constitutional rigidity to an extreme.

JOHN BURGESS

Often recognized as the founder of the academic discipline of political science in America,[14] John Burgess, an Amherst graduate, finished his own education in Europe before creating the graduate program in political science at Columbia University. He issued his *Political Science and Comparative Constitutional Law* in 1890, being strongly influenced like Christopher Tiedeman, by German political theory and, especially, by the philosophy of Hegel.[15] In looking at Article V of the Constitution, Burgess specifically noted that he could not "sympathize with that unreserved commendation . . . indulged in by Mr. Joseph Story and other commentators."[16] Burgess explained:

When I reflect that, while our natural conditions and relations have been requiring a gradual strengthening and extension of the powers of the central government, not a single step has been taken in this direction through the process of amendment prescribed in that article, except as the result of civil war, I am bound to conclude that the organization of the sovereign power within the constitution has failed to accomplish the purpose for which it was constructed.[17]

Burgess connected this putative failure of Article V to "the artificially excessive majorities required in the production of constitutional changes," pointing out that "it was possible for less than 3,000,000 of people to successfully resist more than 45,000,000 in any attempt to amend the constitution under the present process."[18] Burgess feared that such rigidity exposed the nation to "revolution and violence," and he noted that "the safeguards against too radical change must not be exaggerated to the point of dethroning the real sovereign."[19]

Burgess's solution to such rigidity was an amending scheme utilizing "repetition of vote."[20] Specifically, Burgess wanted two successive joint sessions of Congress (a mechanism that would have severely undercut the role of the Senate, whose members were, until the ratification of the Seventeenth Amendment in 1913, appointed by the state legislatures) to be able to propose amendments. Such amendments would be subject to ratification by majority vote of the state legislatures meeting in joint assemblies, each legislature weighted according to its strength in the electoral college, an absolute majority being required.[21] Although admitting that the existing constitution text would appear to require that the new process be limited, like the old, to withdrawing equal state suffrage in the Senate from future amendments, Burgess, like Tiedeman, argued that the nation should not on such matters be "strictly held by the intentions of the framers," but "that present conditions, relations and requirements should be the chief consideration, and that, when the language of the constitution will bear it, these should determine the interpretation."[22]

WOODROW WILSON

One of the earliest advocates of cabinet government in the United States along British lines,[23] Woodrow Wilson, political scientist, college administrator, and future U.S. president, saw the amending process as an obstacle in the path of reform. He seemed to waiver, however, between the view that additional amendments should be added to the Constitution and the view that many changes could be effected through judicial interpretations and presidential assumptions of greater powers.[24] In an early work, *Congressional Government*, Wilson referred to the amending process as "so slow and cumbersome" that it could be moved by "no impulse short of the impulse of self-preservation, no force less than the force of revolution."[25] In what is generally considered to be his most mature political writing, Wilson further faulted the American system of checks and balances for being based on an outdated Newtonian model rather than on a more Darwinian scheme.[26] Citing Montesquieu's scheme, Wilson noted: "The trouble with this theory is that government is not a machine, but a living thing. It falls, not under the theory of the universe, but under the theory of organic life. It is accountable to Darwin, not to Newton."[27] Interestingly, Wilson argued that "it is easier to write of the President than of the presidency," reasoning that "the government of the United States has had a vital and normal organic growth and has proved itself eminently adapted to express the changing temper and purposes of the American people from age to age."[28]

Writing about the relation between the state and national governments, Wilson further noted:

The Constitution cannot be regarded as a mere legal document, to be read as a will or a contract would be. It must, of the necessity of the case, be a vehicle of life. As the life of the nation changes so must the interpretation of the document which contains it change, by a nice adjustment, determined, not by the original intention of those who drew the paper, but by the exigencies and the new aspects of life itself.[29]

Wilson, while clearly recognizing limits on judicial interpretation, saw the difficulty of amendment as a key prod to judicial action.

The process of formal amendment was made so difficult by the provisions of the Constitution itself that it has seldom been feasible to use it; and the difficulty of formal amendment has understandably made the courts more liberal, not to say more lax, in their interpretation than they would otherwise have been.[30]

Warning that judges "should never permit themselves wilfully to seek to find in the phrases of the Constitution remedies for evils which the federal government was never intended to deal with,"[31] Wilson had noted that "change as well as stability may be conservative," and had called for "a process, not of revolution, but of modification."[32]

HERMAN AMES

In 1897, Herman Ames, then a historian at the University of Pennsylvania, published a comprehensive survey of amendments proposed in Congress during the Constitution's first hundred years.[33] As part of this outstanding study in which he identified over seventeen hundred proposed amendments, Ames reviewed several unresolved issues surrounding Article V and concluded that the Framers' hopes for the amending process had not been fulfilled. Acknowledging that many of the proposals he had reviewed were "trivial or impractical" while others had "found a place in that unwritten constitution which has grown up side by side with the written document," Ames suggested that the central reason why a mere fifteen amendments had been ratified, the last three of which "were carried only after a civil war," was attributable to "the insurmountable constitutional obstacles in their way."[34] Acknowledging that "a rigid constitution has its excellencies," Ames asked whether or not there was "a limit to the degree of rigidity desirable?"[35] Without specifying what majorities he would advocate, Ames argued that the reason the amending process had proven "unwieldly and cumbrous"[36] was because "the majorities required are too large," allowing, by the 1890 census, "for eleven States with a population of less than 2,350,000 to defeat any constitutional amendment although it was desired by the more than 60,000,000 inhabitants of the other states."[37] Ames concluded his book with an ominous warning from Professor Burgess about the danger of revolution and violence when the amending mechanism did not prove adequate.[38]

HENRY B. HIGGINS

The title of an article by Australian Henry B. Higgins, "The Rigid Constitution," suggested that his critique of the amending process was also influenced by terminology that had been introduced by Lord Bryce and followed by others.[39] Noting that "the federal constitution has become practically unalterable," Higgins observed, "Except as the result of the volcanic upheaval of the great Civil war and by the use of such devices after the war as were, to say the least, unprecedented, there has been no change since 1804."[40] Like other observers of the period, Higgins believed that constitutional rigidity had led to judicial creativity, so much so that he argued that "the constitution has not merely been unfolded by the courts; it has been amended by the courts."[41]

Higgins was particularly fond of metaphors, several of which he applied to the amending process. In regard to the need for judicial expansions of the Constitution, Higgins thus noted:

A tree may grow notwithstanding the iron band bound around it as a sapling; but it grows deformed, stunted, wanting rondure and completeness. It is better that the sap should run up within the trunk than that suckers and parasites should thrive without. Constrained, as they were, by the iron band of the constitution, too much of the energy of the political leaders has been spent on barren questions of interpretation of a written document, in ascertaining what a dry piece of parchment means rather than what the people need.[42]

Responding to an earlier analogy that had been used by supporters of the amending process, Higgins observed that Jameson "in likening the provisions for amendments to safety-valves, happily added that the force needed to induce motion should not be that which is necessary to explode the machine."[43] Similarly, Higgins adopted two analogies when arguing that

to prevent rash "tinkering" it is not necessary . . . to forbid the repair of holes or fractures; much less is it necessary, with a society expanding so enormously, to put its fundamental law within a wall of concrete and thus restrain it from its natural growth.[44]

Perhaps not aware that he was using a Jeffersonian analogy,[45] Higgins was amazed "that so great a nation has so long submitted to be fettered in its

movements by a garment made for it in its infancy."[46] Higgins clearly favored a less rigid amending process although he was unsure whether the
weight of extraconstitutional interpretation would lead the people to "pull
down the constitution and replace it" or whether, by "some almost super-
human effort of patriotism and self effacement all parties may unite to amend
the amending power."[47]

J. ALLEN SMITH

In *The Spirit of American Government*,[48] J. Allen Smith, then a professor
of political science at the University of Washington, offered a scathing
critique of the U.S. Constitution from the Progressive perspective, challenging what he considered to be the document's aristocratic and undemocratic features and calling for measures to take away the privileged
political and economic status of the ruling elites.[49] In his study, Smith clearly
identified the amending process as one of the elements that contributed to
the undemocratic nature of the Constitution.

But undemocratic as the system was, it was not sufficiently undemocratic to suit
the framers of the Constitution. It was no part of their plan to establish a government
which the people could control. In fact, popular control was what they were seeking
to avoid. One means of accomplishing this was to make amendment difficult, and
this accordingly was done. We need not be surprised that no provision was made
for its original adoption, or subsequent amendment by direct popular vote.[50]

Both this lack of direct popular participation and the extraordinary majorities required for amendments demonstrated to Smith that, while the Constitution "nominally provides for amendment," it really makes such
amendments "an impossibility."[51] Smith argued that neither the Bill of
Rights nor the Civil War amendments had significantly modified the Constitution. While many important changes had been proposed, none had ever
been adopted, the proposal and ratification stages both being too onerous.
Smith pointed out that the two-thirds majority required to propose amendments was greater than any president had received since 1828, while the
three-fourths majorities needed for ratification "effectively precludes the
possibility of any important amendment."[52] Indeed, by Smith's account,
amendment was actually easier under the Articles of Confederation in that,
since the Congress was "the court of last resort for passing on the constitutionality of its own legislation," this Congress could amend the Articles
"by the ordinary processes of law-making" in a way that the present Congress, subject to judicial review, could not.[53]

Comparing the U.S. Constitution unfavorably with the constitutions in
Britain, France, Australia, and Switzerland which showed "the general tendency at the present time to make the majority supreme," Smith argued

that "a constitution is in no proper sense the embodiment of the will of the people unless it recognizes the right of the majority to amend."[54] The only checks on amendment that would be necessary in a truly democratic society are those "calculated to insure the deliberate expression of the popular will."[55]

In a subsequent chapter on the judiciary, however, Smith professed to see some hope in the unused convention option in Article V, which he saw as opening "the door to the most revolutionary changes in our political arrangements."[56] This body might indeed do for the majority what the convention of 1787 had done for the minority: "A new Federal constitution might be framed which would eliminate the whole system of checks on the people and provide for the direct ratification by a majority of voters, as has already been done in the case of most of our state constitutions."[57] If this was too much to expect, perhaps the threat of such a convention could, at least, serve as a prod to needed changes.

> It is possible, if not indeed probable, that a serious and concerted attempt by the people to force changes in the Constitution by this method would sufficiently alarm the opponents of democracy to convince them of the wisdom and expediency of such amendments as would appease the popular clamor for reform without going too far in the direction of majority rule. To prevent the complete overthrow of the system, which might be the outcome if the states were compelled to assume the initiative in amending the Constitution, the minority may accept the inevitable, and, choosing what appears to them to be the lesser of two evils, allow Congress to propose such amendments as the people are determined to bring about.[58]

Smith's hope on this point was indeed so great as to call into question whether the Framers had been as antidemocratic or as wily in carrying out their putative antidemocratic schemes as he portrayed them to be.

HERBERT CROLY

Herbert Croly, the influential author of *The Promise of American Life*,[59] was another progressive spokesman who joined in calls for an easier amending process. While crediting the difficulty of the amending process with contributing to the stability of the political system in the early years of the republic, in *Progressive Democracy* Croly now portrayed Article V as "the most formidable legal obstacle in the path of progressive democratic fulfillment."[60] Croly advocated the adoption of the plan advocated by Senator LaFollette whereby amendments submitted "by a majority of both houses of Congress or by one-fourth of the states" would become law when approved "by a majority of all the voters voting, provided that this majority is distributed throughout a majority of the states."[61]

Not only did Croly view the difficulty of the amending process as undemocratic, but, like others of the same time period, he also associated this difficulty with the assumption of increased powers by the courts, powers that had allowed "a small band of lawyers . . . to convert their political preferences into law under the cover of constitutional construction."[62] Croly perceived, somewhat prematurely it turned out, that the courts were sanctioning ever greater legislative interferences with individual liberties under the rubric of state police powers. While legislative power was more accountable and thus less threatening than judicial power, Croly argued that "public opinion has never exhibited any intention of allowing essentially wilful political instruments, like Congress or the state legislatures, to become all-powerful within their respective jurisdictions."[63] The cure for such democracy was, in characteristic Progressive fashion, more democracy. The "golden hoard" of democracy should "no longer be locked up in an inaccessible safe which cannot be opened except by conforming to a most complicated and difficult ritualistic combination," but should "be placed directly in the custody of the people themselves," allowing them "to realize their own responsibility."[64]

MUNROE SMITH

Munroe Smith, a prominent political scientist and colleague of John Burgess at Columbia University, offered his critique of the constitutional amending process in an article published in the wake of the congressional proposal of the income tax amendment. The title of Smith's article, "Shall We Make Our Constitution Flexible?" suggested that he too was influenced by the earlier classification introduced by Lord Bryce.[65] Smith argued that, while amendments were not terribly difficult to adopt in the early years of the republic, population changes made such amendments much more difficult from 1820 forward.[66] Given the role of the proposed Sixteenth Amendment in restoring a prior practice rather than in initiating innovations, Smith thought it was possible that it would be ratified, although he also said, "The rejection of this amendment, indeed, would go far to prove that formal change of the Constitution is impossible."[67] In the meantime, the difficulty of amendment was leading to judicial attempts to bend the existing document to new exigencies, attempts with undesirable consequences.

Evasion of the law does not create respect for the law, and the lack of respect for the law is already one of our national vices. Further, the attempt to evade the law and justify its evasion is unfavorable to intellectual integrity, to straight thinking and honest speech, on the part of our legislators, and also, in second instance, on the part of our judges.[68]

In Smith's view, the difficulty of amendment reinforced and contributed to the ineffectiveness of American political parties which, in his day, "have no use for principles because they would not be able to put them into practice."[69] Such parties of principle—apparently on the British model—could be aided by an easier amending mechanism.

If a party that can carry a Presidential election by a fair majority of electoral votes could also amend the Constitution, a strong national party might well be formed with a programme more radical than Mr. Roosevelt's—a programme which men of conservative temper would probably term socialistic. Under such conditions, conservatives would no longer be able to rely upon this rigid Constitution and the Supreme Court to protect property interests; they would be forced to organize a party representing their principles.[70]

Smith concluded that "the only line of escape from the existing situation, except through revolution, lies in the amendment of the amending clause of the Federal Constitution."[71]

Citing Burgess's plan of twenty-one years before, Smith argued that it had little chance of adoption because senators would feel that they were being swallowed up in the joint assemblies Burgess had proposed. Smith therefore suggested that amendments should be proposed by "the majority vote of both Houses in two successive Congresses" and ratified by a majority of states, either through legislative approval or approval by the voters of the states, "provided that the ratifying States contain, according to the last preceding enumeration, a majority of the total population of all the States."[72] Smith claimed inspiration for popular ratification of amendments from the state examples and argued that his mechanism would give any party that captured the presidency a "reasonable hope of success, to amend the Constitution."[73] Smith further touted his proposal as a way of ending the veto on amendments that could then be exercised by any section containing one-fourth or more of the states.[74]

FREDERIC B. JOHNSTONE

Thirteen months after Smith's article, Frederic B. Johnstone of the Chicago bar published an article in which he also indicated his belief that the constitutional amending process was too difficult.[75] Changes in the Constitution of 1787 had been made, for the most part, not "by amendment" but "by construction."[76] Such construction, however, carried dangers and was unnecessary.

Neither the court nor the instrument gains respect when by construction it is forced to speak a language different from that which the plain meaning of the words convey. Wresting unspecified power from an ancient grant would seem almost a waste of judicial energy. The grantor is alive and might reasonably be expected to make another deed, especially as he would be the real beneficiary of the instrument.[77]

Among the problems ripe for constitutional solution, Johnstone cited "governmental control of commerce and transportation and of public utilities; the concentration of wealth; equitable taxation; the industrial situation; [and] natural resources and their conservation."[78] Whereas the Framers had expected that amendments would be frequently adopted, however, "since the decade in which the constitution was adopted, but five amendments have been made, two of which, of comparatively minor importance, are over 100 years old, and the last three of which were written in blood."[79] The Constitution suffered from "immobility"; like a boiler, it "becomes a source of danger under pressure in the absence of a safety valve."[80] Johnstone believed the primary obstruction blocking the amending machinery was the provision that amendments be proposed by two-thirds votes in both houses of Congress. He therefore suggested that amendments be "*proposed* on the vote of a simple majority in two successive sessions of Congress"; ratification would follow "by the vote of a majority of the people *plus* a majority of the states."[81] Such a model would be similar to that already utilized in Australia and Switzerland and would serve ultimately to "conserve" the Constitution by making it responsive to the living rather than the dead. It is interesting that in commenting on this paper, John Parker Hall, Dean of the University of Chicago Law School, did not explicitly deny that the alternative amending mechanism proposed would be better, although he did argue persuasively that Johnstone had both exaggerated the difficulty of amendment and underestimated the power of the central government to meet contemporary problems.[82]

J. DAVID THOMPSON

In the year after Higgins's article, yet another piece critical of the amending process was published by J. David Thompson, a law librarian at Columbia University.[83] Reviewing the history of amendments in America, Thompson saw a litany of problems.

This ponderous piece of constitutional machine [is] difficult to set in motion and slow and uncertain in its operation, fully justifying its vigorous condemnation by eminent publicists at home and abroad. Certain other serious objections to it are based (1) on the very unequal weight which it gives to public opinion in different parts of the country, and (2) on the preponderating influence given to the state governments as against the people.[84]

Thompson argued that the "predominance of state influence" was a holdover from the Articles of Confederation at variance with the doctrine of popular sovereignty,[85] and he argued that better examples could be found by looking both at the state experiences and at the amending mechanisms in Switzerland and Australia.[86] Citing the earlier proposals of Professors Burgess and Smith, Thompson commended the latter arguing, however, that state experience had demonstrated that there was no need for votes by two successive legislatures, and contending that good draftsmanship "could be attained more directly and effectively by the establishment of the proposed legislative drafting bureau for Congress."[87] In a proposal that would have bypassed the Senate, which represented the federal interests to which he so objected, Thompson did provide that, where the two houses of Congress disagreed, provision might be made so that "amendments could be proposed by majority vote of *one* house in two successive Congresses, as an alternative to proposal by majority vote of both houses in one Congress."[88] Moreover, Thompson preferred direct popular ratification of amendments to action through state legislatures or conventions and thought it important that states be able to initiate new ideas more freely. Thompson therefore advocated a measure introduced by Senator LaFollette in the previous session of Congress.

The Congress, whenever an absolute majority of both houses shall deem it necessary, or on application of ten states by resolution adopted in each by the legislature thereon or by a majority of the electors voting therein, shall propose amendments to this constitution to be submitted to each of the several states to the electors qualified to vote for the election of Representatives, and the vote shall be taken at the next ensuing election of Representatives in such manner as the Congress prescribes. And if in a majority of the states a majority of the electors voting approve the proposed amendments, and if a majority of all the electors voting also approve the proposed amendments, they shall be valid, to all intents and purposes, as part of this constitution.[89]

M. A. MUSMANNO

While a number of writers mentioned the plan introduced by Senator LaFollette, there were, in fact, a number of plans introduced in Congress during this time period to make the amending process easier.[90] Some eighteen proposals were introduced from 1911 to 1929, most with the intention of liberalizing the process. Four plans dating from 1911 forward were designed to make the proposal of amendments easier by transmitting copies of amendments desired by one state to others for prompt action.[91] Even more proposals concentrated on the ratification phase. A resolution introduced in 1913, for example, would have permitted amendments to be proposed by congressional majorities and ratified by two-thirds of the states.[92] Some also favored calling a convention at the request of smaller numbers of states and/or of ratifying amendments by popular vote.[93] In addition to proposals that Senator LaFollette introduced in 1912 and 1913, a member of Congress from Kansas proposed in 1913 that majorities in both Congress and the state legislatures should be sufficient to adopt amendments.[94] Senator Owens of Oklahoma favored a somewhat similar plan, proposing that amendments be ratified by "a majority of those who vote on the measure in a majority of congressional districts and a majority of all the votes cast therein."[95] He also favored a plan whereby voters would be furnished with a pamphlet explaining the pros and cons of such amendments. Senator

Cummins of Iowa favored a scheme whereby legislatures of sixteen states could propose amendments, and two-thirds of the states could ratify them.[96] Other schemes called for initiating amendments by popular vote or so ratifying them.[97]

In his book compiling such proposals, M. A. Musmanno, a Pennsylvania lawyer and future judge, does not appear to have taken a position on the desirability or undesirability of such plans, although, writing in 1929, he was aware from the experience of the Progressive Era—during which four amendments had been adopted in relatively short order[98]—that the U.S. Constitution was not as "rigid" as some had earlier portrayed it as being. Not surprisingly, then, in an article from the same year as his book, Musmanno, having cited earlier criticisms by Wilson, Smith, and Bryce, argued that "the difficulties which surround the process of change" help contribute to "the excellence of the original instrument."[99] Musmanno's analogy made it clear that the American system should be judged differently from that in Britain:

A constitution is to be either a fountain as in the United States or a running stream as in England. In the former we go to the well for power; in the latter, new channels are added and connected to the main stream until they penetrate every field of endeavor.[100]

Having reviewed numerous proposals that had been introduced in Congress—many unnecessary and others potentially harmful—Musmanno was pleased "that hundreds and hundreds of proposed amendments fall harmlessly and ineffectively like flakes of snow in a fire."[101]

REACTIONS AND IMPLICATIONS FOR THE PRESENT

It would indeed appear that, by the time of Musmanno's study, criticism of the amending process had abated and the Constitution as a whole had generally come to be regarded in a more positive light.[102] As Chapter 9 of this book reveals, many conservative commentators had reacted quite negatively to the adoption of the Progressive Era amendments, even arguing that there had been no constitutional power to adopt them and that the courts should void them. While these arguments eventually proved futile, the apparent ease with which the putatively rigid Constitution had been amended and lingering doubt at least about the wisdom of one of the amendments must have led to reconsideration of earlier criticisms.[103] In 1922 an author said that the idea "that the machinery of amendment provided by the Fathers was so slow and cumbersome that it was impossible as a practical matter to secure a change by that method except under stress of war or great popular excitement" had been "exploded."[104] Similarly, in

1925, Margaret Klinglesmith of the University of Pennsylvania Law School took direct aim at earlier criticisms of the rigid Constitution, which she associated, not altogether inaccurately, with foreigners.

The foreign critics of our Constitution after finding that one after the other [of] the fatal flaws in that instrument, which were to cause the failure of the scheme for self government set up by it, in some limited or unlimited number of years, had not resulted in what they could claim to be utter failure, united in declaring that the Constitution must fail as soon as it became certain that it was practically unamendable.[105]

Klinglesmith classified such critiques as part of "the ephemeral literature" of the period prior to the Progressive Amendments,[106] and favorably contrasted the stability of the national Constitution with that of the states. Klinglesmith declared:

Because it has been shown that the Constitution is not rigid, that it can be amended, it is by no means shown that it is easy or desirable that every sort of legislation, rejected by the states, or declared unconstitutional by the Supreme Court of the United States, should be made a part of the National Constitution by way of amendment.[107]

Klinglesmith rather praised the amending process for preserving the distinction between ordinary and fundamental law and favored no changes.

It would appear that opinion in America since Klinglesmith's day has generally sided with her judgment. Thus, an article appearing the next year and authored by Justin Miller, a professor of law at the University of Minnesota, actually concerned itself with arguing against a change in the Constitution that would make the amending process more difficult.[108] There was some sentiment around the time of Franklin Roosevelt's Court-packing plan for liberalizing the amending process,[109] but New Deal programs were eventually effected through other mechanisms. Moreover, while there is contemporary agreement that amendments are quite difficult to effect,[110] and occasional concerns that changing demographics might have made the amending process more difficult than it was in the past,[111] the consensus seems to be that amendments are still possible and that basic constitutional protections should not be overly subject to popular whims.[112] A Yale law professor, Akil Reed Amar, has recently argued that the Constitution can be amended by referenda outside Article V mechanisms,[113] but his view has been the subject of sharp criticism.[114] Somewhat less controversial is the suggestion that Congress should use its present constitutional power to declare that amendments should be ratified by state conventions rather than by state legislatures.[115] Given the recent defeats of the Equal Rights Amendment[116] and the proposal that would have given the District of Columbia official representation in Congress,[117] there is, of course, always the possibility that, if the nation continues too long without the successful ratification of new amendments, earlier questions about the adequacy of the process will once again become more frequent and persistent.

NOTES

1. See, for example, *Marbury v. Madison*, 5 U.S. 137, 176 (1803), and *Barron v. Baltimore*, 7 Peters 243, 250 (1833). To the extent that Marshall was referring to the convention mechanism for constitutional amendment, his views may not have been that much different from other contemporaries, James Madison in particular. See Chapter 2 of this book.

2. The views of the Anti-Federalists and Sidney George Fisher are respectively treated in Chapters 2 and 6 of this book.

3. Of special concern was whether states had the right to rescind pending constitutional amendments. For details of this controversy, see Joseph B. James, *The Ratification of the Fourteenth Amendment* (Macon, GA: Mercer University Press, 1984), pp. 277–304. This issue is still a live one. See John R. Vile, "Permitting States to Rescind Ratifications of Pending Amendments to the U.S. Constitution," *Publius: The Journal of Federalism* 20 (Spring 1990), pp. 109–22.

4. Advocates of the same cause were also arguing for more flexible interpretations of the Constitution in a development well documented in Thomas H. Peebles, "A Call to High Debate: The Organic Constitution in its Formative Era, 1890–1920," *University of Colorado Law Review* 52 (Fall 1980), pp. 49–104. For a good example of this approach, see Frank Goodnow, *Social Reform and the Constitution* (New York: Burt Franklin, 1970; reprint of 1911 edition). Goodnow cites the difficulty of constitutional amendment on page 4. Also see Hannis Taylor, "Elasticity of Written Constitutions," *The North American Review* 182 (February 1906), pp. 204–14, and Hannis Taylor, "Legitimate Functions of Judge-Made Law," *The Green Bag* 17 (October 1905), pp. 557–65. In this latter piece, Taylor joins other writers examined in this chapter in critiquing the amending process:

> Nothing is more generally admitted in the politics of this country than the fact that any reform is practically hopeless that depends upon the amendment, under normal conditions, of the Constitution of the United States. Experience has shown that the ponderous machinery provided can only be moved by the giant hand of revolution. (p. 563)

5. James Bryce, *The American Commonwealth*, 2 vols., 3rd ed. (New York: Macmillan, 1906).

6. A. V. Dicey, *Introduction to the Study of the Law of the Constitution*, 8th ed. (London: Macmillan, 1926), pp. 123–24, thus noted that "the terms 'flexible' and 'rigid' " were "originally suggested by my friend Mr. Bryce," but added that the terms were "used throughout this work without any connotation of praise or of blame."

Dicey's central amending analogy, which may or may not have been original with him, was that of a sleeping sovereign:

> Under a federal as under a unitarian system there exists a sovereign power, but the sovereign is in a federal state a despot hard to raise. He is not, like

the English Parliament, an ever-wakeful legislator, but a monarch who slumbers and sleeps. The sovereign of the United States has been roused to serious action but once during the course of more than a century. It needed the thunder of the Civil War to break his repose, and it may be doubted whether anything short of impending revolution will ever again raise him to activity. But a monarch who slumbers for years is like a monarch who does not exist. A federal constitution is capable of change, but for all that a federal constitution is apt to be unchangeable. (p. 145)

A footnote notes, however, the ease with which the Seventeenth Amendment had been only recently adopted.

Abbott C. Lowell argued that Bryce's distinction between flexible and rigid constitutions might best be regarded "as one of degree rather than of kind," although he did put the United States on the "rigid" end of the scale. See *The Government of England*, (New York: Macmillan, 1909), vol. 1, p. 6.

7. W. F. Willoughby, *The Government of Modern States*, rev. ed. (New York: D. Appleton-Century, 1936), p. 131, thus seems to use fairer terminology when he contrasted constitutional "flexibility" with constitutional "stability."

8. Bryce, *The American Commonwealth*, p. 370.

9. Ibid., p. 369.

10. Ibid., p. 370.

11. Like the idea of a "rigid" constitution, this warning against "tinkering" seems common to the time. Michael Kammen, *A Machine That Would Go of Itself: The Constitution in American Culture* (New York: Alfred A. Knopf, 1987), p. 205, cites a warning in a speech given in 1912 by Attorney General George Wickersham about "Constitution tinkering." Also see L. White Busbey, "Tinkering the Constitution," *The Unpopular Review* 5 (January 1916), pp. 127–47, and Jos. R. Long, "Tinkering With the Constitution," *Yale Law Journal* 24 (May 1915), pp. 573–89.

12. Bryce, *The American Commonwealth*, pp. 370–71.

13. James Bryce, "Flexible and Rigid Constitutions," *Constitutions* (Germany: Scientia Verlag Aalen, 1980; reprint of New York and London 1905 edition).

14. Albert Somit and Joseph Tanenhaus, *The Development of American Political Science: From Burgess to Behavioralism* (Boston: Allyn and Bacon, 1967), pp. 11–21.

15. John W. Burgess, *Selections from Political Science and Comparative Constitutional Law* (Farmingdale, NY: Dabor Social Science Publications, 1978). Information about Burgess is contained in the introduction by Richard Pious.

16. Ibid., p. 20.

17. Ibid., pp. 20–21.

18. Ibid., p. 21.

19. Ibid., p. 22.

20. Ibid.

21. Ibid.

22. Ibid., pp. 23–24. Writing in 1923, Burgess proposed eliminating all methods of amendment to the Constitution except by constitutional convention, thus keeping "the Sovereign power separate from and supreme over the Government." Apparently, Burgess saw this method as the only one for slowing or reversing the advance of state power and assuring that the best minds would prevail:

Constitutional Amendments are matters of such fundamental and vital importance that they should be drafted and voted on only by men of the highest
quality as jurists, publicists and statesmen, men chosen by the original holders
of the suffrage and chosen for that purpose primarily and alone. No mixing
of the subjects of Amendment with any other subjects, making compromises
instead of principles out of them, should be tolerated.

See John W. Burgess, *Recent Changes in American Constitutional Theory* (New York:
Arno Press and the New York Times, 1972, reprint of Columbia University Press,
1922), pp. 112–14.

23. See John R. Vile, *Rewriting the United States Constitution: An Examination of
Proposals From Reconstruction to the Present* (New York: Praeger, 1991), pp. 30–32.

24. For these ambiguities in Wilson's thought, see Christopher Wolfe, "Woodrow Wilson: Interpreting the Constitution," *The Review of Politics* 41 (January 1979),
pp. 121–42. For a critique of Wilson's views by a contemporary thinker who thought
all changes in the Constitution needed to be effected by amendment, see J. M.
Dickinson, "Centralization by Construction and Interpretation of the Constitution,"
The Albany Law Journal 69 (1907), pp. 98–108.

25. Woodrow Wilson, *Congressional Government* (Boston: Houghton Mifflin,
1885 and 1913), p. 242.

26. Woodrow Wilson, *Constitutional Government in the United States* (New York:
Columbia University Press, 1961; reprint of 1908 edition). Also see Wilson's essay,
"What is Progress?" *The New Freedom*, intro. William E. Leuchtenburg (Englewood
Cliffs, NJ: Prentice-Hall, 1961), pp. 25–45, especially pp. 40–42.

27. Wilson, *Constitutional Government*, p. 56.

28. Ibid., p. 57.

29. Ibid., p. 192.

30. Ibid., p. 193.

31. Ibid., p. 195.

32. Ibid., p. 194.

33. Herman Ames, *The Proposed Amendments to the Constitution of the United
States During the First Century of its History* (New York: Burt Franklin, 1970; reprint
of 1896 edition). Judging from the numerous subsequent writers who observed how
frequently amendments had been proposed and how rarely they had been ratified,
Ames's study appears to have had an important impact on contemporary thinking.
His book was awarded a prize by the American Historical Association in 1897. See
Who's Who in America, 1906–1907, ed. John Leonard (Chicago: A. N. Marquis,
1906), p. 33.

Walter F. Dodd also published a book entitled *The Revision and Amendment of
State Constitutions* (Baltimore, MD: Johns Hopkins University Press, 1910), which
may also have been important in that it indicated that most state constitutions were
more easily amended than that of the national government. Dodd does not appear,
however, to have dealt in any significant way with Article V, limiting discussions
in his book to state constitutions.

34. Ames, *The Proposed Amendments to the Constitution*, p. 301.

35. Ibid., p. 303.

36. Ibid., p. 304, quoting John Marshall in *Barron v. Baltimore*, 7 Peters 761
(1833).

37. Ibid., p. 304.

38. Ibid.

39. Henry B. Higgins, "The Rigid Constitution," *Political Science Quarterly* 20 (March 1905), pp. 203–22.

40. Ibid., p. 203.

41. Ibid., p. 210.

42. Ibid., pp. 215–16.

43. Ibid., p. 218.

44. Ibid., p. 219.

45. See Thomas Jefferson, *The Works of Thomas Jefferson*, ed. Paul Leicester Ford (New York: G. P. Putnam's Sons, Knickerbocker Press, 1905), vol. 12, p. 12.

46. Higgins, "The Rigid Constitution," p. 222.

47. Ibid.

48. J. Allen Smith, *The Spirit of American Government* (Cambridge, MA: Belknap Press, 1965; reprint of 1907 edition).

49. Smith's critique bears many resemblances to the critique that would follow by Charles Beard in *An Economic Interpretation of the Constitution of the United States* (New York: Macmillan, 1935).

50. Smith, *The Spirit of American Government*, p. 43.

51. Ibid., p. 48.

52. Ibid., p. 57.

53. Ibid.

54. Ibid., p. 63.

55. Ibid., p. 64.

56. Ibid., p. 346.

57. Ibid., p. 347.

58. Ibid., p. 348. As a matter of fact, the threat of a constitutional convention does appear to have prodded a number of amendments, including the Seventeenth Amendment, which led to direct election of U.S. senators. See Dwight W. Connely, "Amending the Constitution: Is This Any Way to Call for a Constitutional Convention?" *Arizona Law Review* 22 (1980), pp. 1015–16. Also see Bruce M. Van Sickle and Lynn M. Boughey, "A Lawful and Peaceful Revolution: Article V and Congress' Present Duty to Call a Convention for Proposing Amendments," *Hamline Law Review* 14 (Fall 1990), pp. 37–38.

59. Herbert Croly, *The Promise of American Life* (Indianapolis: Bobbs-Merrill, 1965).

60. Herbert Croly, *Progressive Democracy* (Indianapolis: Bobbs-Merrill, 1965; reprint of 1909 edition), p. 230.

61. Ibid., p. 231.

62. Ibid., p. 234.

63. Ibid., p. 236.

64. Ibid., p. 237.

65. Munroe Smith, "Shall We Make Our Constitution Flexible?" *The North American Review* 194 (November 1911).

66. Ibid., p. 658. W. F. Willoughby made a similar point, arguing that, when there were only thirteen states, "it was far less difficult to get the required action than at the present time when there are forty-eight States and the two houses of Congress have a membership of 96 and 435 in the Senate and House of Represen-

tatives respectively." See Willoughby, *The Government of Modern States*, rev. ed. (New York: D. Appleton-Century, 1936), p. 153.

67. Ibid., p. 659.

68. Ibid., pp. 660–61.

69. Ibid., p. 661.

70. Ibid.

71. Ibid., p. 663.

72. Ibid., p. 667. Emphasis omitted.

73. Ibid., p. 669.

74. Ibid., p. 671.

75. Frederic B. Johnstone, "An Eighteenth Century Constitution," *Illinois Law Review* 7 (December 1912), pp. 265–90. In this same year, the Progressive platform had pledged itself "to provide a more easy and expeditious method of amending the Federal Constitution." See *National Party Platforms, 1840–1964*, comp. Kirk H. Porter and Donald B. Johnson (Urbana: University of Illinois Press, 1966), p. 176.

76. Johnstone, "An Eighteenth Century Constitution," p. 273.

77. Ibid., p. 274.

78. Ibid., p. 275.

79. Ibid., p. 281.

80. Ibid., pp. 282.

81. Ibid., pp. 283–84.

82. James P. Hall, " 'An Eighteenth Century Constitution'—a Comment," *Illinois Law Review* 7 (December 1912), pp. 285–90.

83. J. David Thompson, "The Amendment of the Federal Constitution," *Academy of Political Science* 3 (1913), pp. 65–77.

84. Ibid., p. 69.

85. Ibid., p. 70. David R. Dow, "When Words Mean What We Believe They Say: The Case of Article V," *Iowa Law Review* 76 (October 1990), pp. 56–61, argues that modern proponents of popular sovereignty, most notably Bruce Ackerman and Akil Reed Amar, also forget the federal nature of the Constitution.

86. Thompson, "The Amendment of the Federal Constitution," pp. 70–71.

87. Ibid., p. 75.

88. Ibid.

89. Ibid., p. 76.

90. The increasing number of proposals was noted by Jacob Tanger, in "Amending Procedure of the Federal Constitution," *American Political Science Review* 10 (November 1916), pp. 698–99. Tanger noted that "this later phase in the development of the movement for popular government bids fair to produce results of far-reaching importance" (p. 699).

91. Proposals are found in M. A. Musmanno, *Proposed Amendments to the Constitution* (Washington, DC: Government Printing Office, 1929).

92. Ibid., p. 192.

93. Ibid., pp. 193–94.

94. Ibid., pp. 194–95.

95. Ibid., p. 195.

96. Ibid., p. 196.

97. Ibid., pp. 197–204.

98. These were the Sixteenth Amendment, constitutionalizing the national in-

come tax, the Seventeenth Amendment, providing for direct popular election of senators, the Eighteenth Amendment, providing for national alcoholic prohibition, and the Nineteenth Amendment, extending the right to vote to women. See Alan P. Grimes, *Democracy and the Amendments to the Constitution* (Lexington, MA: Lexington Books, 1978), pp. 65–100.

99. M. H. [*sic*] Musmanno, "The Difficulty of Amending Our Federal Constitution: Defect or Asset?" *American Bar Association Journal* 15 (1929), p. 506. Musmanno is citing an earlier quotation by Bryce.

An article signed "Michael Angelo Mussman," apparently the same individual, takes a similar position. See "Is the Amendment Process Too Difficult?" *The American Law Review* 57 (1923), pp. 694–705.

100. Ibid., p. 506.

101. Ibid., p. 508.

102. Kammen, *A Machine That Would Go of Itself*, p. 228, notes, for example, that both Charles Beard and J. Allen Smith took a more positive view of the Constitution in their writings during this period.

103. The Eighteenth Amendment, providing for national alcoholic prohibition, was eventually repealed by the adoption in 1933 of the Twenty-first Amendment. For a discussion of this issue, see David E. Kyvig, *Alcohol and Order: Perspectives on National Prohibition* (Westport, CT: Greenwood Press, 1985).

104. Charles W. Pierson, *Our Changing Constitution* (Garden City, NY: Doubleday, Page, 1922), p. 45.

105. Margaret C. Klinglesmith, "Amending the Constitution of the United States," *University of Pennsylvania Law Review* 73 (May 1925), p. 359.

106. Ibid., p. 360.

107. Ibid., pp. 368–69.

108. Justin Miller, "Amendment of the Federal Constitution: Should it be Made More Difficult?" *Minnesota Law Review* 10 (February 1926), pp. 185–206. The proposal Miller examined was one proposed by Senator Wadsworth of New York and Congressman Garrett of Tennessee which limited the powers of states to ratify amendments by adding the following provision to Article V:

> Provided, That the members of at least one house in each of the legislatures which may ratify shall be elected after such amendments have been proposed; that any state may require that ratification by its legislature be subject to confirmation by popular vote and that, until three-fourths of the states have ratified or more than one-fourth of the states have rejected or defeated a proposed amendment, any state may change its vote. (p. 186)

109. Lester B. Orfield, *The Amending of the Federal Constitution* (Ann Arbor: University of Michigan Press, 1942), p. 168.

110. See, for example, Mary F. Berry, "How Hard It Is to Change," *New York Times Magazine* (September 13, 1987), pp. 93–98.

111. Peter Suber, "Population Changes and Constitutional Amendments: Federalism versus Democracy," *Journal of Law Reform* 20 (Winter 1987), pp. 409–90.

112. See, for example, Ruth B. Ginsburg, "On Amending the Constitution: A Plea for Patience," *University of Arkansas at Little Rock Law Journal* 12 (1989–90), pp. 677–94.

113. Akil Reed Amar, "Philadelphia Revisited: Amending the Constitution Out-

side Article V," *The University of Chicago Law Review* 55 (Fall 1988), pp. 1043–1104. Similarly, Bruce Ackerman, conscious of Progressive precedents, has proposed adding a new method of constitutional amendment that would allow for ratification by national referenda. See *We the People: Foundations* (Cambridge, MA: Belknap Press, 1991), pp 54–55.

114. John R. Vile, "Legally Amending the United States Constitution: The Exclusivity of Article V's Mechanisms," *Cumberland Law Review* 21 (1990–91), pp. 271–308, and David R. Dow, "When Words Mean What We Believe They Say: The Case of Article V," *Iowa Law Review* 76 (October 1990), pp. 1–66.

115. Willard H. Pedrick and Richard C. Dahl, "Let the People Vote! Ratification of Constitutional Amendments by Convention," *Arizona Law Review* 30 (1988), pp. 243–56. For an earlier article with this same theme, see George S. Brown, "The People Should be Consulted as to Constitutional Changes," *American Bar Association Journal* 16 (1930), pp. 404–6.

116. See Mary F. Berry, *Why ERA Failed: Politics, Women's Rights, and the Amending Process of the Constitution* (Bloomington: Indiana University Press, 1986), and Jane J. Mansbridge, *Why We Lost the ERA* (Chicago: University of Chicago Press, 1986).

117. Clement Vose, "When District of Columbia Representation Collides With the Constitution Amendment Institution," *Publius: The Journal of Federalism* 9 (Winter 1979), pp. 105–25.

Chapter 9

Debates over Substantive Limits on the Amending Process

As Chapter 2 of this book described, the authors of Article V of the Constitution included two entrenchment provisions which sought to enjoin amendments on the subject of slave importation and state suffrage in the Senate. The first came to an automatic end after twenty years; the latter is presumably still in force.[1] As Chapter 4 reveals, however, at least since John C. Calhoun theorists have wondered if there might be other implicit limits on the substance of amendments to the Constitution.

This hope was especially prominent early in the twentieth century when the notion of popular sovereignty as incorporated in the amending process and as exercised by populist and progressive reformers was threatened by a counterrevolutionary effort at constitutional interpretation by those seeking to attach substantive restrictions on the amending process.[2] This battle was part of a wider war aimed at limiting the powers of the national government, and it was waged under such banners as "vested rights," "reserved powers," "states rights," and "substantive due process."[3] Until 1937 those seeking such limitations were winning on many fronts; after 1937 these proponents were beating a hasty, if not always silent, retreat. By 1937, however, those who sought to restrict the amending process had already been defeated, and the story of this skirmish is an instructive chapter in American constitutional history.

THE PHILOSOPHICAL FOUNDATION

Renewed thinking about the possibility that there might be inherent substantive limits on the amending process may well have been rekindled by an article published in 1893 by Thomas Cooley,[4] one of the most influential legal commentators of the nineteenth century.[5] In a review of the amending process, Cooley noted the entrenchment clauses within Article V and proceeded to argue that such clauses were not exclusive but that "there are limitations that are far more important than this, that stand unquestionably as restrictions upon the power to amend."[6] Cooley offered four examples of unconstitutional amendments—an amendment that attempted to detach a certain part of the Union, an amendment that applied different taxing rules to some states, an amendment that established a nobility, or an amendment that attempted to create a monarchy.[7] Pointing out that the first fifteen amendments had all "been in the direction of further extending the democratic principles which underlie our constitution," Cooley argued that amendments "must be in harmony with the thing amended," and he distinguished that which amends a constitution from that which "overthrows or revolutionizes it."[8] Cooley also offered a credible reason why the Founders did not include other stated restrictions on the amending process.

If the makers of the constitution, in limiting this provision [Article V] stopped short of forbidding such changes as would be inharmonious, they did so because it was not in their thought that any such changes could for a moment be considered by congress or by the states as admissible, since in the completed instrument no place could possibly be found for them, however formal might be the process of adoption; and as foreign matter, they would just as surely be declared inadmissible and therefore invalid without an express inhibition as with it.[9]

Cooley proposed an analogy which clearly rested for its force on the notion of higher law.

The fruit grower does not forbid his servants engrafting the witch-hazel or the poisonous sumac on his apple trees; the process is forbidden by a law higher and more imperative than any he could declare, and to which no additional force could possibly be given by re-enactment under his orders.[10]

What is so fascinating about Cooley's arguments is that they were apparently made with no specific reference to any proposed or ratified amendment but simply as a matter of philosophical speculation.[11]

ARGUMENTS OVER THE VALIDITY OF THE FIFTEENTH AMENDMENT

While Cooley viewed all fifteen amendments to the Constitution as democratic and hence as constitutional,[12] there were others who would soon challenge this view. Among them was M. F. Morris, former associate justice of the Court of Appeals for the District of Columbia. The primary target of an article he published in 1909 was the Fifteenth Amendment, which he believed to have "greatly injured our Aryan race and seriously threatened the stability of our Aryan institutions."[13] Morris's racism was evident in his opposition to the "commingling of the races of man upon terms of equality" and in his view that the Aryan and Negro races were respectively "the highest and the lowest of the races in the scale of development."[14]

For Morris, the critical factor in invalidating the Fifteenth Amendment was the distinction between an "amendment" and an "addition" to the Constitution.

This so-called Fifteenth Amendment is not an *amendment*, but an *addition* to the Constitution; and . . . while *amendments* to the Constitution may be enacted by a vote of three-fourths of the States, in accordance with provisions for amendment in Article V of the Constitution itself, yet an *addition* to the Constitution cannot be made, except by the unanimous consent of all the States, which this Fifteenth Amendment never received.[15]

Much like Calhoun had done prior to the Civil War, Morris rested his extraconstitutional distinction on the dangers posed by alternative understandings.[16]

If under the guise of amendment of the Constitution, all this can lawfully be done, what guarantee have the States for their integrity and continued existence? Absolutely none. It will be in the power of three-fourths of the States at any time to destroy the other fourth, to overthrow the whole Federal System, and to establish a centralized despotism.[17]

Recognizing that the Thirteenth Amendment had been ratified by "the inexorable logic of accomplished facts," Morris went on to suggest that parts of the Fourteenth Amendment might be invalid and that, although it had been part of the Constitution for almost forty years,[18] it was not too late to challenge the Fifteenth Amendment in court.[19]

Arthur W. Machen, Jr., evidenced similar sentiment in an article published the next year, rhetorically entitled, "Is the Fifteenth Amendment Void?"[20] Given the intense controversy surrounding adoption of the Civil War amendments, the uncertain status of the Southern states, and several attempted rescissions,[21] Machen might well have focused on questions of constitutional procedure, now approached from a less partisan and more thoughtful light, but his stance was different. He argued that the contents of amendments were subject to two kinds of restraint: "(1) inherent and (2) express."[22] As discussed above, Article V contains two limitations in the latter category—the now superseded slave importation clause and protection for equal state suffrage in the Senate. Machen argued for inherent limitations on the amending process on the basis of this second clause, thus attempting to tie inherent limitations to a specific text.

Accordingly, Machen contended that the Fifteenth Amendment deprived states of their equal suffrage in the Senate by changing their electorates without their consent. Such action was equivalent, in Machen's judgment, "to a compulsory annexation to each state that refused to ratify it of a black San Domingo within its borders."[23] While admitting that the Fourteenth Amendment had also made inroads into state powers, Machen distinguished this amendment first by doubting "whether the elevation of the negroes . . . is more than a matter of sentiment or name" and, second, by separating the civil rights granted by the Fourteenth Amendment from the political rights guaranteed in the Fifteenth.[24] While granting that a constitutional challenge to the Fifteenth Amendment was late, Machen observed that no court decision needed to be overturned if it were voided. In an ironically apt comparison, Machen noted that the passage of thirty-six years had not on an earlier occasion prevented the Court from voiding the Missouri Compromise.[25] In any case, the Fifteenth Amendment had "never been acquiesced in unreservedly" or "been loyally observed except in places where its effect was small."[26]

Machen apparently thought his arguments had a good chance of success,[27] but he might have intentionally overstated his case in the hope that, as in the *Slaughterhouse* cases, the Court would accomplish through limited constitutional construction what he was urging it to do directly.[28] Hence, near the end of the article, Machen argued, "The objections to the validity of the Fifteenth Amendment raised by this article might be obviated if its application within the states could be confined by construction to federal elections for members of the House of Representatives."[29]

The Supreme Court faced arguments similar to Morris's and Machen's in *Myers v. Anderson*,[30] where Maryland's grandfather clause was challenged under the Fifteenth Amendment.[31] The plaintiffs, led by attorney William Marbury,[32] argued:

If construed to have reference to voting at state or municipal elections, the Fifteenth Amendment would be beyond the amending power conferred upon three-fourths of the states by Art. V of the Constitution, and therefore, the Amendment should not receive that construction, it is fairly open to a more limited construction.[33]

Any other interpretation, the plaintiffs contended, would destroy the states,[34] and violate the prohibition "against any amendment which would deprive a State of its equal representation in the Senate without its consent."[35]

In voiding Maryland's grandfather clause, the Supreme Court made no mention of Marbury's arguments. As a partisan in another controversy,

Marbury would soon argue that this silence did not void the substance of his arguments but only their application to this specific case. He suggested that the Civil War amendments had been accepted for fifty years and that "it must be conceded that no court in the world could be blamed for declining to consider objections to their validity after such a long period of universal assent and implied ratification by the whole people of the United States."[36]

ARGUMENTS OVER THE VALIDITY OF THE EIGHTEENTH AMENDMENT: ROUND 1

The occasion for Marbury's new argument was an article that challenged the Eighteenth and Nineteenth Amendments, the first establishing national alcoholic prohibition and the second extending the suffrage to women. Marbury thought that both amendments revealed the danger "that a comparatively small but highly organized and determined minority could cause the legislatures of numbers of states to ratify amendments . . . contrary to the well-known sentiments and wishes of a vast majority of the people of those states."[37] Moreover, Marbury advanced the view that these amendments should be subject to substantive restraints. Marbury's ability to cite plausible precedents (most notably *Collector v. Day* and *Lane County v. Oregon*) in related areas indicated that his arguments were part of a broader constitutional effort, part of which had succeeded.[38] Altogether, Marbury marshalled three arguments for limiting amendments.

Marbury's opening salvo was "that the power to 'amend' the Constitution was not intended to include the power to *destroy* it."[39] Rather, amendments must be designed better to *"carry out the purpose for which it* [the Constitution] *was framed."*[40] An amendment transferring all state powers to raise taxes to the national government would be invalid according to precedents in the taxing cases.[41] Since the language of the amending clause was no broader than that of the taxing provision,

the power to amend the Constitution cannot be deemed to have been intended to confer the right upon Congress . . . to adopt any amendment . . . which would have the same tendency . . . to destroy the states, by taking from them, directly, any branch of their legislative powers.[42]

While Prohibition would itself leave many matters under state control, it marked the first major step in the eventual abolition of the states.[43]

Marbury's second argument advanced from implicit to explicit restraints. That is, he contended that Prohibition deprived each state of its equality in the Senate by opening the door to a destruction of "those functions which are essential 'to its separate and independent' existence as a state."[44] Finally, Marbury took the position, which has parallels in more contemporary arguments,[45] that the Eighteenth and Nineteenth Amendments failed to recognize the difference between constitutional text and ordinary legislation. To raise mere legislation to the status of constitutional law was—and here Marbury was the advocate of constitutional flexibility—to compel one's descendants to live under regulations "which may have become totally unsuited to their changed conditions."[46]

Here Marbury, like Machen before him, faced the problem of distinguishing the Eighteenth and Nineteenth Amendments from the Civil War amendments. Marbury acknowledged that, had substantive questions been raised in a timely manner, the Court "would have given full and careful consideration to these objections."[47] Yet, granting that time had legitimized the Civil War amendments, Marbury interpreted the Court's silence in *Myers v. Anderson* as an indication that "the court left itself free to deal with these considerations whenever they shall arise in future."[48]

Others agreed with Marbury's analysis. Hence, Everett Wheeler argued that an amendment as "revolutionary" as the Eighteenth could (by the analogy of the Union as a compact) "only be effected by the consent of all the states."[49] In obvious reference to the Tenth Amendment, Wheeler contended, "A state that joins the Union under an agreement that local self-government shall be reserved to the states cannot be deprived of this power without its consent."[50] Similarly, another author argued, with seeming obliviousness to *McCulloch v. Maryland*,[51] that the fact that Congress was only to propose amendments it thought necessary "shows that it is not the intent of that article [Article V] to invest congress with unlimited discretion as to the nature of the amendments it may propose."[52] He reasoned that "there can be no valid amendment to the constitution which . . . trenches upon the *internal life* of the several states, as sovereign states, beyond the present provisions of the constitution, until ratified by every state of the union."[53]

Authors of at least three other contemporary articles elaborated on these themes. George Skinner of Princeton University relied primarily on the Ninth and Tenth Amendments. Granting that "no legal limitation can deny the right of revolution which is always without and beyond the law," he argued that, were three-fourths of the states to pass such an amendment, "it would bind only those States which joined in the revolution."[54] A second writer, a member of the New York City bar, argued: (1) that interstate prohibition was not the proper subject of amendment; (2) that such a prohibition would, in any case, require ratification of all the states; and (3) that such ratification could only be given by conventions.[55] This piece was followed by a third article whose author contended that the Eighteenth Amendment infringed inalienable rights and due process, presumably of the substantive type.[56]

ARGUMENTS OVER THE EIGHTEENTH
AMENDMENT IN THE COURTS

While the central arguments raised by Marbury and his supporters dealt with substantive limits on the amending process, the first legal challenge to the Eighteenth and Nineteenth Amendments involved the procedural claim that the amendments were invalid because they had not been ratified by referenda in states, like Ohio, whose constitutions required this. This argument was rejected in *Hawke v. Smith* on the basis of the explicit language in Article V.[57] Aside from dicta in earlier cases,[58] this appears to have been only the second time that the Supreme Court ruled on procedural matters involving the amending process.[59]

Another challenge to the Prohibition amendment, brought to the Supreme Court by seven states, also raised a host of procedural issues.[60] All these procedural claims were rejected by the Court, however, and many of the challenges to the law reflected positions that had been suggested earlier. The arguments made by representatives of Kentucky and New Jersey included most of the contentions advanced by counsel in the other states. Kentucky's case shifted from earlier analysis of the reservations alleged to inhere in the Article V requirement for equal suffrage in the Senate to reliance on the reservations alleged to inhere in the Ninth and Tenth Amendments. The notion that "the power of 'amendment' contained in Article V does not authorize the invasion of the sovereign powers expressly reserved to the States and the people by the Ninth and Tenth Amendments, except with the consent of *all* the States"[61] mirrored both the contemporary interpretation of the Tenth Amendment[62] and a notion of constitutional change reminiscent of John C. Calhoun.

Most interesting was Kentucky's argument from alleged consequences.

If amendment under Article V were unlimited, three-fourths of the legislators would have it in their power to establish a state religion and prohibit free exercise of other religious beliefs; to quarter a standing army in the houses of citizens; to do away with trial by jury and republican form of government; to repeal the provision for a president; and to abolish this court and with it the whole judicial power vested by the Constitution.[63]

The contention that the Founders could not have intended to vest such power in the people was buttressed by dicta in the *Slaughterhouse* cases that such radical constitutional changes should not be posited "in the absence of language which expresses such a purpose too clearly to admit of doubt."[64]

As Kentucky's argument continued, it cited the authority of Curtis's *Constitutional History of the United States*[65] to restrict amendments to subjects already covered by the Constitution and "not to enable three-fourths of the States to grasp new power at the expense of any unwilling State."[66] Like Marbury, the attorneys for Kentucky faced the need of distinguishing the Civil War amendments. They suggested that these amendments dealt with a subject contained in the original Constitution, and "were the result of the arbitrament of war."[67]

Former Secretary of State and Senator Elihu Root, who presented New Jersey's case, contended that the Eighteenth Amendment was invalid because it was an act of legislation. As such, it circumvented majority rule by enabling five percent of the people[68] to prevent future modifications of the law and to freeze a sumptuary policy permanently in the Constitution.[69] Then, in a clumsy effort to distinguish the Eighteenth Amendment from the Thirteenth, Root argued that slavery had been nothing but "the creation of positive law," and that the Thirteenth Amendment did not initiate new policy but merely withdrew the power from individuals to hold slaves. Root noted that the Constitution never intended for state legislatures to have power to "impair substantial rights as freedom of religion."[70] If there were no limits, Root continued, states might "by amendment establish a state religion, or oppress or discriminate against any denomination, or authorize the taking away of life, liberty, and property, without due process of law, etc., etc."[71]

Root's second central argument focused on the preservation of the federal system from the perspective of dual sovereignty. Again Root pointed to possible consequences: "If this amendment be valid, then any amendment which impairs the police powers of the States . . . must likewise be valid."[72] Again, the Civil War amendments required rationalization, and Root distinguished them from the case at hand by contending that, in adopting them, the federal government had only guaranteed a republican form of government to the states as ordained in the Constitution.[73]

Root's colleague took a slightly different tack by arguing that the concurrent powers authorized by the Eighteenth Amendment implied that only legislation mutually agreeable to the nation and the states would be acceptable. In an argument seemingly based on the premise of having his cake and eating it too, Root's colleague argued that states had not intended to relinquish their powers to the national government under this amendment but to answer the question "Shall there be national prohibition without the loss of state control over local affairs?"[74] This attorney used a similar, albeit more plausible argument—"It could not have been intended"—to argue that the Eighteenth Amendment delegated only limited power over non-alcoholic beverages.[75]

Attorneys for the national government made several responses to alleged limits on Article V. First, they argued that this was a political matter inappropriate for judicial resolution.[76] Second, they contended that the Constitution contained many similar provisions, most notably the Thirteenth Amendment, respecting the rights and duties of citizens.[77] Third, the attorneys pointed to the Constitutional Convention's explicit rejection of an amendment preventing infringements on state police powers.[78]

FOLLOW-UP ARGUMENTS ON THE EIGHTEENTH AMENDMENT

While the Court ruled in favor of the government, its brief opinion, authored by Justice Van Devanter, left its reasoning to speculation. On the substantive question, the Court simply noted, "The prohibition of the manufacture, sale, transportation, importation and exportation of intoxicating liquors for beverage purposes . . . is within the power to amend reserved by Article V of the Constitution."[79] While Chief Justice White referred to the duty of citing his thought on the case,[80] he limited his concurring opinion to the meaning of the Eighteenth Amendment and did not comment on alleged substantive limits.

Justice McKenna partially dissented in this case but argued that the Court's conclusions regarding the substantive issue merely "assert the undisputed."[81] Yet both he and the dissenting Justice Clarke accepted an interpretation of concurrent powers that would have severely limited the national government's control over alcohol. Clarke's reference to the Court's courage in the *Slaughterhouse* cases was but one indication of the counterrevolutionary implications of his own interpretation.[82]

For the moment, though, the Court had rejected pleas for implicit substantive limits on Article V.[83] Perhaps the most logical explanation for its decision was made by the author of a response to Marbury's earlier arguments.[84] Openly acknowledging the revolutionary potentialities in the amending process, this author argued:

The only security against the adoption of ill-advised or, if you please, revolutionary amendments is that, in the last analysis, the states themselves are the judges of the necessity for proposed amendments, and the action of three fourths of those states is required. No better security, however, could be devised.[85]

This writer's other arguments paralleled those reviewed elsewhere—the Founding Fathers' rejection of a provision protecting state police powers against amendment and the difficulty of distinguishing the Eighteenth Amendment from the Civil War amendments.[86]

D. O. McGovney followed up on this article and responded to previous publications.[87] Denying that the right to consume alcohol was inalienable, McGovney classified the view that prohibition was not a proper subject for amendment as "an application of the pre–Civil War doctrine of State sovereignty"[88] and went on to demonstrate that the genius of the American system rested on the notion of representative government. As to arguments that the term *amendment* itself served as a substantive limit on Article V powers, McGovney frankly granted that the term contained "an element of euphemism, of conceit in the proposer, an assumption that the proposal is an improvement," but went on to suggest that it referred in fact to any "alteration or change."[89] McGovney closed by noting the Founders' refusal to exempt Article V from possible interferences with state police powers.[90]

Two other articles rounded out this stage of the controversy. One opposed implicit substantive limits on Article V by emphasizing that the result of so limiting the article might well be revolution. The analogy was mechanical, and not altogether original, but effective.

The power to amend is the safety-valve to a nation, and is as necessary to the safety of a state as it is to a boiler. The check, or one check, to it, is the ultimate right to a revolution if it becomes intolerably oppressive and the oppression cannot be thrown off otherwise.[91]

Just because the original Constitution was revered was no reason to believe that the Founders "intended that we should abide by the fundamental principles thereof, forever and a day."[92]

In a second piece, Professor Walter F. Dodd offered a brilliant defense of the *National Prohibition* cases.[93] He recognized that any substantive limits on Article V would deny the people's right "to place in the constitution any thing which the court might itself regard as not properly belonging in the text of a constitution, and would introduce into American constitutional practice a highly undesirable type of judicial control."[94] Dodd further observed that arguments for limits on the amending process ultimately rested on fears that an unlimited amending power "might at some time be unwisely employed."[95]

ARGUMENTS OVER THE VALIDITY OF THE NINETEENTH AMENDMENT

Despite defeats in court and refutations in the law reviews, the Supreme Court had barely ruled on prohibition before William Marbury had tailored his arguments to the woman's suffrage issue. Indeed, Marbury professed to see two hopeful signs in the *National Prohibition* cases. First, he noted that the Court's "distinctly guarded language" did not flatly deny limits to the amending process.[96] Second, he observed that the Court's willingness to render its decision recognized "that the question is a *justiciable*, and not a *political* one."[97]

Still, it was now necessary to distinguish the woman's suffrage issue from the prohibition question, and Marbury's arguments to this end were strained. First, he argued that the Nineteenth Amendment did not merely confer power to extend the vote to women but was a "self-executing" command.[98] By contrast, the Prohibition Amendment "prescribes no penalties for its violation and must depend for its enforcement upon such legislation as Congress may from time to time . . . enact."[99] A close reading of the two amendments indicates that this distinction is specious.[100] Much later in his article, Marbury argued that, while the Prohibition Amendment established a bad precedent, it did not, like the Nineteenth Amendment, "take away wholly or partially, or diminish from the State any power or 'function essential to the independent existence' of a State."[101] Marbury's attempt here is unconvincing in large part because it so closely resembles earlier efforts to distinguish the Eighteenth Amendment from the Civil War amendments.

Since the substitution of but one word would make the Nineteenth Amendment identical to the Fifteenth, Marbury faced even more difficult odds in attempting to show that "the holding void of the Nineteenth Amendment would not necessarily furnish any precedent for a like holding as to the Fifteenth."[102] Here Marbury argued that popular acquiescence—presumably by male voters—had made any challenge to the Fifteenth Amendment untimely and, in fact, amounted to formal ratification by all the states.[103] Thus, Marbury concluded that "the validity of the Nineteenth Amendment may be considered on its merits entirely without reference to either the Fourteenth or Fifteenth."[104]

Aside from these labored arguments, Marbury's points were almost identical to his earlier ones. He placed chief stress on the contention that the amendment destroyed state powers reserved in the Constitution by the guarantee of equal suffrage in the Senate and by the Ninth and Tenth Amendments. Marbury's arguments were in fact linked to his general distrust of popular sovereignty. Hence, he contended that vesting power in the national government to enfranchise women would also recognize a power to say "that only *certain* men or *certain* women should vote."[105] More specifically, "the right to vote might be given to women only, or even to a special class of women only, as to such women as owned no property—the 'proletariat.' "[106] Similarly, Marbury noted that, if the Suffrage Amendment were void, "it will be practically impossible to fix any limit on that power."[107]

Marbury's arguments contrast with those presented by educator and attorney Charles Needham the following year.[108] Needham was also concerned about the erosion of state sovereignty, but he did not believe there was an appeal once the people had expressed their wishes in the amending process.[109] Unlike writers who sought to correct the situation by finding implicit limits on the amending process, Needham called for amending the Constitution to provide that amendments be passed only by constitutional conventions and ratified by a direct vote of the people.[110] Needham offered his proposal not because, like Marbury, he feared popular sovereignty, but because he thought the existing system did not provide for its expression.[111] Needham pointed out that neither the proposing Congress nor the ratifying state legislatures were chosen for their views on any given amendment. Special interest groups, however, secured congressional representatives who would vote their wishes on these matters and were able to apply more pressures to elected congressmen than they would be able to apply to delegates to a convention.

> Members have been compelled to vote upon certain questions by threats that if they did not so vote, groups of voters in their districts would defeat their reelection. Such influences cannot be brought to bear successfully upon delegates in a constitutional convention. The convention has no succession. The delegates are reasonably independent of such influences and considerations.[112]

Less than a year after Needham's proposal, the Court rendered a decision on the Woman's Suffrage Amendment. The case, *Leser v. Garnett*,[113] involved a suit to strike women from Maryland's list of voters on the grounds that women's suffrage conflicted with state law. This time Marbury argued his case in person, but the only real modification in his argument was that, in distinguishing the amendment at hand from the Civil War amendments, he now contended that the Civil War amendments had become valid as a kind of peace treaty.

> It may be true that this involves the contention that the effect of war and the necessity of taking measures to prevent the recurrence of war expands the amending power, but it is submitted that there is nothing unreasonable in that contention.[114]

Marbury still attempted to distinguish the Nineteenth Amendment from the Eighteenth on the dubious ground that suffrage restrictions constituted a novel attack on "the structure of the state government."[115]

As in *Myers v. Anderson* and the *National Prohibition* cases, the Court's decision, now authored by Justice Brandeis, was disappointingly brief. Brandeis focused exclusively on the similarity between the Nineteenth and the Fifteenth Amendments: "This Amendment is in character and phraseology precisely similar to the Fifteenth. For each the same method of adoption was pursued. One cannot be valid and the other invalid."[116] Continuing, Brandeis refused to entertain the notion that the Fifteenth Amendment "was incorporated in the Constitution, not in accordance with law, but practically as a war measure which has been validated by acquiescence."[117] Brandeis further ruled that the ratification of amendments "is a federal function derived from the Federal Constitution; and it transcends any limitations sought to be imposed by the people of a State."[118] As to the argument that certain states had failed to adhere to other state rules,

Brandeis decided that "official notice to the Secretary, duly authenticated, that they had done so was conclusive upon him, and, being certified to by his proclamation, is conclusive upon the courts."[119]

ARGUMENTS OVER THE VALIDITY OF THE EIGHTEENTH AMENDMENT: ROUND 2

While Brandeis's opinion was the third defeat at the bench for arguments for substantive restraints on the amending process, these arguments did not cease. Thus, Brandeis's decision was shortly followed by an article whose author argued that improper amendments would lead to three harms: (1) the adoption of mere legislative proposals under the guise of amendments, (2) the erosion of dual sovereignty, and (3) the destruction of state police powers.[120] Like writers before him, the author concluded that, without limits on the amending process, "the legislatures of three-fourths of the states could impose upon the people of all the states, a national religion, or abolish altogether the right of free speech."[121] Indeed, the states might even abolish the Supreme Court or institute a monarchy.[122]

The author of another article seemed to question the proposed Child Labor Amendment (and perhaps Prohibition).[123] Otherwise, he repeated the familiar claims that amendment implied limitation, that amendments altering the original scheme of government required unanimous state consent and that the absence of substantive restraints would lead to disaster. Perhaps the author's most novel argument was that certain changes could only be accomplished through revolution,[124] a view which, if accepted, might necessitate revolution by reducing the safety-valve function that the amending process provides.

Another set of arguments was offered by law professor and author Selden Bacon[125] who started on familiar grounds by contending that, absent substantive restraints, thirteen hundred men could, under Article V, destroy the nation's fundamental freedoms.[126] Bacon's arguments then took a novel turn that attempted to shift the focus from the Convention of 1787 to the debates over the adoption of the Bill of Rights. On the basis of an ambiguous letter sent by James Winthrop to the Massachusetts Constitutional Ratifying Convention,[127] Bacon argued that the Bill of Rights was designed to limit the scope of future constitutional amendments. While the first nine amendments protected personal rights, the Tenth Amendment addressed itself to limiting governmental powers. Moreover, by the subtle maneuver of Roger Sherman,[128] who had argued for a restriction at the Philadelphia Convention limiting the scope of amendments, those powers reserved to the states and the people were those "not delegated to the United States."[129] But, asked Bacon, what power could this be other than the power of amendment?

All extensions of governmental power over the people and their rights . . . had been taken care of by the Ninth Amendment. What other object could the Tenth Amendment have . . . than to take care of the wide loop-hole so clearly pointed out by Winthrop of the power of amendment.[130]

For Bacon, then, the Tenth Amendment not only implied limits on Article V but was in fact drafted specifically to limit it.

Bacon's dubious history led him to argue that only conventions could ratify amendments infringing on state police powers. Bacon offered the following rephrasing of the intent of the Tenth Amendment:

If the Federal Government wants added direct powers over the people or the individual rights of the people, it must go to the people to get them; the power to confer any such added direct powers over the people and their individual rights is reserved to the people; and the right, at the option of Congress, to get such added powers from any other source, is wiped out.[131]

On the basis of this argument, Bacon hoped to void the Eighteenth Amendment.[132]

Part of Bacon's article, originally published in the form of a pamphlet, received an answer from Henry Taft.[133] Taft showed that a position similar to Bacon's had been rejected in the *National Prohibition* cases. From a more theoretical standpoint, Taft argued that the authors of the Constitution thought "that three-fourths of the states could be depended upon to check any undue encroachment under Article V."[134] Bacon countered that Taft had misunderstood his position and had failed to come to grips with the specific history of the Tenth Amendment.[135]

Bacon had another chance to explicate his view when, in the case of *U.S. v. Sprague*, he joined several others in arguing against the Prohibition amendment.[136] The unanimous decision of the Court was, however, consistent with earlier precedents. Justice Roberts noted that the justices had been asked to modify Article V so that it would be read "as the one or the other mode of ratification may be proposed by the Congress, as may be appropriate in view of the purpose of the proposed amendment."[137] He rejected this reading on the persuasive grounds that the Framers had avoided such a specification.[138] Moreover, Roberts argued that the only difference between the current case and past Prohibition cases was "one of form rather than of substance."[139]

As to claims that Article V was a grant of power to the United States subsequently limited by the Tenth Amendment, Roberts argued that Article V "is a grant of authority by the people to Congress, and not to the United States."[140] Moreover, in language anticipating Justice Stone's pronouncement in *U.S. v. Darby*,[141] Roberts noted that the Tenth Amendment "added nothing to the instrument as originally ratified and has no limited and special operation as is contended upon the people's delegation by Article V of certain functions to the Congress.''[142] Finally, Roberts made the point that had been so crucial in all previous cases: "Several amendments touch rights of the citizens, notably the Thirteenth, Fourteenth, Fifteenth, Sixteenth and Nineteenth, and . . . these were adopted by the method now attacked.''[143] Once again, proponents of substantive restraints on the amending process were defeated by the extensive counterrevolutionary implications of their arguments.

RENEWED ARGUMENTS

The decision in *U.S. v. Sprague* and less restrictive interpretations of the Tenth Amendment apparently marked, at least for a time, the end of serious contentions that Article V was subject to implicit substantive limits. One of Corwin's students took the issue seriously enough in 1934 to devote several pages to the question.[144] He concluded, however, that "it would be strange indeed if decisions of the Supreme Court based upon an amendable Constitution could operate to limit the power of amendment," and, while proposing the adoption of an amendment more clearly defining the amending power,[145] he rejected the plaintiffs' arguments in *U.S. v. Sprague.*[146]

While such arguments died out for a time, they have been more recently resurrected in a number of articles by prominent and thoughtful political scientists and lawyers.[147] Princeton Professor Walter Murphy, for example, argues that certain provisions of the Constitution are so fundamental, and so essential to human dignity, that an amendment repealing them should be voided by the courts.

Murphy offers two examples of unconstitutional amendments. The first example, which has been affirmed by others, involves restriction of the first amendment. Murphy reasons as follows:

1. Incorporation of the First Amendment into the Fourteenth means that the operative constitutional provision effectively reads: "Neither Congress nor the states, singly or together, can make a law 'abridging' freedom of speech, press, assembly, or religion."

2. Constitutional amendments are law;

3. Therefore it is outside the scope of state and federal legislative powers to amend the Constitution and restrict the First Amendment's protections.[148]

In a second example from another article, Murphy imagines that an "ideology of repressive racism sweeps the country.''[149] Its proponents muster the requisite majorities in Congress and in the states to ratify a constitutional amendment endorsing racial discrimination. If such an amendment were challenged in court, Murphy does "not see how the Justices, as officials of a constitutional democracy, could avoid holding the amendment invalid.''[150]

Murphy outlines three arguments. The first, borrowed from the Federal

Constitutional Court of what was then West Germany, suggests that the Constitution is a unit with "an inner unity" and a commitment to "certain overarching principles and fundamental decisions to which individual provisions are subordinate."[151] In this case, Murphy argues, "the protection of human dignity" would, as a core constitutional value, take precedence over the racist amendment. Murphy adopts a second argument from a court decision in India. He reasons that Americans have chosen "a constitutional democracy which enshrines certain values, paramount among which is human dignity."[152] This value is even more important than the democratic procedures by which it was intended to be secured. "By adopting and maintaining such a system of values, the American people have surrendered their authority, *under that system*, to abridge human dignity by any procedure whatever."[153] Since this Constitution makes "no provision for destroying the old polity and creating a new one . . . its terms cannot supply legitimate procedures for such a sweeping change."[154] Murphy further notes that "constitutional tradition establishes a legitimate process for establishing a totally new system through a convention chosen from the *entire polity*."[155] Murphy's third argument is similar to the previous two. Since "there are principles above the literal terms of the constitutional document," Murphy argues that the racist amendment would be invalid as a denial of "the right to respect and dignity" because it sought to "contradict the basic purpose of the whole constitutional system."[156]

Murphy's arguments have been repeated and elaborated in the wake of a proposed amendment[157] stimulated by the U.S. Supreme Court's invalidation of laws making it a crime to burn the American flag.[158] Thus Eric Isaacson has argued, much like Murphy, that the First Amendment prohibition of congressional laws restricting free speech apply also to amendments.[159] He argues that alteration of the First Amendment can proceed only by bypassing Congress through proposals submitted by an Article V convention and subsequently approved by conventions called within the states.[160] Jeff Rosen's argument is even more revolutionary. He argues that the flag burning amendment would be in violation of the unenumerated rights protected by the Ninth Amendment and judicially enforceable in Court.[161] He contends that the only way people could override such a judgment would be to adopt an amendment specifically repudiating the belief that flag burning was a natural right retained by the people under the Ninth Amendment.[162]

CONCLUSIONS AND OBSERVATIONS

It should be clear that the primary issue examined in this chapter was part of a larger controversy over the scope of national powers generally. Would the national government control matters like suffrage, the consumption of alcohol, and child labor, or should these matters be left to the states? Those who thought the matter had been settled by the Civil War underestimated the resiliency of the federalism issue.[163] It mattered little that one's position on the subject seemed so frequently to hinge on whose ox was being gored; it was nonetheless alive. Even as, in more recent times, the matter has been buried under such slogans as "cooperative federalism," it has reemerged, and sometimes in high places.[164]

While the states would have been the immediate beneficiaries had the proponents of limits on Article V proved successful, the ultimate beneficiary would probably have been the Supreme Court. Not only would the Court have the awesome power of judicial review, but it would also have the power to annul modifications of the Constitution that might—as in the case of several amendments that have been adopted—have been ratified with the very intent of overturning the Court's decisions. This would have shifted sovereignty from the people acting under Article V processes to the courts[165] and would have undermined representative government. In the long run, such power might isolate the Court from popular sentiment and place it above even the checks and balances to which it must be subject.

This writer believes, both as against the conservative writers in this chapter and more modern-day advocates of substantive limits on the amending process that the people—acting under the authority and according to the forms prescribed by Article V—have the right to make any constitutional changes they desire with the exception of depriving states of their equal representation in the Senate without their consent.[166] It is the power of "we the people" that makes this nation democratic. Article V was constructed to assure that the nation is not to be ruled by transient majorities, by movements that sweep through limited regions of the country, by temporary fears, or by short-lived partisan appeals to racism and political intolerance. If such sentiments dominate the nation over a sustained period of time and with substantive enough force, however, only the refusal by the people's representatives to translate such sentiments into the Constitution can stymie them.[167] If this were not the case, the people might well use force of arms to obtain what they were denied by constitutional forms. In this sense, the amending process is truly what the Framers claimed it to be, that is, an alternative to revolution; to fulfill this function, it must, in effect, permit revolutionary changes if the people indicate through proper forms that they want them.

NOTES

1. This prohibition is not absolute in that it does not prohibit changes in equal state representation in the Senate but only says that such changes cannot be adopted without individual state consent. Presumably, such consent would be difficult, if not next to impossible, to obtain.

2. Just as the progressives had advocated an organic view of constitutional

interpretation, so the conservatives stressed that the Constitution's meaning was static, at least until it was amended. See Thomas H. Peebles, "A Call to High Debate: The Organic Constitution in its Formative Era, 1890–1920," *University of Colorado Law Review* 52 (Fall 1990), pp. 49–104.

3. For reference to some of these developments, see Alfred H. Kelly and Winfred A. Harbison, *The American Constitution: Its Origins and Development*, 3rd ed. (New York: W. W. Norton, 1963), pp. 685–721.

4. Thomas M. Cooley, "The Power to Amend the Federal Constitution," *Michigan Law Journal* 2 (April 1893), pp. 109–20.

5. For Cooley's influence, see Kermit L. Hall, *The Magic Mirror* (New York: Oxford University Press, 1989), p. 222.

6. Cooley, "The Power to Amend," p. 117.

7. Ibid., pp. 117–18.

8. Ibid., p. 118.

9. Ibid., p. 119.

10. Ibid., pp. 119–20.

11. In Thomas M. Cooley, *The General Principles of Constitutional Law in the United States of America* (Farmingdale, NY: Dabor Social Science Publications, 1978; reprint of Little, Brown, 1880), p. 202, Cooley thus noted that "the first ten [amendments] took from the Union no power it ought ever to have exercised, and . . . the last three required of the States to surrender of no power which any free government should ever employ."

12. In addition to the footnote above, see Cooley, "The Power to Amend," p. 118.

13. M. F. Morris, "The Fifteenth Amendment to the Federal Constitution," *North American Review* 189 (January 1909), p. 82.

14. Ibid., p. 83.

15. Ibid., p. 84.

16. In answering Morris's arguments, Albert E. Pillsbury, "The War Amendments," *North American Review* 189 (May 1909), pp. 740–51 made just this point, also arguing however, that the Fifteenth Amendment was germane to the Constitution of 1787 (p. 743) and that an amendment is "a change or alteration, by way either of correction, excision or addition" (p. 741).

17. Morris, "The Fifteenth Amendment to the Federal Constitution," p. 88.

18. This amendment, ratified in 1870, was, of course, largely unenforced. For an earlier suggestion that the amendment should be repealed for this reason, see Goldwin Smith, "Is the Constitution Outworn?" *North American Review* 166 (March 1898), p. 267.

19. Ibid., p. 91.

20. Arthur W. Machen, Jr., "Is the Fifteenth Amendment Void?" *Harvard Law Review* 23 (January 1910), p. 171. For an earlier article by Machen in which he essentially argued for interpreting the Constitution according to the intentions of those who wrote it, see "The Elasticity of the Constitution," *Harvard Law Review* 14 (May 1900), pp. 200–16. This view makes a good contrast with the view of Christopher Tiedeman examined in Chapter 8.

21. Alan P. Grimes, *Democracy and the Amendments to the Constitution* (Lexington, MA: D. C. Heath, 1978). Also see Walter Dellinger, "The Legitimacy of Consti-

381.

382.

386.

388.

393. Where was Justice McKenna when this case was argued?

401.

xt year, the Court rejected a challenge to the Eighteenth Amendment
ged inability of Congress to set a seven-year ratification limit. The
ever, conclude that "the fair inference or implication from Article
ification must be within some reasonable time after the proposal."
oss, 256 U.S. 368, 375 (1921).

erson, "Amending the Constitution of the United States: A Reply
," Harvard Law Review 33 (March 1920), pp. 659–66.

660. Wayne B. Wheeler made a similar argument in a contempor-
In a republican or democratic form of government, the people are
rce of power. They have been called the Court of Last Resort." See
Constitutionality of the Constitution is Not a Justiciable Question,"
rnal 90 (February 27, 1920), p. 152.

, "Amending the Constitution of the United States," pp. 661–62.
McGovney, "Is the Eighteenth Amendment Void Because of its
umbia Law Review 20 (May 1920), pp. 499–518. McGovney taught
of Law at the State University of Iowa.

504.

514.

515.

Washington Williams, "What if Any Limitations Are There Upon
mend the Constitution of the United States?" Virginia Law Register
July 1920), p. 167. Williams is listed as a member of the Baltimore

172.

Dodd, "Amending the Federal Constitution," Yale Law Journal 30
), pp. 321–54. For reasons of organizational clarity, I have dealt with
e even though chronologically it followed the article by Marbury,
ed later in this chapter.

334.

335.

Marbury, "The Nineteenth Amendment and After," Virginia Law
ober 1920), p. 21. While Marbury appears to have been the first to
w that the Nineteenth Amendment was void because of its substantive
had argued that the amendment was a change that was not in accord
ions of the Founders. See Henry St. George Tucker, Woman's Suffrage
l Amendment (New Haven, CT: Yale University Press, 1916). Unlike
ker had argued:

denied and cannot be denied that if the proposed amendment is passed
gress in the constitutional manner and is ratified by three-fourths of

tutional Change: Rethinking the Amending Process," Harvard Law Review 97 (December 1983), p. 397.

22. Machen, "Is the Fifteenth Amendment Void?" p. 170.

23. Ibid., p. 178.

24. Ibid., pp. 182–83.

25. Ibid., p. 190. The reference was, of course, to the Dred Scott decision, 19 Howard 393 (1857), which had ruled the Missouri Compromise unconstitutional and declared that blacks were not and could not be citizens of the United States. This decision was nullified by the adoption of the Fourteenth Amendment.

26. Machen, "Is the Fifteenth Amendment Void?" p. 191.

27. Clement Vose, Constitutional Change: Amendment Politics and Supreme Court Litigation Since 1900 (Lexington, MA: D. C. Heath, 1972), p. 61.

28. 16 Wallace 36 (1873). For a useful interpretation of this case, see Ronald M. Labbe, "New Light on the Slaughterhouse Monopoly Act of 1869," Louisiana's Legal Heritage, ed. Edward F. Hass (Pensacola, FL: Perdido Bay Press, 1983), pp. 143–62.

29. Machen, "Is the Fifteenth Amendment Void?" p. 192.

30. 238 U.S. 368 (1915).

31. For another contemporary case voiding Oklahoma's grandfather clause but upholding the state's use of literacy tests, see Guinn v. U.S., 238 U.S. 347 (1915).

32. Marbury, like Machen, is identified as a Baltimore attorney. For some comments on their connection, see Vose, Constitutional Change, p. 115.

33. 238 U.S. 368 (1915), 374.

34. The chief case relied on by both Machen and Marbury appears to have been Texas v. White, 7 Wallace 700 (1869).

35. 238 U.S. 368, 374. At this point in his argument, Marbury cites Machen's Harvard Law Review article.

36. William L. Marbury, "The Limitations Upon the Amending Power," Harvard Law Review 33 (December 1919), p. 233.

37. Ibid., p. 223.

38. 11 Wallace 113 (1871) and 7 Wallace 71 (1869).

39. Marbury, "Limitations Upon the Amending Power," p. 225.

40. Ibid. Marbury is quoting from Livermore v. Waite, 102 Cal. 113, 119, 36 Pac. 424 (1894).

41. Ibid., pp. 226–27. Collector v. Day has since been overturned by Graves v. New York ex rel. O'Keefe, 306 U.S. 466 (1939). Marbury's interpretation of Lane County v. Oregon appears to have been overstated. See Charles Warren, The Supreme Court in American History (Boston: Little, Brown, 1926), vol. 2, pp. 500–501.

42. Marbury, "Limitations Upon the Amending Process," p. 228.

43. Ibid., p. 229.

44. Ibid.

45. Writing about the proposed amendment to balance the federal budget, for example, Professor Laurence H. Tribe says that "unlike the ideals embodied in our Constitution, fiscal austerity—however sound as a current goal—speaks neither to the structure of government nor to the rights of the people." See Tribe, "Issues Raised by Requesting Congress to Call a Constitutional Convention to Propose a Balanced Budget Amendment," Pacific Law Journal 10 (July 1979), p. 629. For similar

arguments, see Note, "The Balanced Budget Amendment: An Inquiry Into Appropriateness," *Harvard Law Review* 96 (May 1983), pp. 1600–1620.

46. Marbury, "Limitations Upon the Amending Process," p. 230. In a classic work first published in 1925, Herbert Horwill argued that the Eighteenth Amendment was "unconstitutional" in the British sense, that is, in the sense of "something that there is no law to prevent, but that one feels ought not to be done." It was not, however, "unconstitutional" in the American sense in that "it did not conflict with any provision of that instrument drawn up in 1787." See Horwill, *The Usages of the American Constitution* (Port Washington, NY: Kennikat Press, 1969; reprint of 1925 edition), p. 14.

47. Ibid., p. 231.

48. Ibid., p. 233.

49. Everett P. Wheeler, "Validity of the Prohibition Amendment," *Central Law Journal* 88 (February 21, 1919), p. 146. A similar argument has more recently been raised by Ann S. Diamond, "A Convention for Proposing Amendments: The Constitution's Other Method," *Publius: The Journal of Federalism* 11 (Summer 1981), pp. 113–46. This argument is critiqued in John R. Vile, "Ann Diamond on an Unlimited Constitutional Convention," *Publius: The Journal of Federalism* 19 (Winter 1989), pp. 177–83.

50. Ibid. The response to this argument by Chas. O. Andrews is particularly interesting:

> A number of people of the several Southern States, among whom was the father of the writer, undertook to carry out the above idea in the "early sixties" by supporting even with arms the decision of Chief Justice Taney in the famous case of Dred Scott v. Sanford. . . . Since then the question has generally been considered settled that three-fourths of the states can bind all as to amendments, else the 13th, 14th and 15th amendments would probably never have been adopted.

See Andrews, "Legislative Action on Federal Constitutional Amendment Not Reviewable," *Central Law Journal* 88 (April 18, 1919), p. 285.

51. There, of course, Marshall refused to define necessary as "absolutely necessary." 4 Wheaton 316 (1819), pp. 413–15.

52. Frederick G. Bromberg, "Is the Prohibition Amendment Illegal as Not Being Germane to the Purposes of the Union," *Central Law Journal* 88 (March 1919), p. 237.

53. Ibid.

54. George D. Skinner, "Intrinsic Limitations on the Power of Constitutional Amendment," *Michigan Law Review* 18 (December 1919), p. 223.

55. Justin D. White, "Is There an Eighteenth Amendment?" *The Cornell Law Quarterly* 5 (January 1920), p. 114.

56. Everett A. Abbott, "Inalienable Rights and the Eighteenth Amendment," *Columbia Law Review* 20 (February 1920), pp. 183–95.

57. *Hawke v. Smith* (No. 1), 253 U.S. 221 (1920); *Hawke v. Smith* (No. 2), 253 U.S. 231 (1920). The first case deals with the Eighteenth Amendment, the second with the Nineteenth.

58. In *Luther v. Borden*, 48 U.S. 1, 39 (1849), Chief Justice Taney wrote:

In forming the constitutions of the Independence, and in the various ch been made, the political department posed constitution or amendment v State, and the judicial power has fol

59. The first was *Hollingsworth v. Unit Court decided that the president's approva tutional ratification. For a review of this an to the amending process, see Edward S. C stitutional Law of Constitutional Amend 1951), pp. 185–213. Also see Homer Clark, Process," *Virginia Law Review* 39 (June 19

60. *National Prohibition* cases, 253 U.S. contention that Congress had not made ar necessity, that Article V required a vote rather than two-thirds of a quorum, and th in order for amendments to be effective.

61. 253 U.S. 350, 357–58.

62. Alpheus T. Mason and William *Introductory Essays and Selected Cases*, 6th e 1978), p. 139.

63. 253 U.S. 350, 358.

64. Ibid. Attorneys for Rhode Island change "would bring about a constitution

65. An article by F. W. Grinnell up consisted in large part of quotations from Kind of Amendments to the Federal Con Rhode Island Case—The Views of George Amendment," *Massachusetts Law Quarterl*

66. 253 U.S. 350, 359.

67. Ibid.

68. This figure was Root's estimate o the states. This argument, which is rem Calhoun, continues to fascinate lawyers example, Theodore Sorenson estimates t to propose amendments, "then thirty-fo population could call the convention, tv the population could propose new amend less than 40 percent of the population cou Campaign to Rewrite the Constitution,"

69. 253 U.S. 350, 362.

70. Ibid., p. 365.

71. Ibid.

72. Ibid., p. 367.

73. Ibid.

74. Ibid., p. 371.

75. Ibid., p. 377.

76.

77.

78.

79.

80.

81.

82.

83.

based on
Court di
V is that
See *Dillo*

84. W
to Mr. M

85. It
aneous ar
the ultim
Wheeler,
Central L

86. Fr

87. D
Contents?
at the Co

88. Ib

89. Ib

90. Ib

91. G
the Power
6 (new ser
bar.

92. Ibi

93. W.
(February
this article
which is co

94. Ibic

95. Ibic

96. Wil
Review 7 (
advance the
content, ot
with the int
by Constitu
Marbury, T

It is n
by Co

the States, that it becomes a part of the Constitution of the United States . . .
and . . . such an amendment would be legal and constitutional. (p. 51)

97. Marbury, "The Nineteenth Amendment and After," p. 21.
98. Ibid., p. 2. Here Marbury appears to be transforming an argument that
Elihu Root had made in the *National Prohibition* cases. See 253 U.S. 350, 362–63.
99. Marbury, "The Nineteenth Amendment and After," p. 2.
100.

> Amendment XVIII: Section 1. After one year from the ratification of this
> article the manufacture, sale, or transportation of intoxicating liquors within,
> the importation thereof into, or the exportation thereof from the United States
> and all territory subject to the jurisdiction thereof for beverage purposes is
> hereby prohibited. Section 2. The Congress and the several States shall have
> concurrent power to enforce this article by appropriate legislation. [Section
> 3 not germane]
>
> Amendment XIX: The right of citizens of the United States to vote shall
> not be denied or abridged by the United States or by any State on account
> of sex. Congress shall have power to enforce this article by appropriate
> legislation.

101. Marbury, p. 22. Emphasis omitted. Marbury is criticizing the language of
a Supreme Court decision.
102. Ibid., p. 19.
103. For a rejection of the argument that only the passage of time had validated
the Civil War amendments, see Frierson, "Amending the Constitution of the United
States," p. 662.
104. Marbury, "The Nineteenth Amendment and After," p. 20.
105. Ibid., p. 15. Note that Marbury's argument would extend equally to a
constitutional provision which extended the right to vote to men!
106. Ibid., p. 17.
107. Ibid., p. 20.
108. Charles Needham, "Changing the Fundamental Law," *University of Pennsylvania Law Review* 69 (March 1921), pp. 222–36.
109. Ibid., p. 224.
110. Ibid., p. 236.
111. Ibid. Needham's openness to constitutional change is shown by his willingness to entertain the possibility of calling an amending convention every ten
years. For comparison, see Chapter 4 of this book, which discusses Jefferson and
constitutional change.
112. Ibid., p. 235.
113. 258 U.S. 130 (1922).
114. Ibid., p. 134.
115. Ibid., p. 133.
116. Ibid., p. 136.
117. Ibid.
118. Ibid., p. 137.
119. Ibid.

120. A. M. Holding, "Perils to be Apprehended From Amending the Constitution," *The American Law Review* 57 (July–August 1923), p. 488.

121. Ibid., p. 484.

122. Ibid.

123. Sampson Child, "Revolutionary Amendments to the Constitution," *The Constitutional Review* 10 (January 1926), p. 29. Child says he raised the question of the constitutionality of the Child Labor Amendment only to be told that "the question was settled by the prohibition cases." Later, on page 35, he seems to question the Prohibition amendment. On pages 34–35, Child cites an article by George Steward Brown, "Perpetual Covenant of the Constitution," *The North American Review* (January 1924), which cites five possible amendments that would be substantively invalid. They deal with the national initiative and referendum, abolition of the Senate, destruction of the Senate's equal status in Congress, transfer of certain Senate powers to the House, and "making Congress the final judge of its own powers."

124. Ibid., p. 27.

125. Selden Bacon, "How the Tenth Amendment Affected the Fifth Article of the Constitution," *Virginia Law Review* 16 (June 1930), pp. 771–91. Bacon is identified as a member of the New York bar.

126. Ibid., p. 771.

127. Ibid., p. 775.

128. Ibid., p. 778, fn. 19.

129. Ibid., p. 777.

130. Ibid., p. 778.

131. Ibid., p. 782.

132. Ibid., p. 783. For another contemporary expression of the view that the Eighteenth Amendment was invalid, see Archibald E. Stevenson, *States' Rights and National Prohibition* (New York: Clark Boardman, 1927). Also see Francis X. Hennessey, *Citizen or Subject?* (New York: I. P. Dutton, 1923). The appendix of this book makes reference to the "alleged" Eighteenth Amendment.

133. Henry Taft, "Amendment of the Federal Constitution: Is the Power Conferred by Article V Limited by the Tenth Amendment?" *Virginia Law Review* 16 (May 1930), pp. 647–58. Taft is listed as a member of the New York bar.

134. Ibid., p. 651.

135. Bacon, "How the Tenth Amendment," pp. 783–87.

136. 282 U.S. 716 (1931).

137. Ibid., p. 731.

138. Ibid., p. 732.

139. Ibid., p. 733.

140. Ibid.

141. 312 U.S. 100 (1941), pp. 123–24

The [tenth] amendment states but a truism that all is retained which has not been surrendered. There is nothing in the history of its adoption to suggest that it was more than a declaration of the relationship between the national and state governments as it had been established by the Constitution before the amendment or that its purpose was other than to allay fears that the new national government might seek to exercise fully their reserved powers.

For comments on this case, see Alpheus T. Mason, *Harlan Fiske Stone: Pillar of the Law* (New York: Viking Press, 1956), pp. 555–56.

142. 282 U.S. 716, pp. 733–34.

143. Ibid., p. 734.

144. William A. Platz, "Article Five of the Federal Constitution," *The George Washington Law Review* 3 (November 1934), pp. 38–41. This issue is also treated briefly in Corwin and Ramsey, "The Constitutional Law," pp. 186–90.

145. Platz, "Article V of the Federal Constitution," p. 40.

146. Ibid., p. 42–43.

147. In addition to the works discussed here, see William F. Harris, *The Interpretable Constitution* Ph.D. diss., Department of Politics, Princeton University, 1985, pp. 227–82, and Sanford Levinson, *A Constitutional Faith* (Princeton, NJ: Princeton University Press, 1988), pp. 149–51.

148. Walter Murphy, "The Art of Constitutional Interpretation: A Preliminary Showing," *Essays on the Constitution of the United States*, ed. M. Harmon (Port Washington, NY: Kennikat, 1978), p. 151.

149. Walter Murphy, "An Ordering of Constitutional Values," *Southern California Law Review* 53 (1980), p. 755.

150. Ibid.

151. Ibid. The material cited is quoted directly from the German court decision.

152. Ibid., p. 756.

153. Ibid.

154. Ibid., p. 757.

155. Ibid.

156. Ibid.

157. For a useful discussion of this amendment, see Robert J. Goldstein, "The Great 1989–1990 Flag Flap: An Historical, Political, and Legal Analysis," *University of Miami Law Review* 45 (September 1990), pp. 19–106; and Murray Dry, "Flag Burning and the Constitution," *The Supreme Court Review 1990*, ed. Gerhard Casper, Dennis J. Hutchinson, and David A. Strauss (Chicago: University of Chicago Press, 1991), pp. 69–103.

158. *Texas v. Johnson*, 109 S. Ct. 2533 (1989), and *United States v. Eichman*, 110 S. Ct. 2404 (1990).

159. Eric A. Isaacson, "The Flag Burning Issue: A Legal Analysis and Comment," *Loyola of Los Angeles Law Review* 23 (January 1990), p. 595.

160. Ibid., p. 599.

161. Jeff Rosen, "Was the Flag Burning Amendment Unconstitutional?" *The Yale Law Journal* 100 (1991), pp. 1073–4. An obvious problem with Rosen's argument is that the right of freedom of speech is not an unenumerated right but is directly protected by the First Amendment. Symbolic speech is not, of course, specifically mentioned there.

162. Ibid., p. 1092. Isaacson's and Rosen's views are critiqued in this author's unpublished paper entitled "In Defense of the Constitutionality of the Amendment to Prevent Desecration of the American Flag" (1991).

163. Alpheus T. Mason correctly argued that federalism has inaugurated a continuing debate in American history. See Mason, *The States Rights Debate: Antifederalism and the Constitution*, 2nd ed. (New York: Oxford University Press, 1972), pp. 189–95.

164. See, for example, the decision by Justice Rehnquist in *National League of Cities v. Usery*, 426 U.S. 833 (1976). For the way that a number of Burger Court justices were influenced by their views of Federalism, see Charles M. Lamb and Stephen C. Halpern, eds., *The Burger Court: Political and Judicial Profiles* (Urbana: University of Illinois Press, 1991).

165. Fritz W. Scharpf, "Judicial Review and the Political Question: A Functional Analysis," *Yale Law Journal* 75 (March 1966), p. 589: "I do not find it paradoxical to insist that judicial review in a democracy remains defensible only to the extent that the Court itself will be defenseless against the processes through which the community may assert and enforce its own considered understanding of its basic code."

166. See John R. Vile, "Limitations on the Constitutional Amending Process," *Constitutional Commentary* 2 (Summer 1985), pp. 373–88. Also see Douglas Linder, "What in the Constitution Cannot be Amended?" *Arizona Law Review* 23 (1981), pp. 717–31.

I also believe that the prospect of amendments that would seriously undercut important freedoms is relatively slight. See John R. Vile, "Proposals to Amend the Bill of Rights: Are Fundamental Rights in Jeopardy?" *Judicature* 75 (August/September 1991) 62–67.

167. At the Constitutional Convention, Benjamin Franklin thus noted that "there is no form of Government but what may be a blessing to the people if well administered for a course of years, and can only end in Despotism, as other forms have done before it, when the people shall have become so corrupted as to need despotic government, being incapable of not other." Max Farrand, *The Records of the Federal Convention of 1787*, (New Haven, CT: Yale University Press, 1966), vol. 2, p. 642.

Selected Bibliography

BOOKS

Ackerman, Bruce. *We the People: Foundations*. Cambridge: Belknap Press of Harvard University Press, 1991.

Ames, Herman. *The Proposed Amendments to the Constitution of the United States During the First Century of its History*. New York: Burt Franklin, 1970. Reprint of 1896 edition.

Aquinas, Thomas. *The Political Ideas of Saint Thomas Aquinas*. Ed. D. Bigongiari. New York: Hafner Press, 1953.

Arendt, Hannah. *On Revolution*. New York: Viking Press, 1965.

Aristotle. *The Politics of Aristotle*. Ed. Ernest Barker. New York: Oxford University Press, 1958.

Bacon, Francis. *The Essays or Counsels, Civil and Moral of Francis Bacon*. Ed. Samuel H. Reynolds. Oxford: Clarendon Press, 1890.

————. *The Works of Francis Bacon*. Ed. James Spalding, Robert L. Ellis, and Douglas D. Heath. New York: Garrett Press, 1968. Reprint of 1874 edition.

Bagehot, Walter. *The English Constitution*. Garden City, NY: Doubleday, n.d.

Bailyn, Bernard. *The Ideological Origins of the American Revolution*. Cambridge, MA: Belknap Press of Harvard University Press, 1967.

Barber, Sotirios A. *On What the Constitution Means*. Baltimore: Johns Hopkins University Press, 1984.

Beard, Charles. *An Economic Interpretation of the Constitution of the United States*. New York: Macmillan, 1935.

Beatty, Edward C. *William Penn as Social Philosopher*. New York: Octagon Books of Farrar, Strauss and Giroux, 1975.

Becker, Carl L. *The Declaration of Independence*. New York: Vintage, 1970.

Beitzinger, A. G. *A History of American Political Thought*. New York: Dodd, Mead, 1972.

Bemis, Samuel F. *Jay's Treaty*. New Haven, CT: Yale University Press, 1962.

Benson, Randolph. *Thomas Jefferson as Social Scientist*. Rutherford, NJ: Fairleigh Dickinson University Press, 1971.

Berry, Mary F. *Why ERA Failed: Politics, Women's Rights, and the Amending Process of the Constitution*. Bloomington: Indiana University Press, 1986.

Bickel, Alexander. *The Least Dangerous Branch*. Indianapolis: Bobbs-Merrill, 1962.

Bowen, Catherine D. *The Lion and the Throne*. Boston: Little, Brown, 1957.

———. *Miracle at Philadelphia*. Boston: Little, Brown, 1966.

Bryce, James. *The American Commonwealth*. 2 vols. 3rd ed. New York: Macmillan, 1906.

Burgess, John W. *Selections From Political Science and Comparative Constitutional Law*. Farmingdale, NY: Dabor Social Science Publications, 1978.

Burke, Edmund. *Reflections on the Revolution in France*. New York: Anchor, 1973.

Calhoun, John C. *The Correspondence of John C. Calhoun*. Ed. J. Franklin Jameson. Vol. 2 of *Annual Report of the American Historical Association for the Year 1899*. Washington, DC: Government Printing Office, 1899.

———. *A Disquisition on Government and Selections From the Discourses*. Indianapolis: Bobbs-Merrill, 1953.

———. *The Papers of John C. Calhoun*. Ed. Robert L. Meriwether. Columbia: University of South Carolina Press, 1959.

———. *The Works of John C. Calhoun*. Ed. Richard K. Crallé. 6 vols. New York: Russell and Russell, 1968. Reprint of 1851–56 edition.

Carpenter, Jesse T. *The South as a Conscious Minority, 1789–1861*. Gloucester, MA: Peter Smith, 1963. Reprint of 1930 edition.

Ceaser, James W. *Presidential Selection: Theory and Development*. Princeton, NJ: Princeton University Press, 1979.

Chambers, William N. *Political Parties in a New Nation*. New York: Oxford University Press, 1963.

Charles, Joseph. *The Origins of the American Party System*. Williamsburg, VA: Institute of Early American History and Culture, 1956.

Chinard, Gilbert. *Thomas Jefferson: The Apostle of Americanism*. Ann Arbor: University of Michigan Press, 1957.

Chittenden, L. E. *Report of the Debates and Proceedings of the Peace Convention Held at Washington, D.C., February, 1861*. New York: Da Capo Press, 1971. Reprint of D. Appleton, 1864.

Cicero, Marcus T. *On the Commonwealth*. Trans. G. Sabine and G. Smith. Indianapolis: Bobbs-Merrill, 1976. Reprint of 1929 edition.

Combs, Jerald A. *The Jay Treaty*. Berkeley: University of California Press, 1970.

Cooley, Thomas H. *The General Principles of Constitutional Law in the United States of America*. Farmingdale, NY: Dabor Social Science Publications, 1978. Reprint of Little, Brown, 1880.

Corwin, Edward S. *The 'Higher Law' Background of American Constitutional Law*. Ithaca, NY: Cornell University Press, 1965.

Croly, Herbert. *Progressive Democracy*. Indianapolis: Bobbs-Merrill, 1965. Reprint of 1909 edition.

———. *The Promise of American Life*. Indianapolis: Bobbs-Merrill, 1965.

Cunningham, Noble E. *The Pursuit of Reason: The Life of Thomas Jefferson*. Baton Rouge: Louisiana State University Press, 1987.

Current, Richard N. *John C. Calhoun*. New York: Washington Square Press, 1968.

Dennison, George M. *The Dorr War: Republicanism on Trial, 1831–1861*. Lexington: University Press of Kentucky, 1976.

Dewey, Donald O. *The Sage of Montpelier: Madison's Thought, 1817–36*. Dissertation for Ph.D. in history, University of Chicago, 1960.

Diamond, Martin, Winston Fisk, and Herbert Garfinkel. *The Democratic Republic: An Introduction to American National Government*. Chicago: Rand McNally, 1966.

Dicey, A. V. *Introduction to the Study of the Law of the Constitution*. 8th ed. London: Macmillan, 1926.

Dodd, Walter F. *The Revision and Amendment of State Constitutions*. Baltimore, MD: Johns Hopkins Press, 1910.

Elliot, Jonathan. *The Debates in State Conventions on the Adoption of the Federal Constitution*. 5 vols. New York: Burt Franklin, 1888.

Farling, John E. *The First of Men: A Life of George Washington*. Knoxville: University of Tennessee Press, 1988.

Farrand, Max. *The Records of the Federal Convention*. New Haven, CT: Yale University Press, 1966.

Fisher, Sidney G. *A Philadelphia Perspective: The Diary of Sidney George Fisher Covering the Years 1834–1871*. Philadelphia: Historical Society of Pennsylvania, 1967.

———. *The Trial of the Constitution*. New York: Da Capo Press, 1972. Reprint J. B. Lippincott, 1962.

Foley, Michael. *The Silence of Constitutions: Gaps. 'Abeyances,' and Political Temperament in the Maintenance of Government*. London: Routledge, 1989.

Franklin, Benjamin. *The Papers of Benjamin Franklin*. Ed. William B. Willcox. New Haven, CT: Yale University Press, 1982.

Gilbert, Felix. *To the Farewell Address: Ideas of Early American Foreign Policy*. Princeton, NJ: Princeton University Press, 1961.

Gillespie, Michael A., and Michael Lienesch, eds. *Ratifying the Constitution*. Lawrence: University Press of Kansas, 1989.

Goodnow, Frank. *Social Reform and the Constitution*. New York: Burt Franklin, 1970. Reprint of 1911 edition.

Grimes, Alan P. *Democracy and the Amendments to the Constitution*. Lexington, MA: Lexington Books, 1978.

Guthrie, W.K.C. *The Greek Philosophers: From Thales to Aristotle*. New York: Harper & Row, 1960.

Hale, Matthew. *The History of the Common Law in England*. Ed. Charles M. Gray. Chicago: University of Chicago Press, 1971.

Hall, Kermit. *The Magic Mirror*. New York: Oxford University Press, 1989.

Hall, Kermit L., Harold M. Hyman, and Leon V. Sigal, eds. *The Constitutional Convention as an Amending Device*. Washington, DC: The American Historical Association and the American Political Science Association, 1981.

Halpern, Stephen C., and Charles M. Lamb, eds. *Supreme Court Activism and Restraint*. Lexington, MA: Lexington Books, 1982.

Hamilton, Alexander, James Madison, and John Jay. *The Federalist Papers*. Ed. Clinton Rossiter. New York: New American Library, 1961.

Harris, William F. *The Interpretable Constitution*. Ph.D. diss., Department of Politics, Princeton University, 1985.

Hartz, Louis. *The Liberal Tradition in America*. New York: Harcourt, Brace & World, 1955.

Hoar, Roger S. *Constitutional Conventions: Their Nature, Powers, and Limitations*. Boston: Little, Brown, 1919.

Hobbes, Thomas. *Leviathan*. Ed. M. Oakeshott. New York: Collier Books, 1962.

Hofstader, Richard. *The Idea of a Party System: The Rise of Legitimate Opposition in the United States, 1780–1840*. Berkeley, CA: University of California Press, 1972.

———. *Social Darwinism in American Thought*. Boston: Beacon Press, 1955.

Hooker, Richard. *Of the Laws of Ecclesiastical Polity*. New York: Dutton, 1909.

Horwell, Herbert A. *The Usages of the American Constitution*. Oxford: Oxford University Press, 1925.

Hume, David. *Hume's Moral and Political Philosophy*. Ed. H. D. Aiken. New York: Hafner, 1948.

Hyman, Harold M., ed. *A More Perfect Union: The Impact of the Civil War and Reconstruction on the Constitution*. New York: Alfred A. Knopf, 1972.

———. *New Frontiers of American Reconstruction*. Urbana: University of Illinois Press, 1966.

Hyman, Harold M., and William M. Wiecek. *Equal Justice Under Law: Constitutional Development, 1835–1875*. New York: Harper & Row, 1982.

Jacobs, Clyde E. *Law Writers and the Courts: The Influence of Thomas M. Cooley, Christopher G. Tiedeman and John F. Dillon Upon American Constitutional Law*. Berkeley: University of California Press, 1954.

Jacobson, Gary J. *The Supreme Court and the Decline of Constitutional Aspiration*. Totowa, NJ: Rowman & Littlefield, 1986.

James, Joseph. *The Ratification of the Fourteenth Amendment*. Macon, GA: Mercer University Press, 1981.

Jameson, J. Franklin. *The American Revolution Considered as a Social Movement*. Princeton, NJ: Princeton University Press, 1967.

Jameson, John A. *A Treatise on Constitutional Conventions: Their History, Powers, and Modes of Proceeding*. 4th ed. New York: Da Capo Press, 1972. Reprint of Callaghan and Company, 1887.

Jefferson, Thomas. *Notes on the State of Virginia*. New York: Harper & Row, 1964.

———. *The Papers of Thomas Jefferson*. Ed. Julian Boyd. 20 vols. Princeton, NJ: Princeton University Press, 1950– .

———. *The Works of Thomas Jefferson*. Ed. Paul Leicester Ford. New York: G. P. Putnam's Sons, Knickerbocker Press, 1905.

———. *The Writings of Thomas Jefferson*. Ed. Albert Bergh. Washington, DC: The Thomas Jefferson Memorial Association Monticello Edition, 1904.

———. *The Writings of Thomas Jefferson*, Ed. H. A. Washington. New York: H. W. Darby, 1861.

Jensen, Merrill. *The Articles of Confederation*. Madison: University of Wisconsin Press, 1966.

Kammen, Michael. *A Machine That Would Go of Itself: The Constitution in American Culture*. New York: Alfred A. Knopf, 1987.

Kaufman, Burton I., ed. *Washington's Farewell Address: The View From the 20th Century*. Chicago: Quadrangle Books, 1969.

Kelly, Alfred H., and Winfred A. Harbison. *The American Constitution: Its Origins and Development*. 3rd ed. New York: W. W. Norton, 1963.

Koch, Adrienne. *Jefferson and Madison: The Great Collaboration*. London: Oxford University Press, 1964.

———. *The Philosophy of Thomas Jefferson*. Chicago: Quadrangle Books, 1964.

Kuhn, Thomas S. *The Structure of Scientific Revolutions*. 2nd ed. Chicago: University of Chicago Press, 1970.

Kyvig, David E. *Alcohol and Order: Perspectives on National Prohibition*. Westport, CT: Greenwood Press, 1985.

Lamb, Charles M., and Stephen C. Halpern, eds. *The Burger Court: Political and Judicial Profiles*. Urbana: University of Illinois Press, 1991.

Lee, Charles Robert, Jr. *The Confederate Constitutions*. Chapel Hill: University of North Carolina Press, 1963.

Leoni, Bruno. *Freedom and the Law*. Los Angeles: Nash, 1972.

Levinson, Sanford. *Constitutional Faith*. Princeton, NJ: Princeton University Press, 1988.

Levy, Leonard W. *Original Intent and the Framers' Constitution*. New York: Macmillan, 1988.

Livingston, William S. *Federalism and Constitutional Change*. Oxford: Clarendon Press, 1956.

Locke, John. *Two Treatises of Government*. Ed. Peter Laslett. New York: New American Library, 1965. Reprint of Cambridge University Press, 1963.

Lowell, Abbott L. *The Government of England*. 2 vols. New York: Macmillan, 1909.

Lutz, Donald. *The Origins of American Constitutionalism*. Baton Rouge: Louisiana State University Press, 1988.

MacDonald, William. *A New Constitution for a New America*. New York: B. W. Huebsch, 1921.

Machiavelli, Niccolo. *The Prince and The Discourses*. Intro. Max Lerner. New York: Modern Library, 1950.

Madison, James. *The Writings of James Madison*. Ed. Gaillard Hunt. New York: G. P. Putnam's Sons, Knickerbocker Press, 1904.

Mansbridge, Jane. *Why We Lost the ERA*. Chicago: University of Chicago Press, 1986.

Mason, Alpheus T. *The States Rights Debate: Antifederalism and the Constitution*. 2nd ed. New York: Oxford University Press, 1972.

Mason, Alpheus T., and Gordon E. Baker. *Free Government in the Making: Readings in American Political Thought*. 4th ed. New York: Oxford University Press, 1985.

Mason, Alpheus T., and Donald Grier Stephenson, Jr. *American Constitutional Law*. 8th ed. Englewood Cliffs, NJ: Prentice-Hall, 1987.

Matthews, Richard K. *The Radical Politics of Thomas Jefferson*. Lawrence: University Press of Kansas, 1984.

McClellan, James. *Joseph Story and the American Constitution: A Study in Political and Legal Thought*. Norman: University of Oklahoma Press, 1971.

McDonald, Forrest. *Novus Ordo Seclorum*. Lawrence: University Press of Kansas, 1985.

———. *The Presidency of George Washington*. Lawrence: University Press of Kansas, 1974.

McLaughlin, Andrew C. *A Constitutional History of the United States*. New York: Appleton-Century-Crofts, 1935.

Meyers, Marvin, ed. *The Mind of the Founder: Sources of the Political Thought of James Madison*. Indianapolis: Bobbs-Merrill, 1973.

Miller, Arthur S. *Towards Increased Judicial Activism: The Political Role of the Supreme Court*. Westport, CT: Greenwood Press, 1982.

Montesquieu, Baron de. *The Spirit of the Laws*. Trans. T. Nugent. New York: Hafner Press, 1949.

Musmanno, M. A. *Proposed Amendments to the Constitution*. Washington, DC: Government Printing Office, 1929.

Nelson, Brian R. *Western Political Thought: From Socrates to the Age of Ideology*. Englewood Cliffs, Prentice-Hall, 1982.

Orfield, Lester B. *The Amending of the Federal Constitution*. Ann Arbor: University of Michigan Press, 1942.

Paltsits, Victor H. *Washington's Farewell Address*. New York: New York Public Library, 1935.

Paludan, Philip S. *A Covenant With Death: The Constitution, Law, and Equality in the Civil War Era*. Urbana: University of Illinois Press, 1975.

Parks, William. *The Influence of Scottish Sentimentalist Ethical Theory on Thomas Jefferson's Philosophy of Human Nature*. Ph.D. diss., Department of History, College of William and Mary, 1975.

Peterson, Merrill D. *Adams and Jefferson: A Revolutionary Dialogue*. New York: Oxford University Press, 1976.

———. *Democracy, Liberty, and Property: The State Constitutional Conventions of the 1820's*. Indianapolis: Bobbs-Merrill, 1966.

Pierson, Charles W. *Our Changing Constitution*. Garden City, Doubleday, Page, 1922.

Plato. *The Laws*. Trans. Travor J. Saunders. Baltimore, MD: Penguin Books, 1970.

Plutarch. *The Rise and Fall of Athens: Nine Greek Lives*. Trans. Ian Scott-Kilvert. Baltimore, MD: Penguin Books, 1960.

———. *Selected Lives and Essays*. Trans. Louise R. Loomis. Roslyn, NY: Walter J. Black, 1951.

Pocock, J.G.A. *The Machiavellian Moment*. Princeton, NJ: Princeton University Press, 1975.

Porter, Kirk H., and Donald B. Johnson. *National Party Platforms, 1840–1964*. Urbana: University of Illinois, 1966.

Price, Don K. *America's Unwritten Constitution: Science, Religion, and Political Responsibility*. Cambridge, MA: Harvard University Press, 1985.

Pullen, William R. *Applications of States Legislatures to Congress for the Call of a National Constitutional Convention, 1788–1867*. Master's thesis, University of North Carolina at Chapel Hill, 1948.

Richardson, James D. *A Compilation of the Messages and Papers of the Presidents, 1789–1908*. n.p.: Bureau of National Literature and Art, 1908.

Richter, Melvin. *The Political Theory of Montesquieu*. New York: Cambridge University Press, 1977.

Rosenberg, Gerald N. *The Hollow Hope: Can Courts Bring About Social Change?* Chicago: University of Chicago Press, 1991.

Rossiter, Clinton. *The Grand Convention*. New York: Macmillan, 1966.

Rousseau, Jean-Jacques. *The Social Contract and Discourse on the Origin of Inequality.* Ed. Lester G. Crocker. New York: Simon & Schuster, 1967.

Rutland, Robert A. *James Madison: The Founding Father.* New York: Macmillan, 1987.

Schlesinger, Arthur M., Jr. *The Age of Jackson.* Boston: Little, Brown, 1945.

Schwartz, Barry. *George Washington: The Making of an American Symbol.* New York: Free Press, 1987.

Sheldon, Garrett W. *The Political Philosophy of Thomas Jefferson.* Baltimore, MD: Johns Hopkins University Press, 1991.

Smith, J. Allen. *The Spirit of American Government.* Cambridge, MA: Belknap Press, 1965. Reprint of 1907 edition.

Solberg, Winton. *The Federal Convention and the Formation of the Union of the American States.* Indianapolis: Bobbs–Merrill, 1958.

Somit, Albert, and Joseph Tanenhaus. *The Development of American Political Science: From Burgess to Behavioralism.* Boston: Allyn and Bacon, 1967.

Stimson, Shannon C. *The American Revolution in the Law: Anglo-American Jurisprudence before John Marshall.* Princeton, NJ: Princeton University Press, 1990.

Storing, Herbert J., ed. *The Complete Anti-Federalist.* 7 vols. Chicago: University of Chicago Press, 1981.

Story, Joseph. *Commentaries on the Constitution of the United States.* Intro. Ronald D. Rotunda and John F. Nowak. Durham, NC: Carolina Academic Press, 1987.

Thorpe, Francis N. *The Federal and State Constitutions, Colonial Charters and Other Organic Laws of the States, Territories, and Colonies Now or Heretofore Forming the United States of America.* Washington, DC: Government Printing Office, 1909.

Tiedeman, Christopher. *A Treatise on the Limitations of the Police Powers in the United States.* New York: Da Capo Press, 1971. Reprint of F. H. Thomas, 1886.

———. *The Unwritten Constitution of the United States.* New York: G. P. Putnam's Sons, 1890.

Tocqueville, Alexis de. *Democracy in America.* Ed. J. P. Mayer. Garden City, NY: Doubleday, 1969.

Traynor, Roger J. *The Amending System of the United States Constitution, An Historical and Legal Analysis.* Ph.D. diss., University of California, January 1927.

Trenchard, John, and Thomas Gordon. *Cato's Letters: Essays on Liberty, Civil and Religious, and Other Important Subjects.* 4 vols in 2. New York: Da Capo Press, 1971.

Tucker, Henry St. George. *Women's Suffrage by Constitutional Amendment.* New Haven, CT: Yale University Press, 1916.

Tulis, Jeffrey K. *The Rhetorical Presidency.* Princeton, NJ: Princeton University Press, 1987.

Urofsky, Melvin I. *A March of Liberty.* New York: Alfred A. Knopf, 1988.

Vile, John R. *Rewriting the United States Constitution: An Examination of Proposals From Reconstruction to the Present.* New York: Praeger, 1991.

Vose, Clement. *Constitutional Change: Amendment Politics and Supreme Court Litigation Since 1900.* Lexington, MA: D. C. Heath, 1972.

Wald, Kenneth D. *Religion & Politics in the United States.* New York: St. Martin's Press, 1987.

Warren, Charles. *The Supreme Court in American History*. 2 vols. Boston: Little, Brown, 1926.

Washington, George. *The Writings of George Washington*. Ed. John C. Fitzpatrick. 39 vols. Washington, DC: U.S. Government Printing Office, 1931–1944.

Weber, Paul J., and Barbara A. Perry. *Unfounded Fears: Myths and Realities of a Constitutional Convention*. New York: Praeger, 1989.

White, Morton. *The Philosophy of the American Revolution*. New York: Oxford University Press, 1978.

Willoughby, W. F. *The Government of the Modern State*. Rev. ed. New York: D. Appleton Century, 1936.

Wills, Garry. *Cincinnatus: George Washington and the Enlightenment*. Garden City, NY: Doubleday, 1984.

———. *Inventing America: Jefferson's Declaration of Independence*. Garden City, NY: Doubleday, 1978.

Wilson, Woodrow. *Congressional Government*. Boston: Houghton Mifflin, 1913. Reprint of 1885 edition.

———. *Constitutional Government in the United States*. New York: Columbia University Press, 1961. Reprint of 1908 edition.

———. *The New Freedom*. Intro. William E. Leuchtenburg. Englewood Cliffs, NJ: Prentice-Hall, 1961.

Witt, Elder. *A Different Justice: Reagan and the Supreme Court*. Washington, DC: Congressional Quarterly, 1986.

Wolfe, Christopher. *Judicial Activism: Bulwark of Freedom or Precarious Security?* Pacific Grove, CA: Brooks & Cole, 1991.

Wood, Gordon S. *The Creation of the American Republic, 1776–1787*. New York: W. W. Norton, 1969.

ARTICLES AND ESSAYS

Abbott, Everett A. "Inalienable Rights and the Eighteenth Amendment." *Columbia Law Review* 20 (February 1920), 183–95.

Ackerman, Bruce A. "Constitutional Politics/Constitutional Law." *Yale Law Journal* 99 (December 1989), 453–547.

———. "The Storrs Lectures: Discovering the Constitution." *Yale Law Journal* 93 (May 1984), 1013–72.

Adair, Douglass. " 'Experience Must Be Our Only Guide'," History, Democratic Theory, and the United States Constitution." In Douglass Adair, *Fame and the Founding Fathers*. Ed. Trevor Colbourn. New York: W. W. Norton, 1974, 107–23.

Amar, Akil R. "Philadelphia Revisited: Amending the Constitution Outside Article V." *The University of Chicago Law Review* 55 (Fall 1988), 1043–1104.

Andrews, Chas. O. "Legislative Action on Federal Constitutional Convention Not Reviewable." *Central Law Journal* 88 (April 18, 1919), 285–88.

Bacon, Selden. "How the Tenth Amendment Affected the Fifth Article of the Constitution." *Virginia Law Review* 16 (June 1930), 771–91.

Barker, William T. "A Status Report on the 'Balanced Budget' Constitutional Convention." *John Marshall Law Review* 20 (1986), 29–96.

Berry, Mary F. "How Hard It is to Change." *New York Times Magazine* (September 13, 1987), 93–98.

Bradley, Harold W. "The Political Thinking of George Washington." *The Journal of Southern History* 11 (November 1945), 469–86.

Brennan, Thomas. "Return to Philadelphia." *Cooley Law Review* 1 (1982), 1–82.

Brennan, William. "The Constitution of the United States: Contemporary Ratification." *South Texas Law Review* 27 (Fall 1986), 433–45.

Bromberg, Frederick G. "Is the Prohibition Amendment Illegal as Not Being Germane to the Purposes of the Union." *Central Law Journal* 88 (March 28, 1919), 237–38.

Brown, George S. "The People Should be Consulted as to Constitutional Changes." *American Bar Association Journal* 16 (1930), 404–6.

Bryce, James. "Flexible and Rigid Constitutions." In James Bryce, *Constitutions*. Germany: Scientia Verlag Aalen, 1980. Reprint of New York and London 1905 edition.

Busbey, L. White. "Tinkering the Constitution." *The Unpopular Review* 5 (January 1916), 127–47.

Cahn, Edmond. "An American Contribution." *Supreme Court and Supreme Law*. Ed. Edmond Cahn. Bloomington, IN: Indiana University Press, 1977, 1–25.

Child, Sampson. "Revolutionary Amendments to the Constitution." *The Constitutional Review* 10 (January 1926), 27–35.

Clark, Homer. "The Supreme Court and the Amending Process." *Virginia Law Review* 39 (June 1953), 621–52.

Connelly, Dwight W. "Amending the Constitution: Is This Any Way to Call for a Constitutional Convention?" *Arizona Law Review* 22 (1980), 1011–36.

Cooley, Thomas M. "The Power to Amend the Federal Constitution." *Michigan Law Journal* 2 (April 1893), 109–20.

Corwin, Edward S., and Mary L. Ramsey. "The Constitutional Law of Constitutional Amendment." *Notre Dame Lawyer* 26 (Winter 1951), 185–213.

Dellinger, Walter. "The Legitimacy of Constitutional Change: Rethinking the Amending Process." *Harvard Law Review* 97 (December 1983), 380–432.

Diamond, Ann S. "A Convention for Proposing Amendments: The Constitution's Other Method." *Publius: The Journal of Federalism* 11 (Summer 1981), 113–46.

Diamond, Martin. "The Revolution of Sober Expectations." *America's Continuing Revolution*. Garden City, NY: Anchor Books, 1970, 23–40.

Dickinson, J. M. "Centralization by Construction and Interpretation of the Constitution." *The Albany Law Journal* 69 (1907), 98–108.

Dodd, Walter F. "Amending the Federal Constitution." *Yale Law Journal* 30 (February 1911), 321–54.

Dow, David R. "When Words Mean What We Believe They Say: The Case of Article V." *Iowa Law Review* 76 (October 1990), 1–66.

Dry, Murray. "Flag Burning and the Constitution." *The Supreme Court Review* 1990, ed. Gerhard Casper, Dennis J. Hutchinson, and David A. Strauss. Chicago: University of Chicago Press, 1991, 69–103.

Finkelman, Paul. "James Madison and the Bill of Rights: A Reluctant Paternity."

The Supreme Court Review 1990, ed. Gerhard Casper, Dennis J. Hutchinson, and David A. Strauss. Chicago: University of Chicago Press, 1991, 301–47.

Fisher, Louis. "Social Influences on Constitutional Law." *Journal of Political Science* 15 (Spring 1987), 7–19.

Fisher, Sidney G. "Duties on Exports," *North American Review* 101 (July 1865), 147–62.

Frierson, Wm. "Amending the Constitution of the United States: A Reply to Mr. Marbury." *Harvard Law Review* 33 (March 1920), 659–66.

Gaugush, Bill. "Principles Governing the Interpretation and Exercise of Article V Powers." *The Western Political Quarterly* 35 (June 1982), 212–21.

Ginsburg, Ruth B. "On Amending the Constitution: A Plea for Patience." *University of Arkansas at Little Rock Journal* 12 (1989–90), 677–94.

Goldstein, Robert J. "The Great 1989–1990 Flag Flap: An Historical, Political, and Legal Analysis." *University of Miami Law Review* 45 (September 1990), 19–106.

Grey, Thomas C. "Introduction." Christopher Tiedeman. *The Unwritten Constitution*. Buffalo, NY: William S. Hein, 1974. Reprint.

————. "Origins of the Unwritten Constitution: Fundamental Law in American Revolutionary Thought." *Stanford Law Review* 30 (May 1978), 843–93.

Grinnell, F. W. "Limitations on the Kind of Amendment to the Federal Constitution Provided for by Article V—The Rhode Island Case—The Views of George Tichnor Curtis—The Origin of the Tenth Amendment." *Massachusetts Law Quarterly* 5 (February 1920), 116–31.

Gunther, Gerald. "Constitutional Brinkmanship: Stumbling Toward a Convention." *American Bar Association Journal* 65 (July 1979), 1046–49.

Hale, Matthew. "Considerations Touching the Amendment or Alteration of Lawes." *A Collection of Tracts Relative to the Law of England*, ed. Francis Hargrave. Dublin: Printed for E. Lynch et. al., 1787, 249–89.

Hall, James P. " 'An Eighteenth Century Constitution'—a Comment." *Illinois Law Review* 7 (December 1912), 285–90.

Hall, Kermit. "The Monster That Almost Ate Washington: Historical Reflections on Calling a Second Constitutional Convention." Paper prepared for annual meeting of Southern Political Science Convention, Savannah, Georgia, November 1, 1984.

Halper, Louise A. "Christopher G. Tiedeman, 'Laissez-Faire Constitutionalism' and the Dilemmas of Small-Scale Property in the Gilded Age." *Ohio State Law Journal* 51 (1990), 1349–84.

Hamburger, Philip A. "The Constitution's Accommodation of Social Change." *Michigan Law Review* 88 (November 1989), 239–327.

Harris, J. William. "Last of the Classical Republicans: An Interpretation of John C. Calhoun." *Civil War History* 30 (September 1984), 255–67.

Higgins, Henry B. "The Rigid Constitution." *Political Science Quarterly* 20 (March 1905), 203–22.

Holding, A. M. "Perils to be Apprehended From Amending the Constitution." *The American Law Review* 57 (July–August 1923), 481–97.

Isaacson, Eric A. "The Flag Burning Issue: A Legal Analysis and Comment." *Loyola of Los Angeles Law Review* 23 (January 1990), 535–600.

Johnstone, Frederic B. "An Eighteenth Century Constitution." *Illinois Law Review* 7 (December 1912), 265–90.

Kay, Richard S. "The Illegality of the Constitution." *Constitutional Commentary* 4 (Winter 1987), 57–80.

Kean, Thomas H. "A Constitutional Convention Would Threaten Rights We Have Cherished for 200 Years." *Detroit College Law Review* 4 (Winter 1986), 1087–91.

Keough, Stephen. "Formal & Informal Constitutional Lawmaking in the United States in the Winter of 1860–1861." *The Journal of Legal History* 8 (December 1987), 275–99.

Kirk, Russell. "Edmund Burke and the Constitution." *The Intercollegiate Review* 21 (Winter 1985–86), 3–11.

Klinglesmith, Margaret C. "Amending the Constitution of the United States." *University of Pennsylvania Law Review* 10 (February 1926), 185–206.

Kocher, Paul H. "Francis Bacon on the Science of Jurisprudence." *Essential Articles for the Study of Francis Bacon*. Ed. Brian Vickers. Hamden, CT: Archon Books, 1968.

Kyvig, David E. "The Road Not Taken: FDR, the Supreme Court, and Constitutional Amendment." *Political Science Quarterly* 104 (Fall 1989), 463–81.

Lee, R. Alton. "The Corwin Amendment in the Secession Crisis." *The Ohio Historical Quarterly* 70 (January 1961), 1–26.

Leuchtenburg, William E. "The Origins of Franklin D. Roosevelt's 'Court-Packing' Plan." *The Supreme Court Review*. Ed. Philip B. Kurland. Chicago: University of Chicago Press, 1966, 347–400.

Levinson, Sanford. "A Multiple Choice Test: How Many Times Has the United States Constitution Been Amended? (a) 14; (b) 26; (c) 420 ± 100; (d) all of the above." Paper delivered at the American Political Science Association in 1990 and scheduled for publication in forthcoming issue of *Constitutional Commentary*.

———. "On the Notion of Amendment: Reflections on David Daube's Jehovah the Good." *S'Vara: A Journal of Philosophy and Journalism* 1 (Winter 1990), 25–31.

———. " 'Veneration' and Constitutional Change: James Madison Confronts the Possibility of Constitutional Amendment." *Texas Tech Law Review* 21 (1990), 2443–61.

Linder, Douglas. "What in the Constitution Cannot be Amended?" *Arizona Law Review* 23 (1981), 717–31.

Lipkin, Robert J. "The Anatomy of Constitutional Revolutions." *Nebraska Law Review* 68 (1989), 701–806.

Long, Jos. R. "Tinkering With the Constitution." *Yale Law Journal* 24 (May 1915), 573–89.

Machen, Arthur W., Jr. "The Elasticity of the Constitution." *Harvard Law Review* 14 (May 1900), 200–216.

———. "Is the Fifteenth Amendment Void." *Harvard Law Review* 23 (January 1910), 169–93.

Marbury, William. "The Limitations Upon the Amending Power." *Harvard Law Review* 33 (December 1919), 223–35.

————. "The Nineteenth Amendment and After." *Virginia Law Review* 7 (October 1920), 1–29.

Markman, Stephen. "The Jurisprudence of Constitutional Amendments." *Still the Law of the Land*? Ed. Joseph S. McNamara and Lisse Roche. Hillsdale, MI: Hillsdale College Press, 1987.

Martin, Philip L. "Madison's Precedent of Legislative Ratification for Constitutional Amendments." *Proceedings of the American Philosophical Society* 109 (February 1965), 47–52.

Mayer, David N. "The Jurisprudence of Christopher G. Tiedeman: A Study in the Failure of Laissez-Faire Constitutionalism." *Missouri Law Review* 55 (Winter 1990), 93–161.

McDonald, Forrest. "A Founding Father's Library." *Literature of Liberty* 1 (1978), 4–15.

McGovney, D. O. "Is the Eighteenth Amendment Void Because of its Contents?" *Columbia Law Review* 20 (May 1920), 499–518.

Meador, Lewis A. "The Council of Censors." *The Pennsylvania Magazine of History and Biography* 22 (1898), 265–300.

Miller, Justin. "Amendment of the Federal Constitution: Should it be Made More Difficult?" *Minnesota Law Review* 10 (February 1926), 185–206.

Morris, M. F. "The Fifteenth Amendment to the Federal Constitution." *North American Review* 189 (January 1909), 82–92.

Murphy, Walter. "The Art of Constitutional Interpretation: A Preliminary Showing." *Essays on the Constitution of the United States*. Ed. M. Harmon (Port Washington, NY: Kennikat, 1978), 130–59.

————. "An Ordering of Constitutional Values." *Southern California Law Review* 53 (1980), 703–60.

Musmanno, M. A. "The Difficulty of Amending Our Federal Constitution: Defect or Asset?" *American Bar Association Journal* 15 (1929), 505–8.

————. "Is the Amendment Process Too Difficult?" *The American Law Review* 57 (1923), 694–705.

Needham, Charles. "Changing the Fundamental Law." *University of Pennsylvania Law Review* 69 (March 1921), 222–36.

Nordham, George W. "A Constitutional Door is Opened for Amendment." *Texas Bar Journal* 51 (September 1988), 804–6.

Pedrick, Willard H., and Richard C. Dahl. "Let the People Vote! Ratification of Constitutional Amendments by Convention." *Arizona Law Review* 30 (1988), 243–56.

Peebles, Thomas H. "A Call to High Debate: The Organic Constitution in its Formative Period." *University of Colorado Law Review* 52 (Fall 1980, 49–104.

Pillsburg, Albert E. "The War Amendments." *North American Review* 189 (May 1909), 740–51.

Pious, Richard M. "Introduction." Christopher Tiedeman. *The Unwritten Constitution*. Farmingdale, NY: Dabor Social Science Publications, 1978.

Platz, William A. "Article Five of the Federal Constitution." *The George Washington Law Review* 3 (November 1934), 17–49.

Pope, James G. "Republican Moments: The Role of Direct Popular Power in the American Constitutional Order." *University of Pennsylvania Law Review* 139 (December 1990), 287–368.

Powell, H. Jefferson. "The Original Understanding of Original Intent." *Harvard Law Review* 98 (March 1985), 885–948.

Rakove, Jack N. "Inspired Expedient." *Constitution* 3 (Winter 1991), 19–25.

Rees, Grover III. "The Amendment Process and Limited Constitutional Conventions." *Benchmark* 2 (1986), 67–108.

Riker, William H. "Sidney George Fisher and the Separation of Powers During the Civil War." *Journal of the History of Ideas* 15 (June 1954), 397–412.

Roche, John R. "The Founding Fathers: A Reform Caucus in Action." *The American Political Science Review* 55 (December 1961), 799–816.

Rosen, Jeff. "Was the Flag Burning Amendment Unconstitutional?" *The Yale Law Journal* 100 (1991), 1973–92.

Rovere, Richard. "Affairs of State." *The New Yorker* (March 19, 1979), 136–43.

Sager, Lawrence G. "The Incorrigible Constitution." *New York University Law Review* 65 (October 1990), 893–961.

Scharpf, Fritz W. "Judicial Review and the Political Question: A Functional Analysis." *Yale Law Journal* 75 (March 1966), 517–97.

Sherry, Suzanna. "The Founder's Unwritten Constitution." *The University of Chicago Law Review* 54 (Fall 1987), 1127–77.

Silva, Edward T. "State Cohorts and Amendment Clusters in the Process of Federal Constitutional Amendments in the United States, 1969–1931." *Law and Society Review* 4 (1970), 445–66.

Skinner, George D. "Intrinsic Limitations on the Power of Constitutional Amendment." *Michigan Law Review* 18 (December 1918), 213–25.

Smith, Edward P. "The Movement Towards a Second Constitutional Convention in 1788." *Essays in the Constitutional History of the United States in the Formative Period, 1775–1789.* Ed. John F. Jameson. Boston: Houghton, Mifflin, 1909, 46–115.

Smith, Munroe. "Shall We Make Our Constitution Flexible?" *The North American Review* 194 (November 1911), 658–73.

Sorenson, Theodore. "The Quiet Campaign to Rewrite the Constitution." *Saturday Review* (July 15, 1967), 17–20.

Stathis, Stephen W. "The Twenty-Second Amendment: A Practical Remedy or Partisan Maneuver?" *Constitutional Commentary* 7 (Winter 1990), 61–88.

Taft, Henry. "Amendment of the Federal Constitution: Is the Power Conferred by Article V Limited by the Tenth Amendment?" *Virginia Law Review* 16 (May 1930), 647–58.

Tanger, Jacob. "Amending Procedures of the Federal Constitution." *American Political Science Review* 10 (November 1916), 689–99.

Taylor, Hannis. "Elasticity of Written Constitutions." *The North American Review* 182 (February 1906), 204–14.

———. "Legitimate Functions of Judge-Made Law." *The Green Bag* 17 (October 1905), 557–65.

Thompson, J. David. "The Amendment of the Federal Constitution." *Academy of Political Science* 3 (1913), 65–77.

Tribe, Laurence H. "Issues Raised by Requesting Congress to Call a Constitutional Convention to Call a Balanced Budget Amendment." *Pacific Law Journal* 10 (July 1979), 627–40.

Van Sickle, Bruce M., and Lynn M. Boughey. "A Lawful and Peaceful Revolution:

Article V and Congress' Present Duty to Call a Convention for Proposing Amendments." *Hamline Law Review* 14 (Fall 1990), 1–115.

Vile, John R. "The Amending Process: Alternative to Revolution." *Southeastern Political Review* 11 (Fall 1983), 49–95.

———. "American Views of the Constitutional Amending Process: An Intellectual History of Article V." *The American Journal of Legal History* 35 (January 1991), 44–69.

———. "Ann Diamond on an Unlimited Constitutional Convention." *Publius: The Journal of Federalism* 19 (Winter 1989), 177–83.

———. "Constitutional Interpretation and Constitutional Amendment: Alternate Means of Constitutional Change." *Research in Law and Policy Studies*. Vol. 3. Ed. Stuart Nagel. Greenwich, CT: JAI Press, 1992.

———. "Ideas of Legal Change: Precursors to the Constitutional Amending Process." *Southeastern Political Review* 15 (Fall 1987), 3–26.

———. "In Defense of the Constitutionality of the Amendment to Prevent Desecration of the American Flag." Unpublished manuscript, 1991.

———. "Jefferson's Views on Governmental Change: An Alternative Perspective on Prevalent Madisonian Caution." *Texas Journal of Political Studies* 12 (Fall/Winter 1989–90), 48–75.

———. "John C. Calhoun and the Constitutional Amending Process: Article V and the Theory of Concurrent Majorities." *Midsouth Political Science Journal* 9 (1988), 64–76.

———. "John C. Calhoun on the Guarantee Clause." *South Carolina Law Review* 40 (Spring 1989), 667–92.

———. "Legally Amending the United States Constitution: The Exclusivity of Article V's Mechanisms." *Cumberland Law Review* 21 (1990–1991), 271–308.

———. "Limitations on the Constitutional Amending Process." *Constitutional Commentary* 2 (Summer 1985), 373–88.

———. "Permitting States to Rescind Ratifications of Pending Amendments to the U.S. Constitution." *Publius: The Journal of Federalism* 20 (Spring 1990), 109–22.

———. "Proposals to Amend the Bill of Rights: Are Fundamental Rights in Jeopardy?" *Judicature* 75 (August/September 1991), 62–7.

———. "The Supreme Court and the Amending Process." *Georgia Political Science Association Journal* 8 (Fall 1990), 33–66.

Vose, Clement. "When District of Columbia Representation Collides With the Constitutional Amendment Institution." *Publius: The Journal of Federalism* 9 (Winter 1979), 105–25.

Weber, Paul. "Madison's Opposition to a Second Convention." *Polity* 20 (Spring 1989), 498–517.

Webster, Noah [Giles Hickory, pseud.]. "On Bills of Rights." *The American Magazine* 1 (December 1787), 13–15.

Weinbert, Albert. "Washington's 'Great rule' in its Historical Evolution." *Historiography and Urbanization*. Ed. Eric F. Goldman. Port Washington, NY: Kennikat Press, 1941, 109–38.

Wheeler, Everett P. "Validity of the Prohibition Amendment." *Central Law Journal* 88 (February 21, 1919), 145–6.

Wheeler, Wayne B. "The Constitutionality of the Constitution is Not a Justiciable Question." *Central Law Journal* 90 (February 27, 1920), 152–53.

White, Justin D. "Is There an Eighteenth Amendment?" *The Cornell Law Quarterly* 5 (January 1920), 113–27.

Williams, George Washington. "What if Any Limitations Are There Upon the Power to Amend the Constitution of the United States?" *Virginia Law Register* 6 (new series) (July 1920), 161–74.

Wolfe, Christopher. "Woodrow Wilson: Interpreting the Constitution." *The Review of Politics* 41 (January 1979), 121–42.

CASES

Baker v. Carr, 369 U.S. 186 (1962)
Barron v. Baltimore, 7 Peters 243 (1833)
Calder v. Bull, 3 Dallas 386 (1798)
Chisholm v. Georgia, 2 Dallas 419 (1793)
Collector v. Day, 11 Wallace 113 (1871)
Dartmouth College v. Woodward, 17 U.S. 518 (1819)
Dillon v. Gloss, 256 U.S. 368 (1921)
Dred Scott v. Sandford, 19 Howard 393 (1857)
Ex Parte Merryman, 17 Fed. Case No. 9487 (1866)
Furman v. Georgia, 408 U.S. 238 (1972)
Garcia v. San Antonio Metropolitan Transit Authority, 469 U.S. 528 (1985)
Graves v. New York ex rel O'Keefe, 306 U.S. 466 (1939)
Gregg v. Georgia, 428 U.S. 153 (1976)
Guinn v. United States, 238 U.S. 347 (1914)
Hawke v. Smith (No. 1), 253 U.S. 221 (1920)
Hawke v. Smith (No. 2), 253 U.S. 231 (1920)
Hollingsworth v. United States, 3 Dallas 378 (1798)
Home Building & Loan Association v. Blaisdell, 290 U.S. 398 (1934)
Hurtado v. California, 110 U.S. 516 (1884)
Lane County v. Oregon, 7 Wallace 123 (1870)
Leser v. Garnett, 258 U.S. 130 (1922)
Livermore v. Waite, 102 Cal. 113 (1894)
Lochner v. New York, 198 U.S. 45 (1905)
Luther v. Borden, 48 U.S. 1 (1849)
Marbury v. Madison, 5 U.S. 137 (1803)
McCulloch v. Maryland, 17 U.S. 316 (1819)
Myers v. Anderson, 238 U.S. 368 (1915)
National Labor Relations Board v. Jones & Laughlin Steel Corporation, 301 U.S. 1 (1937)
National League of Cities v. Usery, 426 U.S. 833 (1976)
National Prohibition cases, 253 U.S. 350 (1920)
Oregon v. Mitchell, 400 U.S. 112 (1970)
Pollock v. Farmers' Loan & Trust Company, 158 U.S. 601 (1895)
Reynolds v. Sims, 377 U.S. 533 (1964)
Slaughterhouse cases, 16 Wallace 36 (1873)
Texas v. Johnson, 109 S. Ct. 2533 (1989)

Texas v. White, 7 Wallace 700 (1869)
United States v. Darby, 312 U.S. 100 (1941)
United States v. Eichman, 110 S. Ct. 2404 (1990)
United States v. Sprague, 282 U.S. 716 (1931)

Index

ABOUT THE AUTHOR

JOHN R. VILE is Professor and Chair of the Department of Political Science at Middle Tennessee State University in Murfreesboro. He has written articles for numerous scholarly journals and magazines and has contributed essays to *The Oxford Companion to the Supreme Court of the United States*. He is also the author of *Rewriting the United States Constitution: An Examination of Proposals from Reconstruction to the Present* (Praeger, 1991).